A Profile of Jewish Believers in the UK Church

A Profile of Jewish Believers in the UK Church

Jonathan Allen

WIPF & STOCK · Eugene, Oregon

A PROFILE OF JEWISH BELIEVERS IN THE UK CHURCH

Copyright © 2018 Jonathan Allen. All rights reserved. Except for brief quotations in critical publications or reviews, no part of this book may be reproduced in any manner without prior written permission from the publisher. Write: Permissions, Wipf and Stock Publishers, 199 W. 8th Ave., Suite 3, Eugene, OR 97401.

Wipf & Stock
An Imprint of Wipf and Stock Publishers
199 W. 8th Ave., Suite 3
Eugene, OR 97401

www.wipfandstock.com

PAPERBACK ISBN: 978-1-5326-3995-1
HARDCOVER ISBN: 978-1-5326-3996-8

Manufactured in the U.S.A. 01/30/18

Contents

	Preface	iii
	Abbreviations and Acronyms	v
	Glossary of Terms	vii
1	Introduction	1
	Supersessionism	4
	Messianic Judaism	8
	Research Methodology	11
	Nomenclature	15
2	Data Analysis—the First Cut	17
	Published Writing	17
	Academic Studies	26
	The Main Interviews	28
	The Academic Interviews	70
	Emergent Themes	72
3	Defining the Spotlights	75
	What is Jewish Identity?	75
	What Makes a Jewish Identity?	78
	Identity Theory and Social Identity Theory	82
	Participation and Identity Construction	91
	Social Memory Theory	94
	Translation Theory	107

4	The Theological Framework	119
	A Biblical Mandate	*119*
	The One New Man Ecclesiology	121
	The Olive Tree Analogy	133
	Counting All Things Loss	141
	All are One	143
	Andrew Walls and the Ephesian Moment	146
	David Woods and "Distinction Theory"	147
	Messianic Jewish Scholars	149
	Embrace and Engagement	*151*
	Volf's Drama of Embrace	152
	Alex Jacob's "Models of Engagement"	154
	The Sanders Four Step Process	157
5	The Data Revisited	161
	Respondent Vignettes	*162*
	Specific Issues	*196*
	Answering the Questions	*199*
6	Putting It All Together	211
	Conclusions from Interview Data	*212*
	Why Do JBYs Attend Church?	*218*
	Why Might Messianic Jewish Congregations in the UK be Unsafe?	*220*
	Connecting with Messianic Jewish Scholarship	*221*
	Nurturing Messianic Jewish Identity	*228*
	A Way Forward	*230*
	Bibliography	233
	Scripture Index	249
	Index	253

Preface

This book evolved out of the work undertaken for my doctoral studies at Trinity College, Bristol. It addresses a largely unasked and—as I was to discover during the process of three and a half years' research—somewhat unpopular question: where are all the Jews in church? Given that the early church as described in the book of Acts is entirely Jewish and the church has been actively converting Jews for the following two millennia, we might expect to find that there was a significant and recognizable contingent of Jewish people in the church by now. Moreover, given that it isn't difficult to find many flavors of black church, as well as lots of Chinese, Korean and Filipino churches in London and the larger cities of the UK, we might expect to find a healthy number of Jewish or Jewish-friendly churches in the same places or in areas of Jewish population. Not only is neither expectation approaching reality within the range of church expressions in the UK, but there seems to be opposition to the question being asked. Jews are simply not expected to retain any of their Jewish religious or cultural expressions on coming to faith in Messiah—a strange position indeed given that the Bible was written almost exclusively by Jewish people, about Jewish people and, in most cases, for Jewish people. Christianity was born out of Second Temple Judaism and expresses itself in so many terms and expressions taken from that time: covenant, redemption, forgiveness, salvation, and so on.

This book, however, is not an historical account of how we got to this curious position. Rather it is a survey or a profile of what it is like to be a Jew in the UK church today, based on a series of interviews conducted in the last few years with Jewish believers either still in or with significant experience of, life in churches in the UK. The interviews also included some Gentile Christians both leading or attending churches that are attended by Jewish believers. The group also included some Jewish believers who themselves lead Gentile churches. While the survey is not definitive and cannot be extrapolated to address the whole of the UK or assumed to reflect the lives of every Jewish believer in a UK church, it does paint a sharp picture of the feelings of, and difficulties experienced by Jewish believers and the pressures under which they live, in or on the edge of the church. It is certainly a reliable indication that many Jewish believers in church are not happy and that the church is failing to benefit from the riches that could be available for all to share were the biblical mandates correctly understood and implemented today.

As a latecomer to the field of academic studies—having been a chartered engineer specializing in language analysis, compliance and translation software all my professional career, while being a part-time theologian and teacher for more than twenty years—the transition to full-time study and academia was actually easier than I had feared. I was welcomed in to the research community at Trinity College by Dr. Justin Stratis, the Director of Postgraduate Studies and most especially by my doctoral supervisor, Dr. Howard Worsley. Howard and I worked hard to define the research question and we talked about the issues of inclusion and assimilation in many ways. My external supervisor, Dr. Richard Harvey, recommended more books than I ever found the time to read, and made valuable suggestions and contributions throughout the process.

My long-suffering family put up with the obsessions, distractions and other antisocial research and writing habits that I am told are all too normal for those undertaking doctoral research, and allowed me to plunder the family coffers for the necessary funds to undertake the program as an independent student. They also helped read and critique the various drafts of ideas, papers and chapters as the research drew together.

The research, and this book resulting from it, are dedicated to the generations of Jewish believers in Yeshua who have struggled with church and, although their efforts are almost unseen, made a difference so that some of us today have less explaining to do and more liberty to be ourselves as part of the remnant of Israel that still follows Yeshua, the Jewish Messiah.

Rockbeare, December 2017

Abbreviations and Acronyms

BMJA	The British Messianic Jewish Alliance
CME	Continuing Ministerial Education
CMJ	The Church's Ministry Among Jewish People
CRS	Chain Response Sampling
GTM	Grounded Theory Method
JBY	Jewish Believer in Yeshua
MJ	Messianic Jew
MJish	Messianic Jewish
MJism	Messianic Judaism
NT	New Testament
OT	Old Testament
TGA	The Gateway Approach

Glossary of Terms

Bar-/Bat-Mitzvah Literally: son or daughter of the commandment. A ceremony where a girl (typically aged twelve) or a boy (typically aged thirteen) demonstrates their ability to lead and take part in the synagogue prayer services, by leading some of the prayers, chanting a portion of Hebrew Scripture, and giving a short talk or *drash* about the passage.

Christian Zionism Although commonly used to refer to Christian support for the State of Israel, this denotes the doctrine that the return of Jews to the Promised Land will fulfill biblical prophecy and inaugurate the end times.[1]

Hebrew Christianity Allows "a Jew who [has] 'converted' to Christianity to retain some measure of Jewish (Hebraic) culture and identity," while attending and participating fully in Gentile church as a primary locus of identification. "Hebrew Christianity denies that its link with ethnic Judaism requires *Torah* observance and favors a stronger connection with historical Christianity."[2]

---

1 See Kessler and Wenborn, *Dictionary of Jewish-Christian Relations*, 453.
2 Harvey, *Mapping Messianic Jewish Theology*, 10, 18.

Messianic Judaism	"A movement of Jewish congregations and congregation-like groupings committed to Yeshua the Messiah that embrace the covenantal responsibility of Jewish life and identity rooted in the Torah, expressed in tradition, renewed and applied in the context of the New Covenant."[3]
Yeshua	The original Hebrew name for Jesus in English transliteration

---

[3] "Defining Messianic Judaism," UMJC, accessed 6:50pm, 26 Dec 16, http://www.umjc.org/core-values/defining-messianic-judaism/

Introduction

By way of starting, this chapter introduces the subject of and reason for the program of research from which the profile is built. It defines some key terms and discussion partners before giving a brief overview of the methodology used to conduct the research. This latter can safely be skipped by those whose interest lies in the data itself.

This work began several years ago when I was editing one of Dr. Daniel Juster's articles for publication in *Charisma* magazine.[1] Titled, "When Jews Assimilate into the Christian Faith," it laments that although there are a significant number of Jewish believers in Yeshua (JBYs) in the church, they are "often strongly resistant to the Messianic Jewish call . . . assimilating into the Gentile world" without strengthening the saved remnant of Israel and, on the contrary, "weakening the numbers of the Jewish people."[2] Although Juster had expressed this concern on a number of occasions before, he went on to offer a solution to Paul's challenge for the church to "make Jewish people jealous" (Romans 11:11).

> I am convinced that the answer is a shift in the pastoral leadership of the churches. Church leaders must adopt a doctrinal foundation that insists that their Jewish members identify and live as Jews. This was anticipated in R. Kendall Soulen's book, *The God of Israel and Christian Theology*. In this monumental study, Soulen approvingly quotes Jewish Orthodox theologian Michael Wyschogrod, who argues that we will not see full repentance for anti-Semitism in churches until the pastors of the churches teach their baptised Jewish members that they are called to live Jewish lives based in the Torah (I would add, obviously as interpreted by the New Testament). Without church leaders teaching the reality of the Jewish calling, Jewish Christians in the church will not take that call seriously.[3]

Arguing that the church's early position differs from what later became its standard view,[4] Wyschogrod claims that, "Had the church believed

---

1   See the magazine website: http://www.charismamag.com
2   Juster, "When Jews Assimilate."
3   Ibid.
4   Wyschogrod and Berger, *Jews and Jewish Christianity*, 64.

that it was God's will that the seed of Abraham not disappear from the world, she would have insisted on Jews retaining their separateness, even in the church.'"[5] Soulen, in turn, recommends that "The church, for its part, should repent of having turned its back upon the original determination of the Council of Jerusalem, where the Jewish obligation to maintain Jewish identity was universally presupposed."[6] Answering a question about the low response rate of Jewish people to Christian evangelism[7], Mark Kinzer quoted Elias Friedman, saying, "God is not allowing Jews to become Christians *en masse* because the Jews would disappear."[8] How, Kinzer asked, would the prophecy of Zechariah —"Thus says the L-RD of hosts: In those days ten men from the nations of every tongue shall take hold of the robe of a Jew, saying, 'Let us go with you, for we have heard that G-d is with you'" (Zechariah 8:23)—be fulfilled if Jews have become indistinguishable from Gentiles?

My own personal experience suggests that Juster's fears are well-founded so, following other articles by Juster—"Do we want the Jew to disappear?",[9] "Jews in Christian Churches"[10]—it seemed appropriate to ask whether the claims about loss of Jewish identity could be substantiated and what exactly is the state of Jewish identity among Christians of Jewish descent within the UK church. From there, it is a logical step to considering whether there is a role for a continuing Jewish identity in Jews who have come to faith in Yeshua and, if so, what that ought to look like and how it could be promoted and secured in the face of apparent disregard from the historical church world.

Anecdotal evidence from friends and family, and from others in the Messianic Jewish (MJish) movement, suggested that the church in the UK was almost universally hostile to the continuance or manifestation of any Jewish identity in a church or church-related context. One MJish leader, now leading a congregation in the United States, kept his family out of mainstream church in the UK for three years while studying for his PhD at Cambridge, saying that the church environment was simply "far too corrosive of Jewish identity" for a JBY to feel comfortable or safe attending a church for any length of time. Strong words, certainly, but clearly at variance with Juster's suggestion that there are many JBYs firmly embedded in the church. Perhaps the only way to reconcile the positions is that there are very different ideas about Jewish identity, its

---

5   Wyschogrod, *Abraham's Promise*, 183.
6   Soulen, *The God of Israel*, 171.
7   At a conference at Christelijke Hogeschool, Ede, in 2014.
8   Friedman, *Jewish Identity*.
9   Juster, "Do We Want the Jews to Disappear."
10 Juster, "Jews in Christian Churches."

value or continuation, and appropriate ways in which it can be expressed or manifested.

The research project, then, set out to discover the significance and state of Jewish identity among JBYs in the churches in the UK. Identity theory says that identity can be a negotiated commodity,[11] so the situation depends not only on JBYs themselves but the way they are received or tolerated in the churches and the level of freedom that they feel they have to express their Jewish identity in the church world. Historical and cultural overtones add to the mix. A further complication may be whether church is the primary or dominant religious group in a JBY's social world.[12] Last, but by no means least, is the crucial question of what vision JBYs have for their Jewish identity; what they are trying to achieve for themselves and their families,[13] and how that influences their choices of expression, lifestyle, and participation in their religious communities.

The study sought to assess the current experience of JBYs in the UK church, drawing on church leaders, members, and JBYs outside the church with significant church experience. It was assumed that, although not representative, since the study followed the Grounded Theory Method theoretical sampling procedure towards saturation as time allowed, this would give enough consistent data for an investigative study and to allow a cohesive profile to be built.

This study breaks new ground in two ways. Firstly, the overall subject of the study—the existence of and reception of Jewish identity in Jewish believers in Yeshua within the mainstream churches in the UK—is largely unacknowledged and unexplored territory. Secondly, this study brings together sociology, translation theory, and theology to develop measures for assessing the degree and success of inclusion currently being achieved by JBYs in the UK church.

Before proceeding further, an important term that needs to be defined is "supersessionism"—something that occurred in almost all of the interview data and was clearly much to the fore in many of the respondents' minds and experience.

---

11 Jenkins, *Social Identity*, 19.
12 Stuart Dauermann points out the power of influence that an individual's "community of reference" has over the shape of his or her lifestyle and choices (Dauermann, "Community of Reference").
13 Ikonen, *Daughters of the Vale of Tears*, 56.

Supersessionism

Supersessionism or, as it will more frequently be called in this study, replacement theology, is the belief or teaching that the church has replaced or superseded Israel[14] as the chosen people of God. The *Dictionary of Jewish-Christian Relations* says that the two terms are "substantially equivalent" and "sometimes used interchangeably." The entry for replacement theology says:

> Both designate a theological perspective that interprets Christian faith generally and the status of the church in particular so as to claim or imply the abrogation or obsolescence of God's covenant with the Jewish people.[15]

The entry for supersessionism traces the root of the word to the Latin verb *supersedere*, "to sit above or be superior to," and goes on to say that "in recent decades" the term has gained currency in scholarly and theological circles:

> to refer to the traditional Christian belief that since Christ's coming the church has taken the place of the Jewish people as God's chosen community and that God's covenant with the Jews is now over and done.[16]

Both entries date the beginning of supersessionism to the earliest times; the former stating that "Replacement theology took shape during the second century CE,"[17] the latter that "supersessionism has stood at the centre of Christianity's understanding of its relationship to the Jewish people from antiquity until recent times."[18] Both implicate Irenaeus, Tertullian, Justin Martyr, Marcion, and Augustine as being complicit in the process.

At the beginning of his groundbreaking book, *The God of Israel and Christian Theology*, R. Kendall Soulen provides an easy definition:

> According to this teaching, God chose the Jewish people after the fall of Adam in order to prepare the world for the coming of Jesus Christ, the Saviour. After Christ came, however, the special role of the Jewish people came to an end and its place was taken by the church, the new Israel.[19]

---

14 Smith, "Introduction," 2.
15 Soulen, "Replacement Theology," 375.
16 Soulen, "Supersessionism," 413.
17 Soulen, "Replacement Theology," 375.
18 Soulen, "Supersessionism," 413.

Introduction

Soulen describes three kinds of supersessionism: economic, punitive, and structural.[20] Economic supersessionism asserts that both Israel and the church depend exclusively on Messiah for their salvation. Whereas Israel is said only to correspond to Messiah in a typological or prefigurative way, a physical or carnal way, the church corresponds in a definitive and spiritual way. When Yeshua came, he made the type obsolete, replacing physical Israel with the spiritual church. Everything in "the economy of salvation in its Israelite form becomes obsolete and is replaced by its ecclesial equivalent." Israel is not declared temporary and obsolete because of its sinfulness, but because by definition its only role was to prepare the ground for the reality of the spiritual, permanent and universal salvation brought by Yeshua.

Punitive supersessionism names the position that, "God abrogates God's covenant with Israel on account of Israel's rejection of Christ and the gospel." In effect, God is punishing the Jewish people because they have rejected his Messiah and refused to accept the truth and effect of the Christ event.

Lastly, in Soulen's definitions, structural supersessionism "unifies the Christian canon in a manner that renders the Hebrew Scriptures largely indecisive for shaping conclusions about how God's purposes engage creation in universal and enduring ways." By foregrounding a standard Christian biblical narrative consisting of just four pieces: creation, the fall, the Christ event, and the end times, the Hebrew Scriptures are completely ignored with the exception of Genesis 1–3. The Jews as a distinct people are no longer required in the overall story of the Bible because the Bible has become about individuals getting saved and becoming part of the church.[21]

N. T. Wright also offers three flavors of supersessionism: hard, sweeping, and Jewish.[22] By "hard," Wright refers to that which can be found in some early Christian writers—he particularly mentions passages from the Epistle of Barnabas—teaching that "Jews were now cast off for ever and that gentile believers had replaced them as the people of God." Visualized as a horizontal line with a break in the middle between Israel and gentile Christians, "according to that scheme, Jewish people have no place in the church, so that one has to say that Paul and the others were

---

19 Soulen, *The God of Israel*, 1–2. For a wider overview and history of Replacement Theology and Supersessionism, see the articles by Soulen in Kessler and Wenborn, *Dictionary of Jewish-Christian Relations*, 375–6 and 413–4.
20 Soulen, *The God of Israel*, 29–33.
21 Dauermann, *Keeping the Faith*, 15.
22 Wright, *Paul and the Faithfulness of God*, 806–11.

lucky to make it in before the door slammed shut." Wright thinks it unlikely that this been suggested since the 1950s and "is not normally to be found in contemporary biblical scholarship."

Wright calls his second form of supersessionism, "sweeping," both because of its sweeping acceptance in the church and in scholarship, and because of its sweeping nature. By this he describes the view that the Christ event was of such a radical and apocalyptic nature that it swept away everything that preceded it. This is not discontinuity, Israel has not turned into the church; rather the fresh revelation has swept everything away—including Israel—so that everyone starts again, from the same zero-base footing, and operates on a new and different footing. Now "being Jewish and adhering to the Jewish hope that God would fulfil His long-awaited promises to Abraham, appears to be exactly the wrong kind of thing."

Lastly, Wright sees a third possibility for supersessionism: "Jewish supersessionism." He locates this in the Essene community at Qumran and describes it as:

> the claim that the creator God has acted at last, in surprising but prophecy-fulfilling ways, to launch His renewed covenant, to call a new people who are emphatically in continuity with Abraham, Isaac and Jacob, to pour out His Spirit afresh upon them, to enable them to keep Torah in the new way He had always envisaged . . .

This is a kind of super-Judaism, doing right all the things that Jews had never managed to get right before, replacing or superseding the old corrupt Temple-based Judaism and seeing their leader, the Teacher of Righteousness, as the new Moses.

Stuart Dauermann identifies one more type of supersessionism, which he calls crypto-supersessionism. This is an "unconscious and entrenched cluster of presuppositions held by those who oppose supersessionism" but whose practitioners "affirm the expiration or setting aside of those identity markers"—such as, for example, keeping a kosher diet or observing *Shabbat*—"that formerly applied to the Jewish people." He reports that "its proponents vigorously reject supersessionism while failing to see how their presuppositions and theology rob their Israel-affirming words of substance, leaving religious Israel a hollow shell."[23]

In a paper presented at Trinity College, Bristol, the scholar Susannah Ticciati agrees with Soulen's definitions and points out how the church can be seen as engaging in identity theft in the way it reads and

---

23 Dauermann, *Converging Destinies*, 131.

appropriates the Hebrew Scriptures. "The implied community of readers," she points out, referring for examples to the Psalms, the narrative of the Exodus, and the *Torah* itself, is Israel.

> Thus, for a community to claim these pages as its Scripture is—arguably—to step into the place of Israel, or to claim for itself the name of Israel. Such an argument does not for a minute undermine a Jewish claim on Israel, but it does insinuate Christians in a jarring way in respect of the assumed identification of Israel and the Jewish people. How can Christians who read the Old Testament as Scripture not in some way identity themselves as Israel?[24]

Other commentators describe this as anti-Judaic theology, suggesting that since the Council of Nicea in 325 CE, "all accepted church theology has been built on an anti-Judaic foundation."[25] The church was identified with the "new Israel" or "Israel of God,"[26] replacing the Jews, and was declared to be the kingdom of God that had replaced the kingdom of Israel.[27]

The basic teaching of replacement theology is thus, firstly, that natural Israel, who are the physical seed of Abraham, failed—as documented by the Old Testament—and so have been rejected or cast off: "Jews are no longer special and are like everyone else."[28] Secondly, that the church is a new spiritual Israel—now the spiritual seed of Abraham through Yeshua—and has replaced the old. Thirdly, the physical promises of God to the Jewish people—such as the possession of the Land of Israel—are now to be fulfilled spiritually for and through the church.[29]

Following the claim that Israel has been superseded by the church, the case is also made that "the law of Moses—that ancient charter of the Jewish people—has now been superseded with the coming of Christ. It no longer has a place in redemptive history; its time has passed." Not only has it passed, so is no longer applicable for guiding and regulating the lives or conduct of God's people, but it is now "superfluous with the advent of the Spirit."[30]

Consequently, "the church holds that the preservation of Jewish identity within the new Israel is a matter of theological indifference at

---

24 Ticciati, "The Puzzle of Israel," 2.
25 Gruber, *The Church and the Jews*, vii.
26 Galatians 6:16.
27 Gruber, *The Church and the Jews*, viii.
28 Gibson, *Supersessionism*, 263.
29 Gruber, *The Church and the Jews*, 333.
30 Wilson, "Supersessionism and Superfluity," 235.

best and a mortal sin at worst." This assumption has shaped both the church's standard canonical narrative and doctrinal structure in "fundamental and systematic ways"[31] that are still part of liturgies, lectionaries, interpretations, and training—taught and inherited almost subconsciously—by the church today.[32] As Magnus Zetterholm observes, "The binary ideas that Christianity has superseded Judaism and that Christian grace has replaced Jewish legalism, for example, appear to be essential aspects of most Christian theologies."[33]

Connecting to the idea of repentance mentioned above, Ellen Davis writes:

> One of the forms of repentance most necessary for Christian theological interpreters to exercise, not just personally, but on behalf of tradition, is demonstrating theological respect for and, indeed, gratitude towards Jews.[34]

Supersessionism's implicit demand for assimilation—calling Jews to abandon Jewish tradition and denying the right to express Jewish ethnicity—causes rejection of JBY identity within the mainstream Jewish community, thus complicating efforts to share the gospel into the Jewish world.[35]

Most of the respondents in the interview data are unaware of the term "supersessionism" or of the nuances of the scholarly debate. They present, as will be seen below, a somewhat monochrome view resembling an amalgam of all positions, rather than any particular position, outlined above. Their chosen wording is almost always "replacement theology" so we will most frequently follow their lead.

The next important factor to consider is Messianic Judaism; not that it directly forms a part of this profile, but because it speaks of an alternative to church, is mentioned in a number of the interviews and is how some of the respondents self-identify.

Messianic Judaism

Many of the respondents interviewed have a significant connection with MJism which—where available—offers an alternative to church for

---

31 Soulen, *The God of Israel*, 2–3.
32 Even as recently as 2016, some scholars perpetuate the idea that "Christian" equals "Non-Jewish," that a Christian identity is set over and against a Jewish identity (Tucker and Baker, *T&T Handbook to Social Identity*, 4).
33 Zetterholm, "Paul within Judaism," 34.
34 Davis, "Teaching the Bible Confessionally," 23.
35 Brewer, "Jewish Believers," 257–8.

JBYs, so is described here and elsewhere as a critical partner in understanding the larger JBY picture.

Although the Jerusalem church recorded in the book of Acts was entirely Jewish, as the gospel spread into the Roman Empire and the number of Gentile converts becoming followers of Yeshua grew, the Jewish proportion and influence shrank. The Gentile church leadership strongly deprecated Jewish practice and traditions as part of the Gentile church.[36] There were no Jewish bishops present at the Council of Nicea in 325 CE[37] and it is thought that there were no Jewish churches or groups of believers remaining past the year 400 CE.[38]

From beginnings in the UK in the early-to-mid 1800s, a desire for Jewish fellowship among Jewish believers grew, often hosted and supported by evangelical churches and missionary organizations. These were often termed Hebrew Christian groups, reflecting their close ties to church denominations, seminaries or colleges, and leadership. The MJish movement started growing rapidly in the USA in the late 1960s and has spread to Europe, Russia, and Israel. The growth is variously attributed to a general increase in Jewish awareness and identity since the founding of the state of Israel in 1948, and the 1967 Six Day War.[39]

Contemporary MJism in the USA has been described by Shoshana Feher, Carol Harris-Shapiro, and Francine Samuelson.[40] In the UK, Pauline Kollontai has written three papers based on small-scale surveys[41] and Simon Dein has published an ethnographic study of a MJish congregation.[42] Dan Cohn-Sherbok wrote perhaps the earliest definitive guide to MJism.[43] Writing from within the movement, Dan Juster's early book has been through several editions,[44] while other MJish scholars such as John Fischer[45] and David Stern[46] have contributed work. Richard Harvey has documented the various theological streams within the MJish

---

36 Schonfield, *History of Jewish Christianity*, 62
37 Ponsonby, *God is For Us*, 292.
38 Pritz, *Nazarene Jewish Christianity*, 108; Schiffman, *Return of the Remnant*, 25.
39 Feher, *Passing Over Easter*, 47; Harris-Shapiro, *Messianic Judaism*, 24–5.
40 Samuelson, "Messianic Judaism."
41 Kollontai ("Messianic Jews," "Between Judaism and Christianity," Women as Leaders".
42 Dein, "Becoming a Fulfilled Jew."
43 Cohn-Sherbok, *Messianic Judaism*.
44 Juster, *Jewish Roots*.
45 Fischer, *Olive Tree Connection*.
46 Stern (*Messianic Judaism, Restoring the Jewishness*).

movement.[47] The most recent definitive guide to MJism at a scholarly level comes from David Rudolph and Joel Willitts.[48]

In describing the MJish movement, Feher talks of "consistent inconsistency" as the movement constantly negotiates its positions. Borrowing elements from both the Christian and Jewish worlds while refusing to acknowledge the boundary that exists between Christianity and Judaism, Messianic Jews (MJs) muddy the water and cause offense to both "parent" religions who, typically, are uncomfortable with or refuse to recognize their child. MJs threaten the existing classification system in a way that Jews who convert to Christianity don't, because the former straddle a previously strong boundary, insisting on retaining and exercising both identities.[49] They construct a new coherent identity from two identities that have considered themselves—and each other—as mutually exclusive for many centuries.[50] Intermarriage between MJs and Gentile Christians further blurs both cultural and religious boundaries.[51]

Feher suggests that MJism is an unique religious movement, because it provides "a new conservative religious expression combined with a new ethnic identity," Jewish identity being strengthened beyond a previous cultural-only identity. MJs are considered a threat by the mainstream Jewish communities, not because they are JBYs, but because they deny the Jewish-Christian boundary.[52] MJs challenge the boundaries and beliefs of both Judaism and Christianity.[53] MJism heightens the tension by projecting itself as a Judaism,[54] rather than a Christian denomination, and asserting a Jewish identity that is not a blended tradition.[55]

Today, in the UK, the British Messianic Jewish Alliance (BMJA) is an umbrella group connecting some fourteen MJish fellowships and congregations, as well as several thousand JBYs in church.[56] A few groups meet weekly on *Shabbat* morning, most less frequently; some are open, public meetings, others are closed groups only allowing visitors by invitation or request. The BMJA holds an annual conference. There are

---

47 Harvey, *Mapping Messianic Jewish Theology*.
48 Rudolph and Willits, *Introduction to Messianic Judaism*.
49 Feher, *Passing Over Easter*, 20–1,31.
50 Harris-Shapiro, *Messianic Judaism*, 14.
51 Brewer, "Jewish Believers," 254.
52 Feher, *Passing Over Easter*, 61, 65, 142.
53 Harvey, *Mapping Messianic Jewish Theology*, 1
54 Rudolph, "Messianic Judaism," 35.
55 Harris-Shapiro, *Messianic Judaism*, 14.
56 "The British Messianic Jewish Alliance," accessed 3:40pm 19Aug16, http://www.bmja.net

a number of other independent congregations and smaller groupings of congregations that are not BMJA affiliated.[57]

Christian Friends of Israel (CFI)[58] and Prayer for Israel (PFI)[59] are Christian organizations with many church and individual members and links, focussed on prayer and practical support for Israel. Both produce regular prayer bulletins and reports from Israel and the Middle East and have a political position. Both organize tours to Israel. They do not have a MJish vision and often, though not always, support or encourage evangelism. Although they may have or have had some Jewish leadership, they are predominantly Gentile led and are church based, connected and financed.

The next thing to consider is an overview of the way the data collected and used to build this profile was assembled and managed.

Research Methodology

The research data collected in order to build this profile of JBYs in the UK church was organized using a combination of Grounded Theory Method and The Gateway Approach . Particular attention was also paid to issues of translation: both language and cultural translation have significance in considering the communication between Jewish and Gentile believers in a church context.

The basic premises are twofold. Firstly, there are now, and have been through the centuries since the foundation of the church, Jewish believers in Yeshua (JBYs) in the church. According to the Bible, JBYs *were* the first churches in Jerusalem[60] and continued to be the majority composition of churches for perhaps another ten to twenty years. Gentile believers quickly became the overwhelming majority and the dominant voice in both the church and the churches, a situation that has prevailed until today. Secondly, Jewish identity has not historically propagated or endured in a church context. While there is evidence throughout history of Jewish people becoming believers in Yeshua, joining the church and, often, serving as missionaries to the Jewish people or elsewhere, there has until recently been no record of either them or their children retaining a Jewish identity or any relationship with the larger Jewish world. A Jewish convert to Christianity became just that: a Christian; they, their

---

57 Brewer, "Jewish Believers," 239.
58 "Christian Friends of Israel", accessed 3:56pm 19Aug16, http://www.cfi.org.uk
59 "Prayer for Israel," accessed 3:27pm 19Aug16, http://www.prayer4i.org
60 For example, Acts 2:41.

children, and any future generations became not so much Gentile as amorphous Christian members of the church.

The principal research question concerning the role of ongoing Jewish identity in the UK churches is difficult to approach directly, since the majority of UK churches would either not understand what the question meant or would respond that there was not one. The research process needs, therefore, to build an answer from a number of simpler questions that can be asked of church leaders and members—both Jewish and Gentile—and JBYs currently outside but with some experience of church. Such questions might be, "What is the Jewish experience in church?," "What do JBYs in church think about Jewish identity?," "What does the church think about Jewish identity?," "What is the role of Jewish identity in your church?"

The research works in the interpretivist paradigm: listening to informants and then describing and explaining the social phenomena to which they are responding.[61] Opinion and the answers to the question, "How was it for you?," are essentially a matter of experience and understanding; each respondent provides their own subjective view of the research field as well as the wider world. Individuals have their own story and set of experiences to relate, their own biases, and possibly their own agenda.

Interpretivism implies that each person's information is valid; they relate events, experiences and opinions drawn from within their own value system.[62] Their narratives are essentially unverifiable and significance will be attached to experiences and opinions as they recur in other informants' narratives. While similar results should be expected, this study will not be easily replicable, as it represents a snap-shot in time of opinion and experience.

It follows, therefore, that the aim was to listen to and understand each respondent's data, cross-referencing to other respondents' data to reveal commonalities and to build an overall framework from the different realities each respondent has experienced and the way they report and interpret that reality. Notice that there is essentially a double hermeneutic in play here: this study is trying to interpret the interpretations that the informants report of how they have made sense of the original phenomena they have experienced.[63]

Since this is an area where there has been comparatively little work done and literature published, the decision was taken to use Grounded

---

61 Scott and Morrison, *Key Ideas*, 131.
62 Thomas, *How to Do Your Research Project*, 108.
63 Smith et al, *Interpretive Phenomenological Analysis*, 35–6.

Theory Method (GTM) as the main method for collection and analysis of the field data. Insights from The Gateway Approach[64] (TGA) have influenced interview technique, coding and subsequent analysis.

GTM was developed by Barney G. Glaser and Anselm L. Strauss in the 1960s as a reaction against an obsession with testing and verification rather than what they saw as the sociologist's real work of generating sociological theory.[65] They sought to move away from using qualitative analysis only as a means of proving theories and hypotheses, to deriving and understanding theory directly from the data they collected.[66] The theories or research results are grounded in the collected data, which become the key focus of the research.[67]

GTM data is collected in one or more slices, depending on the richness and number of sources available to the researchers. Each slice may be collected from a different medium; for example: interviews, books, journal and magazine articles and websites. The slices may also differ in orientation, some being snapshots or parallel data, others being longitudinal.[68] The collection of interview data is most often undertaken in a relatively informal style, guided by a schedule of points or areas that the researchers want to explore but led by the informant. In this case, one data slice was a series of informal but fairly detailed interviews, and a second slice was extracted from a series of auto-biographical books written by JBYs in the last twenty or so years.

TGA is a methodology developed by Carolyn Lunsford Mears in 2005 in the wake of the Columbine High School tragedy in Littleton, Colorado, in April 1999. Mears is herself a Columbine survivor. Her son was not physically injured but—like every parent and pupil involved —they were deeply affected by the trauma of the shooting. She developed TGA during the course of documenting and exploring the effect that the tragedy had on parents like herself from her own unique "insider" perspective.[69]

TGA deals, in particular, with two phenomena in particular: the difficulty of communicating with and understanding the experiences of what is essentially a closed group, and overcoming the concern about bias or lack of objectivity when the researcher is themselves effectively part of the group being studied. A number of TGA themes are

---

64 Mears, *Interviewing*.
65 Glaser and Strauss, *The Discovery of Grounded Theory*.
66 Urquhart, *Grounded Theory*, 5.
67 Scott and Morrison, *Key Ideas*, 119.
68 Urquhart, *Grounded Theory*, 18.
69 Mears, "Experiences of Columbine Parents."

particularly significant in the study context: the trauma membrane, the gateway, and oral history techniques.

The trauma membrane, first described by Jacob Lindy in the 1980s, is part of the healing process following catastrophic stress. Defined as "a temporary psychosocial structure, a buffer zone or covering that protects traumatised people in the aftermath of catastrophic stress," it can be formed around individuals or groups in response to stress or trauma applied to individuals, groups, or communities. As in the biological world, its presence implies that there has been a wound; the membrane may be semi-permeable and is not always visible. The trauma membrane appears to allow isolation of trauma events until they can be broken down and processed, but will resist repeated trauma stimuli that threaten to breach the membrane.[70] Mears used the concept of the trauma membrane to describe the way that the Columbine parents isolated themselves from those outside the event, either to prevent further violation or because the reality of the event cannot be understood by others.[71]

TGA provides a gateway between those inside a trauma membrane and those outside, often by means of one or more individuals who have a privileged position within the inside community because of having shared some or all of the trauma. These individuals share vocabulary and experience of the trauma event, so are recognized as insiders by others within the trauma community, and are able to communicate on behalf of those inside with those outside who are seen to lack the relationship and experience. TGA uses oral history techniques to allow narrators to tell their own story. This places the narrator in a position of honor as an expert with value to share and offers positive validation to their experiences. Allowing the narrators' own voices to be explicitly heard, and listening in the context of the cultural background, social setting and community of experience brings the power of the narrators' experiences to the fore and gives memories social meaning.[72]

The act of translation is more common than most people think. It takes place where people with different "first" languages are in communication with each other; either one or the other will translate into the other's first language. It can also take place between speakers who do not speak each others' languages, via a third "intermediate" language. George Steiner argues that translation is implicit in every act of communication, even when the parties to that communication share the

---

70 Martz and Lindy, "Exploring the Trauma Membrane," 27, 29, 30, 35.
71 Mears, "A Columbine Study," 160.
72 Ibid., 160, 164.

Introduction

same first language: "to hear significance is to translate." The history of a language, the means by which it carries nuance and a record of social being, is an essential adjunct to a translation process.[73] Translation can also be seen as a "constant process of updating and elaborating, rather than some kind of physical movement across cultures."[74]

Connecting with the TGA themes above, it is the researcher's job to translate the special or "experience" vocabulary of the closed group into terms that those outside the subject world(s) of the interviewees can understand. In so doing, the researcher has to determine the measure of a respondent's vocabulary and word usage, to detect and report the significance of what the respondent is actually communicating (or not) rather than the simple transcript. This requires translation of vocabulary, culture, and time.[75] The researcher also has to ask his or her questions and interpret each response within the group context of each respondent.

Initial interview scripts were written to explore the issues raised by Juster, Soulen, and Wyschogrod. Data collection continued in line with GTM's theoretical sampling principle until effective saturation, that is: nothing new was being said. The transcripts were then grouped to allow a small sample size with a more particular examination, and the TGA position of privileged access and antecedent knowledge was deployed to select a small subset of three to six of the most significant transcripts in each case for a number of the sample population groups or themes and subject them to a close comparative scrutiny. Lastly, the TGA principle of not obscuring the individual narrators was used to give an active and personal, albeit anonymized, set of voices to the issues being described.

Nomenclature

Please note that, in deference to Jewish and Messianic Jewish custom, unless in a direct quotation, Jesus is always referred to by his Hebrew name, transliterated in English as Yeshua.

So with the decks cleared for action and some basic groundwork defined and established, the next chapter will take an overview of the all important data.

---

73 Steiner, *After Babel*, xii,26.
74 Pym, *Exploring Translation*, 2.
75 Steiner, *After Babel*, 28.

Data Analysis—the First Cut

This chapter will present an overview of the data, summarized in the main category areas and provide an initial voicing for some of the respondent data. It will then move on to consider some potential lenses and spotlights in the two following chapters, before returning to the data for a more detailed examination. The data slice taken from the mainly autobiographical writings of a number of JBYs over the last twenty years comes first, followed by a thin slice of academic papers, then the main interview data. Since many of those interviewed complained that church leaders received little or no training in Jewish issues, the last data slice is of four interviews that were conducted with academic staff currently serving in UK ministerial training colleges. Think of these data slices as the hors doeuvres, the soup or fish, the main course and the dessert.

Published Writing

A small number of JBYs, although some would not identify as such, have written published work—usually autobiographical in nature—from which opinion and quotations will be drawn as if they had participated in the research interview process.

Helen Shapiro

> Helen Shapiro is a JBY who became famous as a singer when she was a teenager in the 1960s, and went on to a singing career lasting over forty years. Born in the East End of London to a typical working-class Jewish family who traced their roots back to the Odessa area of Ukraine, she became a believer in her forties and has been an active singer-evangelist, sharing her testimony in gospel concerts. She now lives in the Greater London area, attending a BMJA fellowship.
>
> Helen describes the moment when she prayed with old friends to invite Yeshua into her life and the immediate challenge to her Jewish identity:

> As we sat back in our seats Penny said, "Well, you're a Christian."
>
> Shock horror. No I was not. To the Jewish mind the word Christian means somebody who hates Jews, an enemy of my people. I could not be identified with all the horrors that had been perpetrated against the Jewish people. I was Jewish. I was happy being Jewish. I did not want to be anything else.[1]

Taken to a lively Anglican church, she enjoyed the contemporary worship, comparing it to the busyness of the traditional synagogue she had known. "Taking what they called 'communion' was the biggest obstacle" although she knew enough from her reading of the gospels to work out the symbolism:

> This being an Anglican [church], when everyone started to queue up and kneel down in front of what looked suspiciously like an altar rail, a little voice in my head was taunting, "How can you do this? You're betraying your people."[2]

Helen relates how it took her over a week to find the London Messianic Congregation, which was to become her spiritual home for a number of years, but writes about churches that are "indifferent or downright anti." One early experience shocked her:

> Not long after I became a believer I visited an evangelical church in Romford where a visiting preacher was speaking in such a derogatory manner about Jewish things I was so offended I practically had to be held down in my seat.[3]

Hugh Montefiore

Hugh Montefiore was born into a Jewish family in 1920, but became a Christian at school in the 1930s. He was an officer in the British Army in India during WWII, before being ordained as an Anglican priest. He served on the faculty at Cambridge University and as a parish priest, before becoming Bishop of Kingston upon Thames and then Bishop of Birmingham.

Although he served as a priest in the Church of England for over forty five years and described himself unashamedly as a Christian, Montefiore retained a clear Jewish identity, writing "As a Jew . . ."[4]

---

1 Shapiro, *Walking Back*, 274.
2 Ibid., 275.
3 Ibid., 279.
4 Montefiore, *On Being a Jewish Christian*, 39.

Data Analysis–the First Cut

in his book, *On Being a Jewish Christian*. He saw a clear bond between Jews and Gentiles:

> If the church and the Jewish people together form the people of God, it follows that there is a close bond between the two, and Christians are in a different relationship to Jews than they are to the adherents of any other faith. I am strongly of this opinion.[5]

He wrote with great affection about the joy and warmth of the Jewish prayer tradition and had "no difficulty in worshipping from time to time in a Jewish synagogue."[6] Nevertheless, he was negative about "Jewish Christian congregations," seeing problems with leadership and relationship with the wider church. He opposed the name "Messianic Jew" because he felt that it gave more emphasis to being Jewish than Christian, and felt unable to join a MJish group in Britain. On the one hand, he wanted to worship with Jews and Gentiles, while on the other, he asked why Gentiles would want to be part of a MJish group, doing Jewish things; his answer: they must be disaffected from the church.[7]

Although he rose in the church to the position of bishop, perhaps Montefiore's comment on becoming a believer in the 1930s describes the wider situation: "It was simply out of the question for Jews to become Christians."[8] He knew another bishop in the Church of England who was so ashamed of his Jewish roots that he never admitted them. He concedes that:

> the vast majority of Jews who have become Christians have simply been absorbed into the predominantly Gentile churches, and even if some of them have retained some Jewish loyalties and love of Jewish customs and spirituality, it is very unlikely that their children will have done so.[9]

Supporting what he saw as "Christians validating the Jewish religion," Montefiore expressed concern that in the church's moves to "affirm Jews and to avoid giving them any offence," Jewish Christians were forgotten—almost wished away—as they "muddy the water" in Jewish-Christian relations.[10]

---

5   Ibid., 59.
6   Montefiore, *Looking Afresh*, 46.
7   Montefiore, *On Being a Jewish Christian*, 73, 162, 164, 175.
8   Montefiore, *Oh God, What Next?*, 2.
9   Montefiore, *On Being a Jewish Christian*, 2, 157–8.
10 Montefiore, *Looking Afresh*, 45–46.

Jenny Berg Chandler

Jenny Berg Chandler is an American Jew, whose family split when her mother came to faith in Yeshua. Spending the second half of her childhood in a MJish context, then marrying a Gentile believer, she spent a number of years trying to come to terms with "church." Her memoir relates how she reintegrated Jewish identity, practice and customs back into her family to establish and pass on Jewish identity to her early teenage children.

Chandler relates that, as a child, "Church was weird and foreign," but she enjoyed Jewish experiences such as walking to services on Friday nights. After marriage, children, and moving from Philadelphia to Florida, she complains about life in church. She misses Jewish things and "is incredibly concerned about our children's lack of Jewish identity. I keep wondering if my kids even understand what it means to be Jewish, since I am raising them in church." Although attending an Anglican church, she writes at the beginning of the book:

> At every Christian holiday I feel like a foreigner who doesn't belong there. At every Jewish holiday I feel let down and sad that I don't celebrate within a community of our own while sharing life-cycle events and annual feasts. Even though I have long been a committed believer in Yeshua, I'd like to publicly admit that for some time now I have wanted way more than what mainstream Christianity doles out. I want my heritage back.[11]

Even as a believer, Jenny feels identity loss. While acknowledging the truth in the evangelical tag-line, "Accept Jesus and you'll never feel lost/alone/empty again"—she says that she is "never devoid of the presence of God"—she feels "weird and sad being a Jew in church" and mismatched:

> The truth is that going to church has always felt un-me, like I need to run home to change my clothes into something that actually fits . . . I have too long pretended that being unconnected to my Jewish culture and identity while doing the Gentile Christian thing isn't a problem.[12]

---

11 Chandler, *Jew in the Pew*, 14, 23.
12 Ibid., 26, 28, 53.

Over the period of her journal, Chandler resolves to introduce Jewish culture and tradition into her family: *Shabbat*, the feasts, and enough Jewish history to understand who they are as Jews:

> The Jewishness I want to instil in my kids is our history, celebrations and food traditions. Without all that, life is just business and it doesn't ground us to who we are and where we came from.[13]

By the end of the memoir, Jenny and her family have integrated a comfortable mix of Jewish practice into their lives and have started attending a MJish congregation an hour's drive away once a month. Some weeks they still attend a Saturday evening service in the local church which feels "much less churchy." In the meantime, Jenny has engaged with the local mainstream Jewish social world[14] and is resolved to accept a blend of the three environments. Her son is about to become *bar mitzvah*.[15]

John Fieldsend

Born Hans Heinrich Feige in Czechoslovakia in 1931, John Fieldsend came to the UK on the *Kindertransport* in 1939. After university, National Service and a year working in industry, he trained for ordination in the Church of England and served in a number of parishes. A deep identity crisis brought him to acknowledge his suppressed Jewish identity: "Hey, I'm Jewish! How on earth have I got here?" He writes:

> I had not only become a *Gentile* Christian; I had become a *very English* Christian. Now I needed to re-inherit not only my Jewish identity, but also my Czech-German identity.[16]

John became part of the Hebrew Christian Alliance of Great Britain[17] and led *Beit Shalom* Messianic Congregation for several years at the same time as his Anglican parish work. At this time, having been "severely taken to task" by church leaders for the congregation meeting on *Shabbat*, he wrote about the pressure placed on churches and JBYs:

---

13 Ibid., 102.
14 In this case, she means Reform or Conservative, not Orthodox.
15 Chandler, *Jew in the Pew*, 250–2.
16 Fieldsend, *A Wondering Jew*, 110–2.
17 Now called the British Messianic Jewish Alliance.

> The . . . most important issue is the pressure now put on the predominantly Gentile church to pressurise Jews into becoming Gentiles, or at least give up an identifiably Jewish lifestyle, in order to become followers of (a very Jewish) Jesus.[18]

In his late fifties, Fieldsend became UK Director for the Church's Ministry Among Jewish people (CMJ). This involved liaison with the Council for Christians and Jews (CCJ), however:

> The leadership made it clear that as long as I insisted in describing myself as a Messianic Jew or a Jewish believer in Jesus I was not eligible for membership. The reason given was that CCJ existed to foster dialogue between the two faiths, and those believers in Jesus who continued to describe themselves as Jews were a threat to the integrity of the dialogue.[19]

Some twenty years later, this position was relaxed in John's case.

Michele Guinness

Michele Guinness is and was raised Jewish, the oldest of three children of a Jewish family, and became a Christian while she was still at school in the sixth form. After university, she married a (Gentile) teacher who later became an Anglican vicar, and she has since had a successful career as a writer and broadcaster.

Experiencing an act of verbal anti-Semitism just a few weeks after becoming a believer, she records that:

> Becoming a Christian so radically shook my sense of identity that it became imperative for me to discover what being a Jew really meant to me. It never mattered before. It was a fact of life, something to be embraced alternately with joy and resignation.[20]

After some years during which her friends assured her, "You're still a Jew, of course, aren't you?," and time becoming involved in church, she came to the conclusion that:

> while Christians patted me on the back and whispered soothingly, "Of course, you're still Jewish," it meant nothing at all. In fact, although it was never actually said, I began to feel that most people hoped I would settle down and become a

---

18 Fieldsend, *Messianic Jews*, 87.
19 Fieldsend, *A Wondering Jew*, 137.
20 Guinness, *Child of the Covenant*, 104.

Gentile as quickly as possible . . . I became a Christian, but not a convert. How I hated the word! Christ was the logical extension of my Jewishness, not an alternative.[21]

Church while at university was lonely, boring, and anti-Semitic. Michele had "tempers, tantrums and explosions, as I wrestled for my identity."[22] She felt that "My Jewishness was treated like theft or drug addiction. It was a habit to be kicked." Some years later, she wrote that "There have been many times in the past when, as a Jew, I have felt culturally alienated from the church." She hopes that her Jewishness has given her "a certain objectivity, which a clergyman's wife might not normally possess."[23]

Engaging with and in church has remained important to Michele, although she has brought her own children up with a strong sense of Jewish identity, celebrating *Shabbat* and the feasts with the active support of her husband,[24] putting their family Friday evening *Shabbat* celebration before church expectations and commitments.[25]

Paul Liberman

Paul Liberman is the grandson of immigrants who came to the USA from Russia in 1894. Raised in the family electrical supply business in Chicago then becoming politically active in the Republican Party, Paul came to faith in the midst of working at a high level in the US federal government, but has always refused the label "Christian." He now leads a MJish congregation in California.

When he first came to faith, he tried attending church, but . . .

> the church hymns really turned me off. I suppose I was visibly squirming in my seat. It all just seemed so *Gentile* . . . In my own mind, it was so *in my face* that I had done something contrary to my people and to my heritage . . . I guess my discomfort at the church was more obvious than I realized.[26]

Liberman reports that when his wife became a believer two years later, she attended church with him just the once and then refused to go again: "I just can't do it. Going to church is just not a very Jewish thing to do." Facing the need to worship as a family and to explain

---

21 Guinness, *Promised Land*, 106, 15.
22 Guinness, *Child of the Covenant*, 109.
23 Guinness, *Promised Land*, 182, 8.
24 Guinness, *Child of the Covenant*, 151–4.
25 Guinness, *Promised Land*, 167–8.
26 Liberman and Wasson, *Don't Call Me Christian*, 164, original emphasis.

to non-believing Jewish relatives and friends, he felt the only thing to do was to start a MJish congregation, with regular Friday night meetings:

> The congregation needed to be immediately recognizable as Jewish! Jewish flavored: Jewish in origin and Jewish in content. Not Gentile—not a church. Being clearly identifiable as Jewish was of paramount importance.[27]

Liberman sees attending church as a matter of giving up "Jewish heritage, identity and culture, becoming a Gentile." His experience with family and friends convinced him that "it was absolutely necessary to maintain and affirm my identity as a Jew." Otherwise, everyone would say that by becoming a believer, "I had 'crossed over' to the 'other' side."[28]

Sarahbeth Caplin

Sarahbeth Caplin, born around the change from Generation X to Millennial, was brought up in a home with a strong Jewish culture. Becoming *bat-mitzvah* at thirteen and searching for God during her teen years, she went to college intending to become a rabbi, but became a believer instead, marrying a Gentile Christian man after college. She is now working on an MA in Creative Writing and has written several books.

Describing herself as "an unusual Christian," Sarahbeth struggles with admitting that she is a Christian, or that she goes to church. She writes:

> Part of me hopes I never get too comfortable "acting Christian." It would feel as if I'd lost whatever strands of Judaism I still have left to claim. My Jewish identity, I quickly discovered, is not something I can easily change like a pair of socks. My Jewish identity is as permanent to me as my skin, hair, eye color, my right-handedness and my blood type. I see the world through Jewish-colored lenses; I don't know how *not* to.[29]

That said, she doesn't now see herself as a Jew:

> Following Jesus always comes with a cost, and for me that cost is giving up my right to call myself a Jew. I've met Christians who insist I can have it both ways—I can call myself a

---

27 Ibid., 203,205.
28 Ibid., 209,211.
29 Caplin, *Confessions of a Prodigal Daughter*, iii.

> Christian by faith, a Jew by heritage—but to insist I'm still Jewish feels intellectually dishonest.[30]

During college years, a visit to a Messianic congregation, although looking Jewish, felt "forced," and she reports that, "This wasn't Jewish. This felt Jew-*ish*." She didn't go again. While agreeing that "it is completely necessary for pastors to educate their congregants about Judaism," she doesn't think this is the way to do it. "Judaism and Christianity evolved in separate directions anyway, and that is the reality we must work with."[31]

In a second book, written a few years later, Caplin's position has moderated and she is now re-forming links with the Jewish world.

> I think Jewish culture says more about me than Christian culture ever did. I still go to church with my husband, but I also started going to Shabbat services at the Jewish Student center on campus, because I missed it; I missed having Jewish friends.[32]

She describes her encounter with evangelical church as "a fish out of water experience," where, although she has met some amazing people, she has also experienced a lot of damage. She ponders whether the latter was something to which her "Jewish upbringing made me particularly vulnerable." At services and Bible study groups, she found herself thinking, "Jews don't say this. A Jew would never say this."[33]

Steve Maltz

Steve Maltz was brought up in a secular Reform Jewish home. He did become *bar-mitzvah*, but without any religious conviction. After a number of years of searching, he became a Christian in 1987. He has written nineteen books, including *How the Church Lost the Way* and his latest, *Hebraic Church*. In his books he argues for the church to abandon what he calls "Greek thinking" and return to "Hebraic thinking." He promotes the idea that the church should stop celebrating feasts with "no biblical derivation" and observe the biblical calendar.

---

30 Ibid., 24.
31 Ibid., 90–91,103.
32 Caplin, *Confessions of a Jewish Skeptic*, 64.
33 Ibid., ii, 8.

> The biblical *modi'im*,[34] that have been largely ignored by the church as part of a campaign to sever themselves from their true Jewish (Hebraic) roots, as a blessing and a regular aid to prompt our memories of the awesome acts of God in biblical history.[35]

Commenting that the early church met as a body of believers, not a "seeker-friendly place for evangelism," because the Great Commission commands the church to "go out and make disciples," so that Paul and the other apostles shared the gospel out in the marketplaces, synagogues and streets, Maltz suggests that :

> Hebraic church should be a place where like-minded believers grow together, worship together and exercise their gifts. It is also a place of discipleship, as what can be more exciting for a new believer than witnessing the blessings of Christians coming together in expectation.[36]

Maltz takes a dim view of the church's history of relating to Jewish people:

> . . . the church has spent most of the last 1900 years not just severing itself from anything Jewish, but relentlessly persecuting the Jewish people themselves, in an on-going airbrushing of history.[37]

. . . and persistently argues that the churches need to seriously engage with the Old Testament, take a good, hard look at the biblical feasts and reject replacement theology.

Although three of these sources are Americans, living in America, they do share thoughts and feelings that are consonant with the interview data, so are included in small measure. More importantly, they provide important triangulation on UK authors and the research data.

Academic Studies

Pauline Kollontai has published three articles about MJs,[38] one of which is based upon research interviews conducted in the UK. In this article,

---

34 Hebrew: appointed times. Used to refer to the biblical feasts in Leviticus 23.
35 Maltz, *Hebraic Church*, 143.
36 Ibid., 160.
37 Ibid., 175.
38 Kollontai ("Messianic Jews," "Between Judaism and Christianity," "Women as Leaders").

she reported on many of the concerns JBYs have in coming to faith: the church's centuries of hostility to Jews, lack of understanding, non-acceptance, prejudice, inability to express their Jewishness, pressure to renounce identity, lack of appreciation, and recognition of Jewish roots. "The opinions expressed show a combination of reasons why Messianic Jews do not choose to join the Christian church."[39]

Simon Dein published a detailed ethnographic study conducted in a BMJA London-based congregation of MJs that also used Chain Referral Sampling (CRS). Dein reports that many of the congregation members also attend "local churches (many of which are Pentecostal) for worship." Most of the Jewish members show strong Jewish identity and come from a more ethnic than religious Jewish upbringing. Like some of the voices on Kollontai's study, many of Dein's respondents speak of an emptiness in Judaism that was answered and filled by belief in Yeshua.[40] However, Dein's study makes no other comment on church membership or attendance.

Esther Foreman wrote a master's dissertation, based upon a number of detailed interviews and a small quantitative survey in two London-based MJish congregations, in which she argued that MJism has created a space between Judaism and Christianity. In this space, she concludes, exist a number of small but independent groups, each with clear group identities and membership, that partake in ritual and lifestyle events in slightly different ways despite their identical theological beliefs and similar charismatic service models. The survey results showed, however, that the groups failed to define a consistent identity for JBYs or Gentile Christians.[41]

Although not a formal academic work, John Fieldsend's *Messianic Jews—Challenging Church and Synagogue* contains a number of interviews and testimonies in which a repeated theme was that, although the church had much to offer, it was like a well-made jacket that didn't fit across the shoulders.[42] A number of informants—some of whom also featured in Dein's work—related varying degrees of discomfort in church: a lack of understanding of Jewishness, a desire for Jewish culture and context, fellowship with other Jews.

---

39 Kollontai, "Between Judaism and Christianity," 4–5.
40 Dein, "Becoming a Fulfilled Jew," 84, 86–7.
41 Foreman, "Messianic Judaism," 80–1.
42 Fieldsend, *Messianic Jews*, 94.

The Main Interviews

A bank of interviews were conducted over a period of eighteen months, in person, by email, or using VOIP software over the Internet. The ages of the respondents ranged from late teens to over sixty, with the highest concentration in the 45–60 age group. The gender distribution was primarily, but not overwhelmingly male. The split by gender seemed to reflect both the gender balance in church and congregation leadership, and the degree to which people felt inclined to give their time for the interview. The split between Jewish and Gentile respondents was almost equal. For this purpose, the definition "Jewish" included those of a Jewish heritage or family background and those who identified in some way as Jewish. Some respondents had a Jewish background but identified as Gentile, so are classified accordingly. The label "Gentile" is used at this stage simply to identify respondents without any Jewish background or heritage rather than "Christian," since many or all of the Jewish respondents would be classed as Christian by the mainstream Jewish world. Those interviewed included both members and leaders of churches or congregations, as well as some academics and others involved in para-church or mission organizations.

Interview Overview

This overview of the interview data groups conversation fragments into common subject areas that make it easier to identify some of the emerging themes.

Many of the Jewish respondents seemed relieved to have someone to tell about their feelings and frustrations, even if positive, as if no-one had ever asked before, or perhaps no-one who understood the issues from a Jewish point of view—perhaps enabling a little lifting of Jewish guilt. Of further interest is that a few Gentile respondents also seemed to experience something of the same emotions.

Self-identity

Statements of identity covered a large spectrum of possible identities and identity-related issues. Some informants immediately proclaimed a firm Gentile identity, with no suggestion of any Jewish heritage or connection, while others declared an unambiguous Jewish identity. Discussion of what exactly was meant by a "Jewish identity" usually came later in the interview. Aware of some of those issues, however, some informants qualified their answers. A significant number of the informants claim either full or partial

Jewish identity based on paternal descent or "Jewish heritage" rather than the Orthodox Jewish definition of maternal descent. Opinions as to whether Jewish identity mattered to them personally varied—some were passionate about being Jewish, while others either dismissed its importance or attempted to deny that it existed.

Jasper, for example, who works full-time for a Jewish missionary agency, sees himself as unambiguously Jewish, insisting that "I won't allow the rabbis to define my identity." He thinks that attempts by the mainstream Jewish community to deny someone's Jewish identity are funny and he is very proud of being Jewish. Claude, on the other hand, despite being halachically Jewish, claimed that "Jewishness has no part of my self-identity"; it is irrelevant to his ministry in the church. Sherry's father was Jewish, but she fiercely defines herself as Gentile; Pip's father, too, was Jewish, yet she openly describes herself as Jewish. Walter talks of "a tenuous non-proven Jewish ancestry" that he would love to be able to prove; while Bethany relates a "family fear of Jewish identity," lest anyone should find out. Carl, a church leader in training, says that he has both a strong emotional connection and a strong sense of belonging to the Jewish people, but admits that he is "not very Jewishly observant."

Calling or Vocation

A number of the informants expressed a sense of calling or vocation, either in church leadership or in mission outreach to Jewish people. Quite a few informants are ordained clergy in a variety of denominations; some are serving in churches, while others work for Jewish missionary agencies. Some see themselves as bridge-builders, as advocates for improving the experience of JBYs in church and as agents to be involved in Jewish-Christian relations. Others recognize a calling to serve in the church, but hide or conceal their Jewish identity to avoid what they see as a glass ceiling for Jewish clergy, an institutional anti-Semitism that would hinder their ministry or career.

Background and Family

The informants come from a wide range of family backgrounds. Jasper, Bethany, and Grant come from families of Holocaust survivors; Jasper's home environment was secular and Pip was brought up as an atheist. Amanda has lived and worked in Israel, so Jewish background and culture feel very normal to her. A Christian upbringing is reported by a number of informants—some including a Jewish heritage and some as children in ministry or missionary families. Claude is very definite about having had no Jewish upbringing, while Bethany's family has experienced a lot of anti-Semitism over the years and so denied their Jewish identity. Rachel, Carl, and Shana were all brought up in MJish families. Stephan and Adam grew up in Reform Judaism. Grant, although brought up as an agnostic and becoming a Christian when he was forty, had no interest in his Jewish identity until four years ago when visiting Israel.

Position

The position of church leader—either the minister or senior leader, or an elder—is well represented (sixteen out of fifty-two) among the informant constituency. Sherry, Benjamin, Walter, Scott, Tom, Judah, Bea, and Bill are, or have been, in leadership in Messianic congregations or fellowships. Past or present workers or leaders with Jewish missionary agencies are also well represented (nine). Carl, Edward, and Serena are trainee church ministers. Many informants either attend, or are members of, churches; while Felix, Andrew, Charles, Brian, and Rosa are also academics. Iain and George are involved in interfaith work or leadership. Micah and Ryan are university students. A degree of overlap between positions is inevitable as some of the informants are, or have been, in several over time.

Church Experience

Although some of the respondents reported being comfortable in church, the majority of these comments were quite negative in tone. On the positive side, Stephan, who is about to start training for ordination in the Church of England, reported that he had been "well received" and was "active in many roles" within his church: a large, active, and charismatic Anglican church. Micah gave the somewhat half-hearted comment that, "it can be alright in church sometimes," although Shana noted that "there are very few good churches around." Less encouraging, Micah also complained that "sermons and messages lack understanding" with misguided and erroneous teaching, and reported that he had sometimes been met with a discouraging silence or "open rudeness." Rather more bluntly, but speaking for more than herself, Juliana said that "Jewish church experience can be very bad."

Bethany admitted that she "always felt like an outsider" in church and that she had been "put out of ministry positions" once her Jewish identity became known. Putting fairly strong cards on the table, Walter said that, in his experience, "anti-Semitism in the church is rising" and that there is very often a marked "anti-Israel attitude"; he blames this on replacement theology. Less aggressively, Hilary's assessment is that the church is too far from both Jesus and its Jewish roots; that it has lost its history, teaching and understanding of God. She and Jean agreed that "there's a lot of replacement theology in the church." Felix, a MJish scholar and activist, reports that, during a time of prayer in a meeting he was leading at a church, he opened his eyes to find a Gentile member of the congregation about to feel his head to look for horns.

Hugh feels that the dividing wall is much in evidence in the mainstream church: "Jewish Christians do not receive a special welcome . . . Gentile Christians do not rejoice at having a Jewish Christian in their midst."[43]

Church-Judaism Conflict

A number of respondents felt that there was conflict between the church and Judaism. Hilary, a Jew whose family escaped from Austria just after the *Anschluss*, but who has been in church for more than thirty years, pointed out that the celebration of communion had been so completely divorced from its original Jewish context—Passover—that "people have no idea why the Lamb of God is important." For George, a JBY who is now an Anglican priest, one of the conflicts is "the sense of sacred and secular space." So much of Judaism, he explained, happens at home—so that all of life is lived in the presence of God, while "we can go to church, we can have our sacred space, but when we come home it is definitely a secular space." For Felix, the church's attitudes to *Shabbat*, *Torah* and idolatry are all areas of open conflict.

Jewish Experience

Experience of Jewish people in general, and of JBYs in particular, among the Gentile respondents was quite varied. Wendy—an ordained Church of England priest—said that, although she had met enthusiasts for both Judaism and Christian Zionism, she had never

---

43 Montefiore, *Looking Afresh*, 45.

encountered a Jewish convert in any of her churches. Ralph, a minister in a popular central London independent church added that:

> Jewish identity in church is not particularly relevant for [us]. There are no prejudices or anti-Semitism in this congregation, but the fact is we have -- no regular attenders from the Synagogue or Messianic churches. We would, of course, gladly welcome such believers if they made their home here, but . . . converted Jews usually choose to gather with fellow Messianic believers in Christ, as this may be more comfortable for them.

In both cases, the use of the term "convert" may show a certain attitude to JBYs, and the latter comment acknowledges that church may not be a comfortable place for them. Jeffrey, a Free Church pastor, has a number of informal family friendships with Jewish families and has worked alongside the Jewish chaplain in a university chaplaincy team. Oscar, another Free Church pastor, is currently friends with a Jewish family, and his children have attended a Jewish faith school. Edward, a trainee priest, has only ever met "a couple of Jews," but Tiffany has attended a MJish congregation and visited Israel. Quentin, on the other hand, knows, and has worked with, many Jewish people; Amanda has lived and worked in Israel. Nevis and Clement, too, have had significant contact with Jewish thought and JBYs.

The background of Jewish respondents also covered quite an extensive range. Pip has many Jewish relatives, while Stephan admitted that his Judaism was "very much cultural-social-ethnic rather than religious" and he "stopped practicing Judaism after my *bar-mitzvah* once it ceased to be compulsory." Juliana still regularly *davens*[44] the synagogue prayer services and observes the biblical festivals, while several JBYs brought up in MJish contexts are familiar with, and still sometimes keep, the rituals of their upbringing. Randall, George and others still keep some elements of the *kabbalat Shabbat*[45] service on a Friday evening, and lighting candles at the start of *Shabbat* happens in some respondents' homes.

Fellowship Groups

A number of the respondents, both Jewish and Gentile, belong to fellowship groups as well as churches. Hilary and Jean attend the bi-

---

44 A Yiddish verb meaning to recite the prayers in the formal liturgy of the *Siddur*.
45 Hebrew: welcoming *Shabbat*.

weekly group run by George on a Tuesday morning. All the attendees have "a strong Jewish interest" although not all the group members are Jewish. Jean explains that they "look at things from a Jewish point of view." Hilary adds that the group tries to keep some elements of the biblical feasts. George confirms that the group usually keeps Passover, although they can't do that every year as it's "difficult to be a church minister and run Easter and do Passover at the same time."

The British Messianic Jewish Alliance serves as an umbrella for a number of fellowship groups that meet once or twice a month on a Saturday afternoon. Each group has a leader and a Hebrew name, but the BMJA insist that all their members must be full members of a church that they attend on a regular basis—the fellowship groups are an add-on, not intended to replace church or be a free standing MJish congregation. Sherry and Bea have led BMJA fellowship groups; other respondents are, or have been, BMJA connected.

Church Attended

A majority of the respondents attend church on a regular basis. While location clearly plays a part in the choice available, the range of churches attended is considerable. The Church of England—both in and outside London, both charismatic and traditional—is quite popular, while Baptist, FIEC,[46] and several flavors of independent evangelical church were mentioned. Pentecostal churches and healing ministries scored a couple of hits, while one MJish congregation and an independent Messianic fellowship (both meeting weekly on *Shabbat*) were also listed. Many of these churches are majority-white, although several have various ethnic groupings—such as African, Caribbean, Polish or sometimes students!—in the congregation; none have any significant Jewish membership except the MJish congregation. Randall reports only one other Jewish person in his church; Quentin thinks there are two or three in his church. Olive, whose church is in a very Jewish area, says that her church and minister have very good relations with the local synagogues and sometimes make a connection to the Jewish feasts in the church teaching and calendar. Most of the other churches are not in areas of any significant Jewish population.

Several of the Jewish respondents do not attend church. Often this follows some dispute with a church over some Jewish practice or principle. One respondent was not allowed to play in a church

---

46 The Federation of Independent Evangelical Churches.

worship band because they kept *Shabbat*; several respondents have been warned off discussing their Jewishness on the grounds that "we don't do that here."

A number of the Jewish respondents are also ordained ministers (in several denominations) and experience various levels of conflict between their Christian calling and duty of service, and their personal preferences as Jews. Some resolve, or intend to resolve, this by working to make the church more friendly and accommodating to JBYs; others report a glass ceiling within their denomination structure that actively Jewish ministers cannot seem to pass.

Ethnicity

A number of the church leader interviews approached the questions about Jewish identity after looking at the more general question of ethnicity in church. These leaders were asked whether they had experience with ethnic minorities—that is, non-white or non-standard-UK population—within their churches, either on an occasional or regular basis.

Serena, a younger minister in a Pentecostal church and herself from a Jewish heritage, explained that her church was very Jesus-focussed so welcomed everyone regardless of background—their ethnicity doesn't matter: everyone is welcomed and loved in the same way. While Serena's church might recognise someone's ethnicity by their appearance or speech, they wouldn't expect to offer any special support. Carol, who leads a charismatic and healing ministry church, was puzzled by the question—as if to say, why would anyone's ethnicity make their need of salvation, healing and deliverance any different? Ivor "never thought of the need to protect ethnicity or identity," but said that his church—a majority-white urban Baptist church—had "a high acceptance of diversity" and would be "surprised if anyone felt under cultural threat." They have had some visitors from Africa attending services in traditional dress and they were well accepted, with both groups feeling comfortable. Jeffrey felt that his church would "welcome some diversity" and said that physical appearance would probably be the most likely clue to an ethnicity. "It is based on relationship," Walter noted: "speaking to people rather than looking to see what you recognize."

In terms of how to help people with an ethnicity settle down in a church, Jeffrey's church want to make everyone feel included and part of what is going on; they specialize in providing explanations for what is happening. As they are a Free Church, there is much less formality and ritual, to explain in a more relaxed atmosphere. The only special provision they make for an identifiable group is that they feed students. Serena's church will offer special support to anyone who seems to be having trouble belonging to the church which would include people from an ethnic background. Walter's congregation only take special measures with Jewish people, whom they always encourage to express their Jewishness by wearing a *kipa*[47] or *tallit*[48] during services.

Jewish Identity

The category of Jewish Identity—generally answers to the questions, "What is Jewish Identity?" "How would you define it?"—had a wide range of answers that ranged from what the respondents thought was the factual or legal answer to the question "Who is a Jew?" to what makes a Jewish identity. Perhaps this illustrates Quentin's suggestion that the church is confused about Jewish identity.

Sherry and Quentin report that by Orthodox *halacha* a person is only Jewish if their mother is orthodoxly Jewish, or if they convert to Judaism under the auspices of an Orthodox *bet din*,[49] and that is the only strict and portable answer.[50] Sherry also concedes that the State of Israel's definition (following the Nuremberg Laws of the Third Reich) of having any one of four grandparents who were Jewish in order to make *aliyah*[51] was in conflict with that. She added that there

---

47 A "*kipa*," also known as a "yarmulke," is worn by Jewish men on their heads as a sign of God's authority over them. Its color and material are often an indicator of denominational or religious affiliation.
48 The "*tallit*" is the prayer shawl worn by Jewish men during prayer services. Its basic design—as a rectangle—allows the *mitzvah* (command) of *tzitzit* (tassels) to be fulfilled as there is a long tassel in each of the four corners.
49 A *bet din*, literally a "house of judgement," is a Jewish religious/legal court.
50 Several respondents pointed out that an Orthodox conversion is not always portable, depending on where it was done. The London *Bet Din* doesn't automatically accept all Israeli Orthodox conversions and similarly, the Israeli Rabbinate won't always accept all UK Orthodox conversions.
51 The process of becoming a citizen of the State of Israel. From the Hebrew root עלה, "to go up or ascend," Jewish tradition holds that Israel is holier than all other nations, so that one ascends in holiness when going to live in Israel. Similarly, one always "goes up" to Jerusalem from anywhere in Israel, both geographically because Jerusalem is in the Judean mountains, and spiritually because Jerusalem is the "city of the great king" (Psalm 48:2 and Matthew 5:35), the "apple of God's eye" (Zechariah 2:8).

are many One-Jewish-Grandparent Jews in the Diaspora, some of whom do identity with, and are accepted by, the Jewish community. Juliana agrees that matrilineal descent is the Orthodox norm, while Clement insists that Jewish identity can only come from the Bible, with Bethany adding that biblical identity is always paternal, and Jasper that the rabbinic definition is unbiblical. Adam, himself *halachically* Jewish, feels that one fully Jewish parent or grandparent is enough.

Another focus of attention for Jewish identity is community acceptance. Scott speaks of "acknowledged participation" in a Jewish community and "recognition by at least some members of that community that you are a member as well." Nevis affirms the importance of "a strong community identity"; it is difficult to be a Jew in isolation. Adam feels that he is quite flexible about Jewish identity and self-identifies as Jewish; he doesn't need community affirmation. Iain, too, supports the principle of self-definition. Bea disagrees; she says that a Jew is someone who is seen and accepted by the community as Jewish. While Juliana says that "Jewish identity is inescapable," she adds that, "community affirmation is important, particularly for converts." Oscar, an independent church pastor, suggests that "Judaism is cultural" and that "Jews can shape what it means for them to be Jewish." Serena agrees; for her, "Judaism can be just cultural without any faith structure." Benjamin, based on his experience growing up in a Jewish community and leading a MJish congregation, says that Jews have a Jewish identity "even if they don't know that they are Jewish or have had no Jewish upbringing." Iain points out that "the church can't do that: a hidden or unknown Christian, an unbelieving Christian."[52]

Another thread that seemed important to a number of respondents was that of the questions of covenant and choice. Stephan proposes that "Jewish identity stems from the Abrahamic covenant," supported by Keith, who is definite that "Jews are chosen, loved and disciplined by God." Hector suggests that Jewish identity is "a matter of belonging to the family," while Randall talks about Jews being "part of a tribal system" and that Jewish identity depends on having performed certain ritual steps: circumcision (although at eight days old, that is hardly a matter of choice), becoming *bar-* or *bat-mitzvah* and marrying under a *chupah*.[53] Ryan, a student and

---

52 That is, someone being a Christian who doesn't know that they are or denies belief in or knowledge of Christianity.
53 It is traditional to get married under a *chupah*, or canopy to symbolize the new home where the married couple will live together and God's covering

relatively young in acknowledging his Jewish identity, talks about "a choice to express being part of the covenant." Juliana says that "Jewish identity has a responsibility, a shared destiny as a people" and that Jews identify as Jews through the *Torah* and by obeying the *mitzvot*.[54]

Jewish Identity Manifestation

This is another large set of responses that arose mainly from how respondents thought Jewish identity was shown or manifested.

Physical appearance generated a number of similar reports. Hector says that in his experience he has seen Jews who had no visible sign of their Jewish identity, but were "proudly Jewish." Others he has met were "wearing clothing styles inherited from previous generations: the whole Hassidic package—dressed in black, hat, *peyot*,[55] etc." Benjamin agrees that Jewish identity "is not always manifest," while Lucy—who lives in an area of high Jewish population—sees lots of Jews "wearing typical ultra-Orthodox clothing." Amanda, who is also in a Jewish area, comments that "Jews of different synagogues each wear their own uniform." Ivor, too, suggests that Jewish people can often wear "particular items of clothing." Perhaps less kindly, Clement picks up on *peyot* and prayer shawls—both of which he considers unbiblical—and notes that Jews "can be easily caricatured." Adam echoes the concern about caricature, but says that "external signs are no guide to the inside person." Other signs—such as dietary issues, keeping the *Torah*, speaking or knowing some Hebrew, traditional food, a sense of humor, scholarship and studying skills, being medical or a musician —were also mentioned by a number of respondents.

Keeping the festivals and *Shabbat* is another frequently mentioned observation. Nevis says that "keeping *Shabbat* and attending synagogue are obvious manifestations of Jewish identity," and Bea would expect to see "some degree of festival keeping" in Jewish people. Keith suggested that the feasts provide a "community

---

over them. It is mentioned in the Bible (Psalm 19:6 and Joel 2:16) and in the rabbinic writings. Practically, it is a piece of cloth supported on four poles; a *tallit* or prayer shawl may be used.

54 Hebrew: commandments.
55 *Peyot* is the Hebrew word for the (usually curled) long uncut strands of hair in front of the ears worn by men to fulfill the commandment, "You shall not round off the side-growth on your head, or destroy the side-growth of your beard" (Leviticus 19:27). *Peyot* are an exclusively male observance.

framework." In that vein, Iain feels that Jews show signs of "belonging to a people" and "being connected to the Land [of Israel]," having "a strong sense of continuity and rootedness." Avi believes that just reading a Jewish newspaper may help Jewish people stay connected with the community.

Juliana expresses concern that "Jews tend to mimic their host cultures," so may risk losing their identity. She feels that Jewish people should live *Torah* fully, "but appropriately for their host culture," adding that JBYs should also live *Torah* "appropriately for the church." Keith is also concerned that Jewish people can be "suspicious of Gentiles" and display something of a "pilgrim mentality at times." Olive has noticed that Jewish people often have a "reserved manner." Grant, himself quite new to his Jewish identity and meeting a fairly stiff wall of opposition in the church he and his wife attend, asserts that there are lots of "Jews hidden in church, without any thought to the relevance and importance of their Jewish identity." Benjamin responds that Jews who "discover" their Jewish identity become learners—sometimes quite obsessively as they race to connect with their Jewish heritage!

Jewish Behavior

Alongside the above manifestations of Jewish identity, a few respondents comment particularly about Jewish behavior. Adam speaks about an "undefinable but unmistakable behavior" and Avi touches on "Jewish temperament and behavior," but Lucy says that while the "majority of Jews are indistinguishable from other people," there is a "minority who can be arrogant and rude." She wonders if this is because they are so used to being told they are "chosen," they have developed an attitude; Keith suggests it is a typical "Israeli Sabra[56] behavior: loud, brash and talking a lot." Carol, who has been involved with deliverance ministry and spiritual counselling for many years, reports that "some Jews have behavioral issues due to identity denial or suppression."

Jewish Identity after Coming to Faith

This block of responses was triggered by questions such as "Does Jewish identity continue after coming to faith in Messiah and, if so,

---

56 Native-born Israelis are often called "sabras," so named after a type of desert cactus that grows in the wilderness areas of the country, and has bright flowers but long and stiff prickles all over.

how?" Apart from one ambiguous "yes and no" answer, all the other responses were various forms of "yes." However, although there were lots of positive explanations about how this should be seen, it was also clear that that "yes" was a theoretical (and juridical) answer as most respondents then qualified their answer with laments about the way that church makes it very difficult, if not impossible, to actualize that identity in practice.

Juliana started by asking "How can anyone ask this question?," adding that "the fact that people do is a matter of concern." It should be a given—as Sherry points out: "circumcision cannot be reversed"—and, echoing Rabbi Adin Steinsaltz: "Once a Jew, always a Jew."[57] Lucy is certain that "a JBY remains Jewish," while Serena adds that "Jews don't become Gentile in order to become Christians." Adam agrees, that when someone becomes a believer in Messiah, there is no change for Jewish or Gentile identity, "both identities remain." Jasper is adamant that "Galatians 3:28[58] doesn't affect Jewish or Gentile identity." Not only is "the distinction between Jew and Gentile clearly maintained" (Clement) but, just as "Jesus is still Jewish" according to Carl, Benjamin asserts that "God wants JBYs to be Jews."

Quentin asserts that many JBYs in church have "no visible sign as they are fully assimilated and, despite a hidden or lingering desire to identify, have no means by which to do so." A Jewish woman in his church even felt it necessary to ask the vicar's permission before doing family genealogical research. Quentin feels that the church "has been really unhelpful, pushing an assimilationist agenda and replacement theology, and denying JBYs permission for identity markers." Lucy says that the "church has expectations of 'normal' Christian behavior" and Bea reports that "Christian groups expect a JBY to drop kosher rules." Carl agrees that "observance won't be easy in church." Hector regrets that, in a church context, many JBYs "drop every Jewish practice and value"; he thinks this is "a great pity, a great mistake." Ryan confirms that JBYs "may suppress their Jewish identity to conform to church." When he became a believer, John reports, his new church and his foster parents "strongly urged

---

57 Steinsaltz, *We Jews*, 53. Drawing on traditional rabbinic interpretations of several Bible verses, Steinsaltz argues that, although a Jew may be a "good Jew" or a "bad Jew" it is impossible to lose Jewish identity because this is not a matter of human choice, but divine choice. However bad or apostate a Jew may be, it is always possible to repent.

58 "There is neither Jew nor Gentile, male nor female, slave nor free, for you are all one in Messiah Yeshua."

upon me that now I was no longer Jewish: I had joined God's new Israel, the church, and I should put my Jewishness behind me."[59]

On the other hand, Nevis observes that "a JBY may become more Jewish than before coming to faith; a JBY's Jewish identity can be awoken and appreciated." His position is colored, perhaps, by the dual observation that "in principle, observance is a matter of choice," but at the same time, there is "a mission imperative for greater observance." As will be seen later, there are a number of respondents who feel that the only purpose for Jewish identity is to provide a vehicle for evangelizing other Jewish people. Amanda suggests that "not many JBYs were religious before coming to faith," and argues that "it is important for there to be JBYs in the church." When JBYs move into their Jewish identity, Nevis explains, they can become very possessive of *Torah* and Jewish tradition: "These are my stories, my things." "Keeping kosher and observing circumcision," Clement notes, become important where they were not before, and Juliana stresses that "keeping *Shabbat*" is essential for many.

Olive reports that there are some church contexts where JBYs feel that it is not safe to identify as Jews. Jeffrey feels that "the church probably wouldn't encourage any continuity," while Grant speaks of "strong pressure to gentilize." It is easy to become frustrated and hurt when the church does not support or encourage one's vision and identity. Amanda adds that it is "difficult for Jewish people to show their faith in Yeshua."

Although a significant number of respondents said that JBYs should be not only allowed, but encouraged, to teach the church about their own stories, the Jewish roots of the Christian faith and Jewish understandings of Scripture—that this is a key part of a JBY's calling and *raison d'être*—Juliana reports that "JBYs can be really hammered in church for being JBYs," while Avi says that it can be "like living in the twilight zone." Stephan has been quite active in his church, teaching and leading groups and services, but as discussed above, Bethany and others have been excluded from ministry because of their Jewishness.

---

59 Fieldsend, *Messianic Jews*, 33.

One Law Position

Several of the respondents either taught or endorsed the "One Law"[60] position; these views were expressed as part of their response to manifestations of Jewish identity after coming to faith in Messiah. Walter relates that in the congregation he leads, "Gentile congregants are expected to keep the kosher dietary laws, to keep *Shabbat* and to observe the biblical feasts." He asserts that "Christian identity is in doing these things." Tom's congregation is criticized by "local Hebrew Christian elements closely bonded to churches" who don't like Tom and his congregation teaching Gentiles to observe *Shabbat* and the biblical feasts.

Standard Church View

Oscar, clearly puzzled by the very question of a continuing Jewish identity, gives what he feels is the "standard" church view. He says that following Hebrews 8:13, "the first covenant is obsolete," so Judaism is only "a cultural lifestyle" and "not a living faith." Adopting a supersessionist tone, he says that "to be a true Jew, one must accept Jesus as Messiah; to be a true part of the body of Israel, one must know Christ." Rejecting any other options, following a tight evangelical interpretation of John 14:6, he insists that "relationship with God is through Jesus alone." Avi, who has had forty or more years' experience ministering in the church, reports a typical church attitude to be, "We're not Jewish, so we don't want all this Jewish stuff." Felix relates how he had almost been physically refused entry to a church as a visiting speaker until rescued by the minister who had invited him. Jenny complains that:

> Church involvement through Sunday school and Youth Group supports our teaching the kids about Jesus but not really in his context; a fact I find baffling. It's as if Jesus was *not* a Jewish man who came from a Jewish family; and talked, ate and worshipped as a Jew and spouted Jewish Scripture.[61]

---

60 The "One Law" position teaches that Jews and Gentiles alike are all obligated to follow the rules of Jewish law as laid out in the *Torah*. This is based on verses such as "One law and one rule shall be for you and for the stranger who sojourns with you" (Numbers 15:16), taking "you" as the Jewish people and "the stranger" as Gentiles grafted into Israel (as per Romans 11:17–24).

61 Chandler, *Jew in the Pew*, 45.

Jewish Attitudes to Yeshua

From her background of living and working with Jewish people in the church in the UK and in Israel, Amanda explains that it is difficult for a Jewish person to trust and have faith in someone they do not know. She added that, "the gospel—as preached by the church—is deficient for Jewish people" as it has been stripped of its Jewish values and context.[62] Oddly, she says, "most Jewish people are proud of Yeshua as one of their own," but are strongly put off having anything to do with church because of "historically bad behavior by the Gentile church"—referring to the various expulsions of Jews from many countries in Europe, the Inquisition, pogroms and forced conversions, and the Holocaust—and "currently bad attitudes by the Gentile church"; the latter including connivance with or participation in anti-Semitism, and particularly towards the State of Israel in such ways as the BDS movement.[63]

Church Jewish Encouragement

These responses generally came from questions about the way in which the church has or has not encouraged JBYs. They roughly split into three groups.

Hector, who leads a church in central London, admits that his church has celebrated a Passover meal and had some Jewish Roots preaching and teaching, but feels that the church is "very novice at this" and doesn't do much to encourage JBYs. Randall, who has a very strong and visible Jewish identity, says that the church should be "more Jewish-friendly." Stephan feels tolerated, but not encouraged, while he feels "the church looks on JBYs as an interesting fringe addition." Edward, who is very mission and youth focussed, admits that "the church could afford to incorporate some Jewish stuff," but worries that "Jewish stuff may be confusing to unchurched people."

Avi, a Jewish man in ordained church ministry, reports that, in his experience, JBYs can be encouraged to preach, can be selected for ministry, and can be licensed as missionaries. It is, nevertheless, diplomatic, he says, to play one's Jewish identity down to avoid

---

62 The main theme of David Stern's book, *Restoring the Jewishness of the Gospel*.

63 Boycott, Divestment and Sanctions: a movement that seeks to influence the political situation in the Middle East, and Israel in particular, by boycotting Israeli products, divesting in companies that do business with or in Israel, and the imposition of sanctions against Israel and Israeli citizens.

being blocked. A second respondent, who wants to remain anonymous on this particular issue, speaks about a glass ceiling, as if the church doesn't feel comfortable trusting JBYs in senior positions. Another anonymous source with a strong Jewish identity reported having both their application to train for ordination and a subsequent offer to work with that denomination at a regional level refused because of that identity.

Clement feels that "the Gentile church has really failed to keep Paul's mandate in Romans" and "should not discourage Jewish identity in JBYs," but instead "accept Jewish identity as it is" as "Jewish identity provides an enduring context for Jesus." Micah agrees, confessing that "the church has not encouraged me" and that "some people try to discourage me" in expressing Jewish identity. He says that "the church does not encourage any visible manifestations" and does not "understand Old Testament rules and their contemporary currency." Going further, John writes about many JBYs "who have been placed under great pressure to give up their keeping of Jewish festivals if they are to be accepted into church membership" and notes that serious questions have been raised within church leadership about his own observances.[64]

A number of churches allow certain Jewish events. Passover demonstrations, usually led by groups such as Jews for Jesus, or evangelistic concerts—such as those given by Helen Shapiro—are acceptable, as is inviting Jewish mission speakers. Olive's church has hosted Hebrew classes taught by a local rabbi and leads regular church trips to Israel. A few churches are more positive; Quentin's church encourages Jewishness, speaking and teaching about Jewishness and Jewish themes, and supporting visible signs of Jewish identity such as wearing a *kipa*. Quentin says that he would be very keen to interview JBYs in the congregation about their faith during services, but only a few of the respondents would feel comfortable with such attention.

Iain, a senior church leader in the London area, thinks that the church should accept *Shabbat* services and reading from the *Torah*: "church should not only be permissive, but should positively encourage Jewish expressions." However, he feels that "these things are not necessary, they may be good and laudable—an appropriate expression of worship—and honor a continuing sense of Jewish identity." Seeing the need for the church to provide space for JBYs as Jews and, at the same time, maintain a healthy tension and

---

64 Fieldsend, *Messianic Jews*, 20.

relationship between different spaces, he wouldn't want to see isolated Jewish expressions that are not connected. He emphasises the need for congregations to interact and be in communion, where "being in communion doesn't abolish identity."

Denominational Attitudes to Jewish Identity

Not every respondent attends, or has been connected with, a church that is part of a recognized denomination, so some respondents were not asked how their denomination felt about JBYs in church; others ignored the question.

Nevis, who is part of the Church of England, has encountered a range of opinion: "some would take no position and would not want to offend; some would be uncomfortable with Jewish identity and would want to negate it; some would want a JBY to reject all Jewish identity and practice; some would not want a JBY to believe in Yeshua." Avi's experience is that most denominations are positive about JBYs, although he was concerned that some denominations have become over-politicized. Maria's denomination is silent or neutral about JBYs and Jewish identity, while Ryan reported that "Calvinist and Reformed churches are bad about Jewish identity and New Frontiers are deeply into replacement theology." While his current church is an exception to the pattern, he admitted that "many JBYs in my church are very Christianized."

Attitude to Christian Zionism

When respondents were asked about their attitude towards Christian Zionism, the majority of the responses were negative. Only Walter openly said that he was a Christian Zionist, although a number of the respondents said that they had a degree of personal sympathy with the underlying Zionist cause.

Hector doesn't "have a problem with the Christian Zionist agenda," but sees Christian Zionists as a mainly Gentile or Gentile-led set of groups and doesn't pass their material on within the church he leads. The idea of Gentile leadership is quite widely held; Avi, Jeffrey, and Ivor—each from very different church contexts—agree, as do two of the Messianic congregation leaders, Benjamin and Walter. A common feeling is that Christian Zionism is a distraction —a view shared by Adam, Jeffrey, Amanda, and Serena, all of whom are church leaders—and Benjamin, Walter, Bea complain that it is not generally well received by church leaders. Jasper added that all pro-Israel ministries are a hindrance in church contexts—his church won't tolerate a PFI⁶⁵ group—and Ivor has actively discouraged Christian Zionism in his church. Iain went as far as to say that "Christian Zionism can be profoundly unhelpful" and can be "a Gentile obsession."

Christian Zionists were accused of "simply using Israel and Jewish identity for their own script," not doing any serious study of their own, "missing the timing and purpose of the gospel," and even "obscuring the sharing of the gospel." Carol and Keith—again, from very different churches—feel that a line should be drawn between Jews and Israel, with "Israel being incompatible with ministry to individuals." Serena comments that Christian Zionists can be very zealous for their cause; sometimes overpoweringly so. Bea reports that Christian Zionism often "seems more political than theological" and can sometimes "engage in aggressive lobbying."

Several voices, however, were more positive in part. Felix said that "Zionism is the right thing from Scripture"; Amanda feels that "the essential message—that Israel is there by divine right—is true." Sherry reports that she has had some good support from Christian Zionists, but that "they don't respond well to attack from critics."

Roger and Tom, two elders of a local independent evangelical church expressed concern over Steve Maltz's books and teachings. They are under pressure from a number of activists in their church to adopt keeping the Jewish feasts; they described one woman who whenever she reads from the Bible always prefaces it with a prayer in Hebrew[66] that they and the rest of the church don't understand. The church has no members with a Jewish heritage and the eldership is worried that the situation may disturb the congregation as a whole and possibly cause a split in the church, although they think the activists have little support.

Work as a Missionary

A number of the respondents have worked or still work for missionary organizations that target the Jewish people. Some of these are Jewish, while others are not. Naturally, they feel strongly that mission—reaching Jewish individuals with the gospel and

---

65 Prayer for Israel—see "Prayer for Israel", accessed 3:27pm 19Aug16, http://www.prayer4i.org/
66 In all likelihood, this is probably nothing more alarming than one of the standard Jewish blessings before reading from the *Torah*, but Tom and Roger feel it is out of place in a standard Gentile church context without either an explanation or a translation being offered.

seeing them come to faith—is their *raison d'être*. Jasper sees his job, his calling in life, as mission: "It's my job to be a witness to the Jewish people." He feels that while the church may take mission in general and mission to Muslims seriously, mission to the Jewish people is unvalued and woefully underfunded. He complains that Jewish mission has a low priority in individual churches and in denominations, and is simply "not attractive to the church." Although he has offered training courses and practical sessions, it is very difficult to get people to attend or churches to host them.

Jewish Reception in Church

This category attracted a very wide range of responses and feeling. While Serena said that "every church should be welcoming," adding that "there shouldn't be any reason why people cannot come," she admitted that "there is a stigma in some churches about Jewish things." Ivor and Keith both hope that JBYs would be met with "love and acceptance." Jasper, speaking as a missionary worker for an organization that believes that JBYs belong in church, and Jeffrey, an independent church pastor, claimed that "Jewish identity is received as any other identity would be." Jasper, although himself Jewish, suggested that "Jewish identity was pretty much irrelevant" and was "just part of the normal baggage." Hilary, too, noted those feelings being held by the church, but in a highly sarcastic tone of voice, indicating her complete disagreement. Bethany confessed that she has long felt "uncomfortable admitting to being a Christian," while that is why Paul's book is titled: *Don't call me Christian*.[67]

Rachel and Grant, among others, reported that there are "several ways that Jewish identity could be received in church." On the positive side, a JBY can be "given a warm welcome and encouraged" (Sherry) or could be "welcomed for who they are" (Lucy). Carl and Avi reported that JBYs "can be loved in church," but warned that they can be "too loved!" Felix reported that he had "been made very welcome in some churches," while Keith suggested that JBYs would be welcomed more in newer types of church and rather less in the older denominations. Oscar, an independent church pastor in an area of low Jewish population, thought that, "A JBY would have an active part to play as a church member." Benjamin, both a mission and congregation leader, who has spoken quite a lot in churches, pointed out the dichotomy that, on the one hand, "Jewish identity is usually

---

67 Liberman and Wasson, *Don't Call Me Christian*.

well received," but on the other hand, "you need to hide Jewish identity to get total acceptance."

More negatively, Bea and Carl pointed out that a JBY—even if relatively ignorant of their Jewish heritage and new in their faith as a believer—can be "deemed an expert on Judaism and the OT." Amanda and Eric confirmed that a JBY can often be put on a pedestal, while Carl and Benjamin both spoke about being the "token Jew" in a church. Adam, Benjamin, and Micah described JBYs "being treated as a trophy" by a church. George commented that "a Jewish convert is a mission success for the church." Sherry agreed that, "a JBY can have a real struggle to survive in church," that it "may be easier to keep a low profile," and even that, "it may be easier to deny being Jewish." Randall reported that he had initially "been received with suspicion" and "felt an outcast," though he later conceded that after a number of years in church, "the church have been very good to me." Shana experienced "suspicion over *Torah* observance," adding that no one tried to understand her position about observing *Torah*, let alone offered any encouragement.

A number of respondents, including clergy, felt that the "clergy are often ignorant about Jewish issues" (Amanda, Quentin, and Carl). Clement said that "clergy can oppose Jewish things and understandings," based on replacement theology, learned attitudes and opinions from the church fathers. Grant spoke of church leaders being very closed and negative. Quentin claimed that many church leaders see Israel and Jewish things as divisive; it is "easier for clergy to go with the flow rather than heading upstream."

Iain shared a senior church leader perspective, starting from the comment that JBYs can "put Gentile Christians in a difficult place." Their existence "messes up Christian-Jewish dialogue," which can make some church leaders impatient, so JBYs can often become the "excluded middle." Iain feels that the strength of Jewish identity is what makes it challenging, as a dual identity is difficult to handle. While aware of the importance of Jewish identity, and affirming that there is a place for JBYs in church, he is concerned about awkwardness and difficulty, asking the question, "What does it mean for the rest of the church?" He feels it is important to be able to say "yes" to JBYs both with and without a continuing Jewish identity, but suggests that JBYs with a continuing Jewish identity need to be the ones who determine whether there is a place for them in church.

Several of the respondents report a bad response to physical signs of Jewish identity. Micah, who "wears a *kipa* and *tzitzit*,"[68] insists that "there are some places that you must hide a Jewish identity." Ryan, who felt comfortable wearing a *kipa* when meeting the author in person, after commenting that "church encourages uniformity" and "isn't receptive to Jews," added that "Jewish appearance [in church] can cause discomfort." Other respondents are less positive. Carl and Benjamin note that "A JBY manifesting Jewish identity in church may have serious repercussions," adding that "a JBY can be kicked out of church once the church knows they are Jewish." Bethany reports that this has happened to her. Juliana had church membership refused and was "expected to repent of being Jewish," leading to her endeavoring to "hide Jewish identity in a church context." Lucy and Bea both explain that "Jewish practice, such as keeping the feasts, is not encouraged." Walter lays out what he sees as the dangers for JBYs: having their Jewishness removed, being paganized, being condemned, and developing self-hate. Carol agrees with Walter's first point, adding that JBYs are "urged to break the kosher dietary laws"[69] and may feel forced to "return to the Synagogue and remain hidden there as secret disciples."

JBYs as Church Leaders

A number of the respondents are church leaders, and reflected both on their own leadership experience and that of others. Adam—an ordained clergyman though not currently serving a church—admits that "even JBY clergy can struggle with church at times." He feels that "JBY clergy are not really accepted by the church" and that "JBY ministry—however good—is simply not recognized." "Jewish identity is seen to be a career/ministry hindrance" and is "hushed up in the same way as gay identity." He worries about the church being "institutionally anti-Semitic," with an "anti-Jewish attitude." Other respondents have already echoed some of the same feelings above.

Iain counters by saying that "there must be no hint of someone being excluded from leadership because of Jewish identity." He feels that, just as church contains a spectrum of Jewish believers, so there must be visible representation for everybody; there must be space for individual identities. He says that he would be perfectly

---

68 The *"tzitzit"* are tassels, worn to fulfil the commandment given in Numbers 15:38–39. They are to be affixed to the corners of a four-cornered garment.
69 Several Jewish respondents reported that they or others they know were challenged, "You're a Christian now, have a ham sandwich!"

comfortable with one of his clergy "wearing a *kipa*" in or out of church, but would insist that they "properly explained why they did so" to their congregation.

Church Accommodation

These responses mainly arose from conversation around what steps the church has taken, or could take, to accommodate JBYs in church.

Maria tells of the PFI group that meets in her church, adding that they have also shown films about Israel and allowed her to speak about the time she spent as a volunteer working in vineyards in Samaria.[70] Hector and Randall have both led Passover meals in churches; Lucy and Carl have attended Passover meals in churches and been at churches that allow someone to speak about Holocaust Memorial Day. Amanda's church holds Hebrew classes and teaches about the Jewish festivals as well as organizing trips to Israel. Olive reports that outside guest speakers from the Jewish world have a novelty value and are well received. Almost all of these accommodations are Israeli or Jewish in nature; they make a distinction between what others may do, but "we" do not. Amanda alone suggests that "church could provide a time for lighting candles on Friday evening," or "have a worship service on *Shabbat*."

Iain suggests that "the mainstream churches have moved beyond assimilation as a policy," but concedes that "there is opposition from a minority," who "try to enforce a rigid definition of identity" based upon "one particular snapshot of tradition."

Church Encouraging Jewish Identity

In contrast to discussion on what accommodations church may have made or could make for JBYs in church, these answers came from conversation around how the church does or could encourage Jewish identity in its JBYs.

Sherry, Jasper, and Avi share their experience that "church does not encourage Jewish identity or practice in any way"; so much so, Sherry adds, that "only a threat to leave might bring change." Jasper agrees that "Jewish identity is discouraged," adding that he left his church for some years over the lack of understanding and communication. Things were "no better when he returned," he remarked, but he felt that he had got better at articulating the issues

---

70 The biblical name for the area known as the West Bank or the settlements.

so that he could force communication. Avi wishes that "there was more encouragement of Jewish identity in church for JBYs."

Amanda, a Gentile church leader who has lived and worked in Israel, talked about the need for a "bridge between JBYs and the church," a way for "both to learn about Yeshua together." She says that "it is important for Jewish people to retain their Jewish identity" and her church has been running joint classes and developing relationships with the Jewish communities in the area. She welcomes Jewish people in her church and takes steps to remind JBYs about their Jewish heritage, encourage them in their faith and doesn't ring them during *Shabbat*. Reporting that they celebrate *Sukkot* by building a *sukka* inside the church, and that they always cater on a *kosher* basis when Jewish visitors might attend, Amanda coyly points out that "all churches could do that." John asks, "If Jesus so celebrated and used the rabbinic elements in these festivals as signs proclaiming His Messianic identity, may not we, His Jewish followers, do the same?"[71]

Carl, a JBY in ordination training, responds that he has been allowed to preach in his church, although he suggests that "churches with older leaders are less likely to be receptive" to JBYs. He feels that church leaders should "understand and welcome Jewish identity," but admits that they will be looking for some freedom, "a release from the Law" and changes in a JBY's life. Michele wonders "whether the church ever really accepted people as they were, or whether we continually forced them to fulfill our expectations."[72]

Carol leads a charismatic church and deliverance ministry that uses Hebrew words in songs for worship and uses "a Jewish musical style to encourage Jewish dancing." Her church has taken a deliberate decision to encourage Jewish identity and offers ministry and support for JBYs whose Jewish identities have been suppressed or abused by their church experiences. Eric's experience is that some JBYs only find their Jewish identities because of being in church.

Micah has tried encouraging Christians to listen to Jews and JBYs, but says that "some Christians just won't listen." Ryan enjoys being part of his church at university, as they encourage him "to witness to the Jewish community and family." They want to "foster wide acceptance of people" and so encourage him "to wear a *kipa*"

---

71 Fieldsend, *Messianic Jews*, 19.
72 Guinness, *Promised Land*, 249.

in church. Sadly, he adds, his "home church have been less understanding."

Jewish Life outside Church

The question, "Should JBYs have a Jewish life outside church, and if so, how?" showed a clear split among the respondents; between those who saw no conflict and those who felt that there was a significant conflict. Also, see "Time Management Conflicts" below.

Juliana, an ordained church leader, insists that she needed to have a "completely separate Jewish life, entirely outside church," adding that "church/Jewish time conflicts can be serious for JBYs." Shana is another separate Jewish life person; for her, "*Shabbat* always comes first," even if it means "missing church stuff on Saturday." Ivor and Olive agree that "conflict could exist," although Ivor also speaks about embracing diversity while warning about the "danger of legalism" if JBYs insisted on doing Jewish things.

Grant and Stephan felt that there was no real conflict. Grant admitted that he didn't keep *Shabbat*, but both he and Stephan use the day for doing Jewish mission work. Avi remarked that a JBY needed time with other Jewish people for evangelism.

Several respondents—such as Lucy, Micah, Ryan, and Grant—celebrate some or all of the Jewish feasts, while Lucy also reports that she doesn't celebrate Christmas; Bethany's "Sunday is a normal working day." Anecdotal reports and the researcher's personal experience show that while this is common practice in the MJish world, church often forces compromise in this area. Although he acknowledges that it is "difficult to always get it right," Micah feels it is "important to align with *Torah*." Ryan attends mainstream synagogue on Friday evening, while George has done occasionally. One step removed, other respondents were happy that JBYs either should (Avi, Olive, Ryan, and Maria) or could (Clement) celebrate the feasts, Clement asserting that "we should live in accordance with Scripture" although "the Christian feasts can be good too." Randall commented that "the church should know about the feasts and festivals" and should "read the Ten Commandments," particularly at *Shavuot*/Pentecost. After pausing, he added seriously, "the church should follow and keep the feasts." Ivor felt comfortable that both JBYs and Gentiles could celebrate *Shabbat*.

As a trainee minister, Carl puts his finger on the dichotomy of being Jewish and in church leadership. He admits that "having a Jewish life outside church will be really difficult" for him and his family, but feels that he will "need contact with other MJs outside church to remain sane." He suggested that he might have to "compromise on dates" to try another day, or skip celebrating a feast if necessary, relying on God for "grace to cover conflicts of call." He and Micah both feel that they need to "negotiate to try and find a way through." In practice, Ryan reports that negotiations over *Shabbat* are difficult. Jasper admits that "as a missionary, Jewish social events are difficult, but possible." While he wouldn't prioritize something Jewish over church attendance, he would "always choose mission over church."

A number of respondents feel that it is unfair that JBYs always have to give in and compromise. They ask, "Why, why should it always be the minority?," expressing doubt that the church would even agree to a 50-50 split. George, who has to perform weddings on Saturdays and lead services on Sundays, tries to keep the spirit of *Shabbat* by making part of the (Jewish) day special. He knows a bishop who has to keep his *Shabbat* observance secret.

Adam, who became a believer after a Reform Jewish upbringing and is now a church minister, said that he "never had any difficulty finding time" but then added a little sheepishly, "in Reform, observance is less demanding." Stephan, who starts ministerial training this year, also comes from a Reform Jewish background and repeats Adam's ease over allocating time; he "attends family Jewish events," but "takes a pragmatic approach on each occasion." Adam adds that he had "never known a church block a Jewish celebration." Olive and Bethany hold the opinion that church events should be prioritized over Jewish events.

Importance of Jewish Identity for Church

Over a quarter of the respondents explicitly said that Jewish identity is either important or vitally important for the church; the majority of the other respondents made supporting comments implying that without using those words.

Hector starts by saying that this is "a significant issue," then adds that "this could be the biggest question for the church today." Hector is joined by Carl, Grant, and Stephan in asserting that Jewish identity in the church has "eschatological implications" and by Avi, Grant, and Shana in concluding that "the majority of the church doesn't see this." He and Clement agree that the Jewish people must be visibly present in church, while he, Nevis, Adam, and Keith all reference Paul's "One New Man" paradigm. Hector feels that both revelation and intercession are more important than education; important though the latter is, God will provide the revelation in his own time. Benjamin and Maria point out that "the church has connection to the Bible without Jewish identity in the church," Benjamin adding that, without Jewish identity, "there is no demonstration of the broken wall." Stephan observes that the church can only have "an incomplete and distorted view of the church without understanding its Jewish origins."

From Hector's suggestion that "church leaders are prejudiced over some biblical texts," Lucy complains about the "distortion of replacement theology," pointing out that "the church is grafted into Israel." She sees replacement theology in seminaries and Bible colleges, and is concerned that "congregations don't know enough to challenge their leaders due to lack of teaching." Jasper says that "Jewish identity is important unless you start discarding Scripture." Sarahbeth notes that "Christians everywhere are in awe of Jesus the Saviour," but she is "inspired by Jesus the Jew. Jesus without Judaism is no Jesus at all."[73]

Describing MJism as "the third plank of the Trinity in church," Amanda worries that, although she can "understand the growth of separate Messianic Jewish congregations," not having those JBYs in church robs "the church of Jewish input." She says that "Jewish approaches to life are more practical than Gentile/Greek ideas," and are "really needed in church." Quentin adds that the "Gentile church needs a partner"; although, historically, "the Gentile church pushed the Jewish partner out," they should now be "arguing for Jewish identity in church." After all, as he and Nevis point out, "Christianity is Jewish—there would be no Christianity without Judaism." Picking up the thread, Nevis talks about a shared story—a common trajectory—adding that "historically, the church doesn't know who she is or where she came from." Clement agrees: "the church is poorer for Jewish identity lost in the past." He affirms God's sovereignty in allowing it to happen, but laments that "the break between Old and New is a bad mistake." For him, even "the title 'Old Testament' is a bad call."

Carl feels that Jewish identity in the church "helps everyone to understand Yeshua, mission, and the Scriptures better." Iain agrees. Serena explains that "Jewish identity has doctrinal significance and is important for the church if it is understood." She and Maria think that "the church needs Jewish identity and a Jewish mindset to

---

73 Caplin, *Confessions of a Prodigal Daughter*, 62.

understand the Bible." After all, as Serena, Iain, Walter, Carol and Stephan agree: "Jesus was a Jew!" Juliana asserts that "the church must acknowledge JBYs as part of the Body of Messiah," noting that "this has profound training implications." This means, she explains, "addressing and integrating JBYs, addressing and facing its past history" because "an exclusive church is not a sign of the kingdom of God." Felix is looking further; he sees "correction of church praxis —worship and liturgy—and elimination of church idolatry: feasts, etc." This, he says, would be "a second reformation to restore the church."

Taking a slightly different tack, Serena—who is Jewish—makes the point that "Jewish identity is part of one's heritage and can't be removed." She thinks that "it shouldn't be removed by church," but wonders whether it should really "become a part of church identity." Iain feels that "the Jewish/Gentile relationship is central to the New Testament and is crucial for interfaith working, diversity, and organizing church life." He is adamant that "we must fix the Jewish/Gentile relationship before being able to help others." Carol sees Jewish identity as a key to ministry: "there will be no powerful church life without the Jewish components." She thinks that "world evangelism is blocked by the absence of the Jewish components." Olive and Benjamin agree that "Jewish identity and presence in the church can help prevent heresy developing"—the church cannot be orthodox without understanding its Jewish background.

Jeffrey, one of the independent Free Church pastors, maintains that although "there's lots of good background" and that Jewish identity can bring a "cultural understanding as background to the gospels"—in which he is joined by Edward—nevertheless insists that "the value today is for understanding the past, only for historical teaching." Jeffrey thinks that "Jewish identity is no different from other national or ethnic identities."

The Importance of Jewish Values for Today

These responses, about Jewish values in today's world, spilled over from the last question set about Jewish identity in a couple of the interviews.

Ivor uses "the Ten Commandments as an example of Jewish values," pointing out that "they have not only been taken up as Christian values, but have been incorporated into Western culture." On the subject of circumcision, a long held and practiced Jewish custom, he first claims that "Paul says circumcision is not important" and points to "modern cultural opposition to circumcision," but then expects a JBY family to circumcise their male children.

Edward is keen to underline that "the Old Testament remains part of the Bible" and deduces that the "the story continues." God isn't finished yet. As Serena says, "The Jews are still God's people."

Jewish Visibility in Church

Two opposing views emerged from conversations around the need, or otherwise, for JBYs to be visible as such in church. Jeffrey is negative: "It is not a priority for Jewish identity and people to be visible in church." Serena is positive; although she is unsure exactly what the meaning or implications of God's continuing relationship with the Jewish people might be, she affirms that "there should be a place for the Jews in church; they should be there." Taking a theological position, Felix states that "if there are no Jews in the church, there is no One New Man," adding that "JBYs must learn to be Jewish in the New Covenant." Walter is sure that "Jewish people have much to say" and could help build relationship. He thinks that it behoves "church leadership to align with Jewish groups," which "might prevent hateful comments."

Translation

Translation was only explicitly mentioned once during the interviews. Olive, who is a professional translator, echoed the words of George Steiner: "everyone is always engaged with a constant translation of self into culture." She paused and then added, "JBYs must translate themselves for both Jews and Christians."

Found in Church

In this category are included both "things" and attitudes that the respondents reported encountering in church, and some experiences that happened in church.

The big three "things"—anti-Semitism, anti-Judaism and anti-Zionism—were reported by eighteen of the respondents, although this was disputed by some others. Carl and Walter define anti-Zionism as "just a modern-day cover for anti-Semitism with a new head." Jasper and Clement counter that "anti-Semitism is rare in church," coming only from "the fringes and people with issues." Randall, Olive, and Pip, too, insist that "anti-Semitism is not found in church." Stephan and Ryan hedge, saying that they have not encountered "personal anti-Semitism" in their churches. Edward suggests that "there is general intolerance of 'the other' rather than specific anti-Semitism." Maria, on the other hand, reports that "anti-Semitism is growing"; Olive has experienced "anti-Semitism among members of Pentecostal churches." Micah has experienced "covert anti-Judaism," which he says comes from "individuals rather than the church as a whole." Although he is not aware of any specific motivation, there is "discomfort at what JBYs both say and wear."

On the other hand, Lucy and Juliana report "discrimination against Jewish people" and "harassment of JBYs in church." Lucy says that discussion of Jewish mission or Jewish roots is rejected and that she was dropped from the prayer/intercession rota after praying for the peace of Jerusalem. Carl thinks that clergy teaching is at fault and complains about Christians who will insist on telling jokes about Jewish people in his presence even when they know he is Jewish. Shana was prevented from "playing in the worship band" and, in spite of reasonable acceptance from her peer group in church, met with "opposition and a lack of understanding from leadership."

Digging a little deeper, Juliana senses "institutional rejection of Jewish identity" (echoed by Carol), a "historical and theological development of anti-Semitism." She claims that the "Gentile church currently gives JBYs no seat at the table," so that the church has a "cultural imbalance," which is why "Messianic Jewish congregations are important." She explains that "JBYs and Gentiles occupy overlapping spaces," and suggests that "a balanced theology would allow a life-giving dialogue."

Replacement theology is reported by several respondents: Clement, Carol, Grant, Maria, and Stephan. Olive says that her church has received "complaints about Jewish content and emphasis." Congregants have told Carol of "feeling vulnerable about being Jewish," while Grant has been shown "active discouragement from leaders." Israel causes "strongly polarized views," with a predominantly "pro-Palestinian position" in Stephan's home church; he says it is difficult to "un-bracket Jewish people and the modern State of Israel."

Found in Messianic Contexts

Only a few respondents mentioned what they found in MJish congregations, technically outside the scope of this study. Lucy, who attends one such congregation regularly as well as church, reports that "everyone is on the same page" and that there is "no discrimination between Jew and Gentile." Benjamin, who was leading a MJish congregation at the time of his interview, says that his congregation fosters "support for Jewish identity," but that there is only a low percentage of Jews in the congregation: 20 to 30 percent. Eric, who has visited almost every MJish congregation or fellowship in the UK, confirms that this is very normal: Gentiles outnumber Jews by two or three to one.

Aspirations for the Church

Asked what aspirations they had for the church, the interviewees produced a range of ideas: teaching and doctrine, practice and custom, mission, and leadership.

In the area of mission, Lucy wants to see more "connection with Jewish roots," promoting and "supporting *aliyah*." Adam is calling the church to "take Jewish evangelism seriously" and to "overcome its prejudice against Jews." He says that the church needs to "change the narrative" and stop "using the Jews as scapegoats."

Stephan was concerned about the church facing up to its own history—"understanding its own heritage and history"—and stopping being hindered "by its own ignorance and ignoring." Olive sees replacement theology as a big issue; needing to be "revoked and expunged," inviting Jewish scholars to come and teach, helping the church to understand, without necessarily supporting, Zionism.

Rachel suggested that the "church needed to delve into the OT more," to "understand more about first century Judaism as context for the gospels." Taking Scripture as a whole more seriously came from Adam: "Old Testament too—in a more holistic way."

Shana's focus was more on praxis: to "throw out the pagan festivals" and "be more accepting of *Shabbat* and the Jewish feasts." Adam says "the church could learn so much by celebrating the feasts." Eric agrees, reporting that some churches he has visited do so in a limited way. Avi feels that the church should recognize and celebrate Passover, in particular, more. Juliana points to the need to "create a safe space for JBYs in church" and "implement safeguarding for JBYs" with "effective safety nets."

Eric says that "clergy need to be committed to life-long study and CME," rolling back "1800 years of history and practice," to "reform the church to the biblical model." Grant wants to "unlock the negativity of blind leadership." Juliana points to the need for "educated and trained ministers" who will "not be neurotic about their JBYs" and be "relaxed about JBYs doing their own praxis."

Jewish-friendly Churches

These answers are responses to an enquiry about Jewish-friendly churches—do the respondents know of any? The responses came mainly from clergy, although some lay people did also respond.

Hector, sited in the central London area, openly admits that he knows of "no Jewish-friendly churches, only a few clergy." He adds that, as far as he knows, he is the only Jewish-friendly person in his church. Amanda said that "some churches are really pretty grotty" and that "some clergy are completely clueless." She feels that there are more Jewish-friendly churches in the Free Church sector, but admits that "not many churches are safe or good places for JBYs." She worries about too much publicity for her church stirring up anti-Jewish feeling within her denomination and notes that JBYs in general "don't need any more spotlight or publicity." Nevis reports that "other clergy are not at all sympathetic," giving a partial reason that "Israel is a very polarizing issue." Clement feels that "churches with liturgy can be welcoming," while Serena, who although Jewish doesn't count herself as a JBY, says that she has "never been in a church which has JBYs in it."

Avi's experience is that there is "good support in some areas." Walter, perhaps a little cynically, says that while "many churches welcome converts," he knows of "no churches who welcome Jewish practice." Black churches and Pentecostal churches, Eric notes, "can be very friendly towards JBYs," but "Reformed churches very much less so"; he feels that "Anglican churches can be very mixed." Olive says that she does "know of some" Jewish-friendly churches and was "glad to be in one," but, like Eric, she thinks that "the Anglican church in the UK is starting to lose the plot." Marie knows "no Jewish-friendly mainline churches," reporting instead "attitudes of disregard, disinterest and apathy." She is worried that "bad attitudes are growing." Micah is blunt: "No church is openly Jewish-friendly."

Amanda and Pip both say that "to JBYs, Gentile church doesn't feel like home," Amanda adding that "Gentile church is very alien to JBYs." Somewhat more bluntly, Sherry states that "JBYs will feel discomfort in church no matter what." While they should "just muck in and offer what they can," they shouldn't "ask for or expect a welcome or help."

Data Analysis–the First Cut

Vision for Jewish Congregants

One of the questions for church leaders asked what vision they had for JBY congregants. This produced quite polarized responses.

On the one hand, Amanda, feeling that "JBYs are all natural leaders," wants JBYs "to have their own identity and be secure in it"—Adam agrees with that last point—including "to celebrate and practice their Jewishness." Amanda is supported by Walter, who wants JBYs to "be able to express their Jewishness freely."

On the other hand, Sherry is adamant that "new believers needed discipling only to follow the Lord Jesus Christ, nothing else," adding that a new JBY is "now in a separate community with a wide gulf from Judaism." While she concedes that "Jewish culture and identity softens the blow to a new believer's family," she is clear that "JBYs will have an identity crisis." She feels that "a new-found observance of *Torah* in a new believer would be false," suggesting that only "later, a JBY can revert to being comfortable among Jews again." Sherry does see value in groups of JBYs meeting together, to "share experiences" and to "pray together," to "empathize and encourage each other," but cautions that "JBYs can develop a group victim mentality." Adam adds that "identity is more important than practice."

In the middle, Hector is saddened that there are "barely any JBYs in the church," and that often, while a Gentile partner can see the need for Jewish identity, their JBY partner isn't interested. He would like his "congregation to be like the One New Man" and regrets that there are "no role models for this in the UK." Serena, while Jewish, presents a very standard Christian set of aspirations: "firm acceptance of Jesus as Lord, being clearly born again, being filled with the Holy Spirit, praying, and studying the Bible." Ivor, suggesting that "JBYs in the church could enrich us," feels that JBYs needed to find out for themselves "what they wanted to do and be." As part of that, he says that JBYs should meet with the main church, not in separate groups. That subject is revisited by more respondents later. Benjamin, who both leads a MJish congregation and works with a missionary organization, was carefully nuanced: he wants JBYs to "grow in their relationship with God" and to "grow in faith and discipleship of Messiah Yeshua"; his choice of wording and nomenclature will be heard differently by church and Jewish audiences.

Discipling in Jewish Identity

Another leadership question here: would you disciple a JBY into their Jewish identity? This question was sparked by Michael Wyschogrod's statement that "Jews who embrace Christ must be persuaded by the church to retain their identity as the seed of Abraham" and "must also remain loyal to the Torah and its commandments."[74]

Eight of the leaders affirm that they would disciple a JBY towards their Jewish identity, encouraging them to develop Jewish practice in various ways: observing the Jewish calendar, keeping the Jewish feasts, avoiding inter-marriage, practicing circumcision. Nevis suggests that the church should "teach into" and "encourage the celebration of Jewish identity." Amanda reports that she has advised JBYs to attend synagogue in order not to lose their Jewish identity, because "Jewish identity is core for JBYs," a "huge part of who they are." Quentin bluntly says that the "church interpretation is aberrant."

While insisting that "JBYs have nothing to prove," Adam would "help JBYs to understand that they are still Jewish." Avi agrees, but notes that "some people can identify as Jewish, but can't or won't change" their lives to reflect that. He would "leave it to the individuals as to where they are comfortable." Keith and Walter would "encourage JBYs to read the Old Testament"; Keith also favors Matthew's gospel and would want to make "courses and mentoring available." Nevis adds that "encouragement in Jewish identity and practice for JBYs is fundamental" and regrets that there are so few "JBYs in church who express their Jewish identity."

Jeffrey sounds a note of caution; he and his leadership team would not initiate or suggest any move towards Jewishness by a JBY, and would not support it in any way unless they were sure that it was wanted by the person themselves. Jenny reports people saying, "Well, you converted so why should it matter?" to her.[75] Conversely, Walter would try to overcome a JBYs resistance not to grow their Jewish identity. Another caution is raised by Eric, who warns about including elements from rabbinic Judaism.

---

74 Wyschogrod, *Abraham's Promise*, 198.
75 Chandler, *Jew in the Pew*, 55.

Data Analysis–the First Cut

What Can JBYs Offer the Church?

Most would like to see JBYs involved in some kind of teaching role, for example, about the Jewish feasts or what Jewish people do, while Shana goes a step further, wanting JBYs to be able to "teach the true meaning of Torah." Hugh feels that "JBYs have been gifts by God to contribute to the Church of God."[76]

Ivor, Edward, and Grant all feel that JBYs would help to foster an understanding of the biblical or Jewish background to Christian faith. Serena thinks that the church would benefit from "a knowledge of Jewish heritage" and seeing a "different type of connection with God" that could "inspire Christians in their faith." She points particularly to the problem of the "Forgotten Father." While perhaps a little cynically suggesting that JBYs could "look forward to being a consultant on Hebrew name pronunciation," Sherry is quite positive about "demonstrating Passover meals in churches, houses and schools" and being able to "promote Jewish issues such as Holocaust Day, synagogue visits and pro-Israel lobbies."

Eric and Grant both want the church to see JBYs as "an eschatological sign—the restoration of Israel and the return of the Lord." Grant adds that JBYs are "the fulfillment of Scripture" and should be involved in "seed sowing" and "organizing Israel tours." Eric, on the other hand, says that JBYs are a "testimony to God's faithfulness" and bring a "witness of continuity," not to mention a "defense against Marcionism." Perhaps more seriously, he added that JBYs can bring a "demonstration of the Jewish rhythm of life." Stephan thinks that JBYs can "help with Jewish outreach" and "help the church to accept cultural diversity."

Time Management Conflicts

These responses arose from following the thread about having a Jewish life outside church and conflicts between observing Jewish time and/or church time.

Serena seems conflicted; she is Jewish herself, but is ordained in a Pentecostal church denomination that demands a lot from its leaders. She starts by observing that "everyone needs time to rest," adding that "the church shouldn't force a break with Jewish heritage." Then she points out that *Shabbat*—Friday evening in particular, but also many events on Saturday—"clashes with youth

---

76 Montefiore, *Looking Afresh*, 46–7.

work." She wonders "which is more important? A strict time of rest or connecting with people?" What, she asks, "is *Shabbat* really for?" Noting that "Jesus healed on *Shabbat*," she concludes that "JBYs could do something else in the same time frame" because "a calling is more important than Jewish time."

Juliana, also Jewish, and also ordained by a Christian church network, is not unprepared to resolve the conflict. She says that "*Shabbat* is my (the minister's) day off," adding that she doesn't "schedule church events in Jewish time." Regretting that "churches always seem to schedule youth work on Friday evening," and that "Childrens' and youth camps are always a problem," she concedes that while "a church member can just make an excuse for not being in church on *Shabbat*," "an official minister of a church must compromise *Shabbat* to attend work stuff." On the other hand, she "won't compromise *Yom Kippur* or the first day of *Pesach*." She tries to work around things, but finds it difficult to get the right balance. On the one hand, stating unequivocally that "you can't cherry pick *mitzvot*"; on the other hand she asks the hard questions, "Will it commend Jews and Jewishness to the church? Will it compromise holiness?" She always had her own "children out of school for *Yom Tov*,"[77] but recognized that she couldn't stop under-eighteens from participating in all youth activities as it might drive them away. Her catch-all question is "Will it inspire love for the *Torah*?"

George, a Jew serving as an ordained priest in the Church of England, explained that his mid-week study group usually keeps Passover, but says that "it's difficult to be a church minister and run Easter and do Passover at the same time." In the year of the interview, they were too close but that was the first year for some time that he hadn't managed to squeeze both in. He is worried about the stress and work levels of other senior leaders alongside him and wants to tell them to rest on *Shabbat*.

Hilary complains that church is always busy and always fills Saturday with "fairs and coffee mornings." She recognizes that they can't happen during the week because people are at work, or on Sunday because of church services, so "the church says 'let's fit them in on Saturday.'" She says that "people need a break and a rest." Jean, who is also Jewish, agrees to compromise *Shabbat* once

---

77 The generic category–"Good Day"–for all of the major festivals: first and last day of *Pesach/Matzah*, *Shavuot*, *Yom Teruah*, *Yom Kippur*, the first day of *Sukkot*, *Shemini Atzeret* and *Simchat Torah*.

a month to help with Messy Church. Hilary, although she was asked, says that she refused. Jean feels that as she is retired, she can take another day as her *Shabbat* on that week.

Edward, a Gentile trainee minister, is interested in the conflict. He says that he "wants to listen and understand, to dialogue with JBYs" in church to try to "offer a midweek alternative." He recognizes "the tension between freedom (in Christ) and a sense of being commanded." Part of the question, he says, is "how do we define what is sacred time?"

Tension between JBYs and Church

The respondents were asked to identify areas of conflict or tension that might arise between a JBY and church. Most of the respondents were certain that there would be some, if not many: "Invariably, yes," say Maria, Stephan, and Sherry; "many incidents," Maria adds.

Serena, starting from the observation that "where there are people, there is always conflict," says that conflict can arise when "church people don't understand Jewish issues and sensitivities;" she has a feeling that the church will too often say, "You're in church now, you must leave that behind." If a church leader is antagonistic towards JBYs, "a JBY may need to move on to find a more sympathetic church." Pip echoes the last point, while Bethany has had to do just that herself. Bea adds that, while some "church leaderships reject Jewish praxis," some "JBYs are over zealous in tackling every issue every time."

Iain is aware of "hostility towards Israel" and what he calls "casual anti-Semitism" in churches, that make church life difficult for JBYs. He suggests that "JBYs need a context where they can meet and encourage each other," warning that "if JBYs feel that their voice or perspective is not heard in church, that can cause hurt." He points out the damage that can be done on "Israel tours run by critical or unsympathetic organizations." Stephan and Shana also see "a failure to deal with or condemn anti-Semitism in the church" as a problem. "Conflict in Israel" remains a trigger for tension; "a pro-Palestinian and anti-Israel agenda" or what Sherry describes as "denominational BDS policies"—while JBYs have a wide range of their own views on the behavior of the State of Israel—make JBYs uncomfortable.

Replacement theology is a frequent cause of conflict; Amanda, Maria, Carl, Eric, and Sherry all mention this. Coupled with this are reports of churches teaching that *"Torah* is irrelevant to believers" or is "damaging to spiritual life and growth." Stephan reports "a downplaying of the Old Testament." Eric knows JBYs who have been "made to feel that being Jewish is a sin" of which they "need to repent." This kind of environment "can lead JBYs to deny their Jewishness" and be "isolated from their Jewish world." Eric, Stephan and Bethany describe JBYs being pushed by the church: "pushed out of their Jewishness" and "pushed into isolation." Grant says this is "the church trying to gentilize JBYs."

Under what Shana reports as "constant pressure to choose between Torah and church," Maria claims that "a JBY is never really at home" in church and asks, "How much conflict can a JBY tolerate?"

CME Requirements

This topic surfaced in many of the interviews: are church leaders adequately trained in the areas of the Jewish world in general, and JBYs in particular? Most respondents, whether clergy or laity, held the opinion that church leaders were not initially provided with adequate training in this field and should be offered it as part of in-service training. In Olive's words: "there needs to be much more Jewish teaching for leadership." Pip, an educated, professional Jewish-and-proud-of-it woman, insisted that "Jewish identity should have training implications." Shana amplifies this: "This definitely needs leadership training . . . but that is no good without the heart in the right place."

Iain, who has some responsibility for commissioning leadership training in the London area, feels that "initial training would be a good idea," although "ongoing formation is probably more useful." He suggests that "balanced tours to Israel that see both the Jewish and Christian side" are important, but concedes that "colleges can resist yet more stuff being packed into their programs." Bea reports that, while "there are some excellent Jewish Studies courses available," there is "very little on Messianic Judaism." Although she says that there has been "talk of founding a Messianic Jewish school, similar to those in the USA," that "could actually lead to greater marginalization" and "probably wouldn't address or help church leaders."

Juliana, who has had a number of encounters with hostile church leadership, explains that "church leaders think they are innocent of anti-Semitism and harassment of JBYs." They genuinely "get upset when they are told what they have said is offensive—they don't see what they say and do as anti-Semitic." She feels that they "desperately need training on anti-Semitism, harassment, etc."

Felix, as an academic, has a list of things that church leaders need to understand: "Israelology, the One New Man, Judaism—not rabbinicism, and Messianic Judaism." Eric, on the other hand, puts his finger on what he sees as four key failings in ministerial training: "inadequate Old Testament teaching; optional or no Hebrew language skills; an unbalanced new focus on evangelizing Islam; and that Jewish focus is an embarrassment—particularly with Islam."

Security

Several respondents in, or with connections to, Jewish areas mentioned security as another thing that church in general doesn't seem to understand here in the UK. "Security is important in the Jewish world," so one church takes "serious security measures" for events involving or inviting the Jewish community. The UK now has quite a lot of "third-generation Holocaust survivors[78] and they have significant levels of fear and paranoia." It is important that church leaders maintain "privacy about who is Jewish" in their congregations unless a JBY church member is open about their Jewishness. One respondent reports that "the church receives antagonism from the Jewish community" and that there is "a risk of JBYs attending church being harassed by the Jewish community." While such threats may be a local phenomenon, church leaders in Jewish areas may be the "subject of negative email campaigns."

Church under Threat

Allied with security, several respondents spoke of the way that the church feels and behaves as if it is under threat. Walter maintains that "the church is threatened by the establishment of the State of Israel." He adds that "the church is also threatened by the fulfillment of prophecy." Ryan reports that the churches—particularly the more strongly evangelical churches—"think that JBYs are stealing the gospel." He points to an occasion when Daniel Boyarin was accused of trying to take the gospel of John away from Christians[79] and suggests that "Evangelical Christianity has such a prescribed interpretation and understanding of Scripture" that a Jewish understanding is taken as heresy, thus preventing engagement.

---

78 That is: grandchildren of Holocaust survivors.
79 Boyarin, *Border Lines*, x.

Jewish Continuity

This was one of the more emotive areas of conversation. Many of the respondents, both Jew and Gentile, saw the question of Jewish continuity—that is, that the children and grandchildren of JBYs should identify as and be recognizably Jewish—as important and under threat (Quentin, Avi, Carol, and Benjamin) or vital (Bethany and Maria). George says that "Jewish continuity is a really challenging question" and "gives me more sleepless nights than anything else." Rachel, Shana, Edward and Carl are actively concerned about being able to pass Jewish identity on to their children. Insisting that "I will pass Jewish identity on to my children," Shana says, "I need a Jewish spouse" but fears that "the church will hinder this or at best be neutral." Claude, who is both *halachically* Jewish and a senior church leader simply denies this: "There is nothing to pass on; there is no continuity."

Carl reckons that while "the church could help with continuity," it "needs to change to become more welcoming and accepting." He, Bea, and Benjamin identify that a "child needs to have a strong working Jewish identity" and he and Bethany recognize that this is "developed through Jewish experience"; then Carl adds that "a strong identity in Messiah must come first." He wants to "join an accepting Jewish community." George admits that "if I could go to the Liberal synagogue and worship as a believer in Jesus Christ, then I would be really comfortable."

On the other hand, Avi, Bethany, and Ryan complain that 'the church is "unhelpful" about Jewish continuity, "in that it sees no need." Stephan suggests that "the church is totally indifferent to Jewish continuity" and "blind to Jewish heritage." Ryan sees ambivalence: "some members would encourage continuity, some would strongly disagree." Micah acknowledges that "argument [about identity] between different Judaisms" doesn't help, but thinks that "the church needs help with getting Jewish identity right."

Bea says that, while "children of JBYs remain Jewish, children of Hebrew Christians can find Jewish heritage very remote." Her experience shows that "children of Hebrew Christians affiliate with the church" while "children of Messianic-Jewish-ly involved parents have a stronger Jewish identity." She says that "outreach to second and third generation JBYs" is needed "to explore their identity." Hilary says that "Jewish continuity gets more important as I get older" but "my children won't talk about it" and hopes that any turn-around when they get older won't be "too late."

Olive, picking up on earlier comments about JBYs teaching the church, somewhat tartly remarks, "then why on earth not their own children?" She thinks that Jewish continuity "would be such a good example to the church" and she would "encourage dual identity." Bethany and Ryan claim that Jewish continuity is "commanded by God" and are joined by Carol and Benjamin in the assertion that "JBYs must maintain praxis—they run a risk of total assimilation if they don't maintain praxis." As a church leader, Carol matter-of-factly states that "church could and should encourage both Jewish praxis and culture."

On the subject of intermarriage, touched upon by a number of respondents, Benjamin explains that "Intermarriage is a very severe threat," about which he says, "the Messianic movement is doing nothing." The church "ensures intermarriage and assimilation," supporting the mainstream Jewish argument that "conversion is destruction of the Jewish people." Avi suggests that any intermarriage situation will need "negotiation for the agreement of the spouse" and that, without a strong Jewish identity, "intermarriage may well be unhelpful." Carl provides an illustration: "a desire for a Jewish son to be circumcised really shocks a Gentile partner."

Repentance Over Anti-Semitism

These responses came from the question about the church's need to repent of historic and continuing anti-Semitism sparked by R. Kendall Soulen and Michael Wyschogrod at the start of the Introduction. Not all interviewees were asked this question, and whether they were asked depended on their answers to previous questions and how helpful the interviewer felt asking the question would be.

Carl feels that if the church repented of anti-Semitism then "we'd see less splits and more united congregations." Avi reports that "some churches have faced up to past Jewish issues" and cites the Vatican II document *Nostra Aetate*, but is sad that "replacement theology is still a majority position." He doubts that church leaders have received enough theological training either to do or to implement such a repentance. Benjamin points out that "the whole church is not responsible for the persecution of Jews" and says that "we need to address the latent anti-Semitism in the church first," before repentance for the past.

Ivor agrees that the church "isn't blameless with regard to anti-Semitism" and that "some of Luther's teaching was pretty outrageous," but points out that "John's gospel can be taken as anti-Semitic." He rejects "Two covenant theology," but wonders if "replacement theology is a loaded term," proposing instead that "the church has evolved from, rather than replaced, Israel" and is "an expression of the New Israel."

Walter and Eric "totally agree with Soulen and Wyschogrod." Walter is concerned that "the church is in danger of repeating the Holocaust." Carol is uncompromising that "the church must stop assimilating JBYs"; she cannot see that there is any "connection between the church repenting about anti-Semitism and JBYs being Jewish."

Taking a more theological line, Clement says that, while "the church is happy to accept a universal Jesus," it "is not happy to accept Jesus' distinctiveness." After all, "Jesus chose to have, use and work with a Jewish identity." Accepting that "difference is not and doesn't mean partiality," the Bible teaches that "the gospel has a clear priority: to the Jew first." Micah agrees: "the gospel belongs to the Jewish people first."

Where Do JBYs Belong?

This question produced three clear answers: in church, in MJish congregations, and in both. Hugh insists that the church is "not complete without the inclusion of both Jews and Gentiles."[80]

Bea starts by saying that "the church has many different expressions" and that "JBYs are called to be part of a worshipping, loving and serving community." She acknowledges that "Messianic Jewish congregations fulfill good and useful roles," but counters that "it is not essential for JBYs to be in Messianic Jewish congregations." Eric joins her to point out that "JBYs need fellowship with other Jews to work on identity and other issues."

Keith and Olive want "JBYs to be part of a mixed church of Jew and Gentile." He, Bethany, and Stephan "would not want to see them in separate Messianic Jewish congregations." Keith teaches that "the New Testament calls for a composite expression of faith" and both he and Bethany make reference to Paul's "One New Man" image.[81] Olive says that "it would be a sign for all believers to be fully integrated and at peace," while admitting that "in some cases, there may need to be separate Messianic Jewish congregations." Avi

---

80 Montefiore, *Looking Afresh*, 46.
81 Ephesians 2:15.

has only ever seen "separate congregations meeting on the different days."

Micah is clear that he thinks JBYs belong "in separate Messianic Jewish congregations." Benjamin agrees, adding that they belong "in the community." Shana would prefer "a good Messianic Jewish congregation or group," but says that "finding a congregation is not easy." Bethany agrees that "finding and being in the right place is not without cost." She wants "to be with like-minded people." Shana would be prepared to compromise: "a congregation plus a sympathetic church where Jewish identity is valued," where "leaders promote biblical precepts and encourage JBYs to teach and share."

Micah, Grant, and Bea agree with the ideal that "it should be possible to maintain a Jewish identity in the Gentile church," but Grant concedes that "now there is hostility and apathy." Micah bases his position on the basis that "the Christian faith is based upon the ancient Jewish covenants" and that "the church should keep biblical feasts and lifestyle." He wants the church to "learn from Messianic Jewish leaders." Pip sees no reason for separate congregations; admitting that "it is impossible to retain a strong Jewish identity in church," she asks, "but why would you want to . . . if church leaders preach the Bible faithfully and never belittle the Old Testament?" Maria, Pip, and Stephan think that "JBYs belong in church—where they are missed and needed," but, like Pip, Maria concedes that it is "extremely difficult to maintain a strong Jewish identity in church."

Grant thinks that "both church and congregation can be good." His ideal is "to attend church weekly and a Messianic congregation monthly." At the same time, he says that "church can be a lonely life for a JBY without others." Carol admits that "most JBYs I know are in Gentile churches."

Eric, who is familiar with the work of Alex Jacob and has "visited all of the Messianic Jewish fellowships and congregations in the UK," reports that they all operate in Jacob's third model; none in the fourth. Stephan adds that his experience of UK MJish congregations is that they are all unsound. He thinks that "JBYs should be treated just like all other converts from other religions: they should be welcomed, and their heritage be embraced, but sects only promote division and arguments."

Jewish Identity in Ministry

A few of the JBYs who are in leadership positions talked about how they used, or showed, their Jewish identity in their ministry roles.

Bethany has been involved in ministering to other JBYs. Avi, who has been an Anglican clergyman for many years, teaches about "the three *regalim* feasts[82] in church," and also teaches "on and around Holocaust Memorial Day." He leads "Passover *seders* in churches," will "build a *sukka* in church" and "brings Jewish humor and heritage into teaching and preaching." He has taught at theological college and considers himself "a catalyst to draw out other Jews." George, who "could easily wear a prayer shawl and sing Psalms in Hebrew," wouldn't wear the shawl in church because "it wouldn't help the congregation . . . who have negative images of Judaism."

The Academic Interviews

One often repeated comment in the main interview stream concerned a wish for more or relevant training for church leaders so that they would have an understanding of the issues and aspirations for, and of, JBYs. A small number of interviews were, therefore, conducted with academics occupying staff positions in Bible colleges to see where this might lead. These interviews, admittedly too few to do more than throw up some indications of feeling and intent and suggest lines for further research, nevertheless seemed to bear out the concerns of the previous interviewees and demonstrate some of the tensions that might be involved.

Four interviews were conducted over the course of several months with currently active staff members at UK Bible colleges or seminaries. Three of the interviewees are male, one is female; three are ordained clergy, one is not; three are at denominational training colleges, one is at an independent college; two are New Testament specialists, one is an Old Testament specialist, one publishes in a wide area including Israel, Jews and JBYs; two of the colleges offer full-time and part-time training, one offers only part-time training, and one provides distance learning; two of the interviewees were also the principals of their colleges; all four are involved in curriculum decisions; all four colleges offer formally validated degrees at BA and MA level, with three different universities.

---

82 The three *regalim* feasts are *Pesach, Shavuot,* and *Sukkot* (Passover, Weeks, Tabernacles), so called because they are all pilgrimage feasts that the *Torah* stipulates Jewish males should attend in Jerusalem (Deuteronomy 16:16). *Regalim* is the plural of *regel,* the Hebrew word for a foot, the only mass form of transport in biblical times. The word is specifically used in the verse: "Three foot-festivals you shall keep to Me in the year . . . " (Exodus 23:14).

All four of the academics felt that it was very important to emphasize the Jewishness of Yeshua, his Jewish setting and context, in their teaching. Rosa, an Old Testament specialist, makes reference to and exposes her students to Jewish commentaries (such as Rashi[83]) in appropriate classes. Andrew, a New Testament specialist, is in contact with the changes in Pauline studies over the last thirty years and keeps students and courses up to date with concepts such as "The New Perspective on Paul"[84] and the "Paul within Judaism"[85] debate. Brian, also a New Testament specialist, spoke of the special relationship between Judaism and Christianity, and the way Christianity was birthed from Second Temple Judaism. Charles alone went as far as "it is essential for Christian leaders to receive training in the area of the Jewish roots of Christianity and the issues faced by Jewish believers in Jesus."

The three denominational academics all gave a similar set of responses to many of the interview questions. Visits to a synagogue, visiting lecturers from the Jewish world, and the incorporation of professional clergy interfaith relationships are all being done to some degree, and would probably be welcomed to a greater extent, subject to time constraints. Contact with MJism, its leaders and contexts is not being done and although theoretically welcome—after all, why not?—is not being pursued and is unlikely to be. Curiously, in spite of their affirmation of the unique relationship between Judaism and Christianity, all three also set Judaism on a level with Islam and the non-Abrahamic world religions: it was spoken of as an interfaith issue and somehow equated with the non-Christian religions. Andrew's college used to provide an hour's content in "World Faiths," but that has now moved to "Professional Ministry and Practice." Rosa suggested that, if training were to be provided to help church leaders understand JBYs, then presumably it would be needed for Christians from Islamic, Hindu and other backgrounds.

For the three denominational academics, training time and priority was the key question. Rosa stressed how much the churches want done in an awfully short time. Brian said that while he'd love to include this, he couldn't do so without taking something else out and both the church and his college would have to take a priority decision between a number of competing subject areas. Andrew's curriculum pressures are "trying

---

83 Rabbi Shlomo Yitzchaki (1040–1105 CE), a French rabbi who wrote commentaries on the Torah, the Prophets and the Talmud, lived in Troyes where he founded a yeshiva in 1067; focuses on the plain meaning (*p'shat*) of the text, although sometimes quite cryptic in his brevity.
84 See, for example, Dunn, *New Perspective*.
85 See, for example, Nanos and Zetterholm, *Paul within Judaism*.

to squeeze a quart into a pint pot." All three felt that the need for training would have to depend on where the trained ministers might be deployed. and so on the number of JBYs they would be likely to meet or need to help. All felt that the church, as a whole, needed a greater awareness of the Jewish roots of the Christian faith, although they were less sure about JBYs.

By contrast, Charles' college has recently launched new course modules exploring Jewish Christian studies, for both laity and leaders. Another academic, not formally interviewed in this research program, while on staff at another independent UK theological institution, had started the first formally accredited UK MA in Messianic Jewish Studies, which ran for some years. Charles has active contacts with MJish leaders and involves MJish events in the curriculum and events run by his college. Without a denominational training schedule to meet, and working mainly by distance learning, Charles' college can offer a much wider choice of course modules from a broader range of providers and faculty. This allows students to follow one of a number of different pathways or emphases through the material provided so that, unlike the denominational colleges who are training denominational church leaders with only a few independent students, Charles' students may already be involved in leadership in a MJish context or be training to do so. While Charles recognizes that anyone coming to faith in Yeshua from a different religion or cultural background will have significant identity issues, he sees the Jewish-Christian relationship and JBY issues as unique.

Emergent Themes

Once detailed analysis of the data had begun, a number of repeated themes emerged. These were voiced by significant subsets of the total sample population and were often present at a lower level in the majority of the interview data.

While there was quite a range of views expressed in each category, the respondents divided into three main groupings: Gentile church leaders with varying amounts of appreciation or understanding of the issues that Jewish people can face in church; Jewish people, both clergy and laity, all of whom reported different degrees of dissonance and unhappiness; and academics who expressed varying levels of sympathy for Jews in church, but were generally constrained against being able to offer greater levels of training to clergy.

Discomfort and Dissonance

With a few exceptions—and even they at times showed traces—the Jewish respondents all showed varying levels of discomfort and dissonance at being in church, perhaps typified by Pip's comment: "Gentile church doesn't feel like home," or Sarahbeth's "fish-out-of-water experience." Even the JBYs in church leadership positions, while confirming their God-given call to be leading a Gentile church and expressing duty of care and appropriate concern for their Gentile congregations, nevertheless expressed wistful feelings about Jewish life and identity. This was perhaps most sharply felt by those in ministerial training who were hoping to retain some expressions and observances of their Jewish identity and bring those into their church ministries.

Lack of Acceptance

Jewish believers in church consistently feel that the church does not understand them or accept them for who they are, and doesn't want to understand Jewish issues and Jewish ways of looking at things. While sometimes this lack of acceptance is expressed by forms of anti-Semitism, anti-Judaism or anti-Zionism or is manifest as distrust, marginalization or disenfranchisement, JBYs often just feel unwanted, vaguely insecure or "different" from everyone else. There are reports of insensitive teaching, based upon replacement theology, and constant, but varying from slight to significant, pressure to assimilate and be like everyone else.

Jewish Continuity

Most JBYs want to maintain at least some of their own Jewish identity and are concerned about how they can do that in an unsympathetic and sometimes hostile, church context. They worry about whether they will be able to pass that identity successfully on to their children and grandchildren. The church is seen as neutral at best, through indifferent and uncaring, to relatively hostile and negative at the worst.

Discrimination

Some JBYs feel that they have been discriminated against in church, despite their best efforts, because of being Jewish. Some Gentile supporters of Jewish identity, thought, and praxis in church report exclusion and hostility from other church members. One informant reported that after a number of years' operation, the chaplaincy of their local university still refused to recognize their Messianic fellowship as a place of worship.

Exclusion from Leadership

Both Jews and Gentiles are concerned about this; many respondents feel that JBYs ought to be in leadership in some churches, should be speaking and teaching within the church as a whole, that the church has a lot to learn—in both senses of the phrase—but that church leaderships, both at congregation level and denominational level are blocking this. While some JBYs have been accepted and ordained as clergy and mission workers, they worry about being "too" Jewish and spoiling either their opportunities for ministry or for future positions.

Identity Conflation

Many respondents reported the difficulty of separating the issue of Jewish identity in the church from modern-day politics and the State of Israel. Churches and church leaders are reluctant to discuss or show favor to JBYs or Jewish issues because of political pressure concerning the Middle East conflict. Some JBYs feel that they are held responsible for the decisions of the government of Israel and penalized accordingly. "Israel," as Calvin Smith points out, "has also become a touch-paper—is symptomatic—of a wider ideological conflict which appears to be brewing . . . here in the United Kingdom"[86] concerning the church's attitude to Islam.

This chapter has considered the field data in a linear manner, presenting a summary of the interviews in roughly the same order as the interviews themselves took. The next two chapters will define some spotlights that can be used to examine the data in a more thematic way and generate questions that can be used to interrogate the data to find out how it correlates with the existing literature and research.

---

86 Smith, "Introduction," 7.

Defining the Spotlights

Having taken a summary overview of the data and its emergent themes, this chapter will describe three sets of spotlights that will be used to examine the data in more detail. It will first ask questions about Jewish identity, then interact with three areas of social science and linguistics—Social Identity Theory, Social Memory Theory, and Translation Theory—and use theoretical applications to build a series of spotlight questions that can be used to interrogate the interview data.

What is Jewish Identity?

> Now therefore, if you will indeed obey My voice and keep My covenant, you shall be My treasured possession among all peoples, for all the earth is Mine; and you shall be to Me a kingdom of priests and a holy nation (Exodus 19:5-6) . . . You only have I known of all the families of the earth; therefore I will punish you for all your iniquities (Amos 3:2).

Moses brings God's commission to the Children of Israel at Mt. Sinai; they are to be his chosen people—chosen from all the other nations and to serve him as priests and a holy nation. The prophet Amos reminds a later generation of Israelites that, because they are known and chosen by God, they are called to a higher standard than any other nations and will accordingly be held accountable for their behavior. The double-edged sword of being God's chosen people has rested heavily upon Jewish people and non-Jewish people alike through the ages.

It has long been a vexed question: who is a Jew? There are almost as many answers as there are Jews![1] Judaism today is "obsessed with the subject of identity." Even after the founding of the State of Israel in 1948, being Jewish is different from being Israeli. Clearly not just a religion, Jewish identity is a "mixture of ethnicity and religion. But in what proportion? And was not the whole more than simply a compound of these two elements?"[2] This phenomenon is echoed by Michael Wood —"there is at the moment an obsession with defining identity, with

---

1   Brewer, *Jewish Believers*, 247
2   Meyer, *Jewish Identity*, 3.

categorising and even trying to measure it and teach it"—but he insists this is not imposed from outside or by an hierarchy, but rather is grown or developed over time:

> Identity doesn't come from the top down . . . it is not genetic, it is not fixed, safe and secure, for it can be reshaped by history and culture; so that it is always in the making and never made; but it is the creation of the people themselves.[3]

This seems to be confirmed by Richard Jenkins' assertion that "identification is not a 'thing'; it is not something that one can *have*, or not, it is something that one *does*."[4] Or, in the vernacular: we are what we do. According to Howard Taylor, "we cannot define Jewishness. It is sustained by the grace of God."[5]

Jewish people have always argued and written prolifically, whether in a physical medium or carried by oral tradition. Dissenting opinions are recorded alongside the majority[6] and communication between an often widespread Diaspora makes use of media important, "to actively construct networks and cultural identities in response to their changing circumstances."[7] It is transmitted texts—and there are many different "types" of texts in many different media: stories, histories, inscriptions, rites, ceremonies, dances, parades, carvings, weavings, tattoos, and coins —that make groups of individuals into a people.[8]

Michael Wyschogrod anchors Jewish identity in the *Torah*:

> For Jews, the Torah is the expression of God's will for the conduct of the Jewish people. It is not only that. It is the telling of the stories that collectively constitute the history and self-understanding of the Jewish people.[9]

Israel is more than a collection of individuals with a set of common values; it is a nation, a people, a corporate identity. Benedict Anderson offers a definition for a nation: "an imagined political community— imagined as both inherently limited and sovereign." Imagined because everyone outside an immediate village context will not know or meet the other members of the nation; limited because it has finite boundaries outside which are others who are not members; sovereign because within

---

3   Wood, *Story of England*, 401.
4   Jenkins, *Social Identity*, 6.
5   Taylor, "Israel," 344.
6   *m*. Eduyot 1:5
7   Nastiti, *Diasporic Community*, 2.
8   Joseph, "Identity," 10.
9   Wyschogrod, *Abraham's Promise*, 161.

the nation, it is in charge of its own affairs; and community because however remote or different they may be, a community projects as a horizontal community of brothers.[10] The Jewish people meet those criteria for nationhood: imagined in that there are Jewish communities the world over, with a variety of different views and traditions, who have never met or will never meet each other, yet all recite the *Sh'ma*[11] and affirm that *Am Yisrael Chai!*;[12] limited because only Jewish people are part of the community and outside are the Gentiles; sovereign because each community takes its own decisions within *halacha* and local tradition yet recognizes the overall sovereignty of the God of Israel; and community because all Jews are part of the people of Israel.

Daniel Langton speaks of the "problem of defining 'Jewishness'", noting that "One tendency, not uncommon among theologians, is to essentialise by classifying people and phenomena as Jewish only in so far as they conform to an assumed essence of a normative Jewishness." What "normative" means is open to debate; it may be described by "theologically derived criteria such as matrilineal descent, conversion to a particular tradition or set of beliefs, adherence to a certain body of law, or a role in salvation history," or by "non-theological criteria such as racial, national or cultural characteristics." This approach, however, depends on validation by an observer, who may be inside or outside the community and may or may not agree with the criteria. Langton shrewdly comments that it also depends on consistency through history —which has been far from the case. He suggests that a second approach, that moves the responsibility for the accuracy of the claim from an observer to the claimant, is self-definition: "the approved method for many social scientists and historians." An individual can build his Jewish identity from some, or all, of the accepted criteria above, or from a variety of other components. Whether such a self-defined Jewish identity will be acceptable to the mainstream Jewish majority is a different matter, but changing perceptions over time mean that some historically accepted Jews would not be considered Jewish by today's standards and vice versa.[13]

---

10 Anderson, *Imagined Communities*, 6.
11 The key assertion of Jewish faith, Deuteronomy 6:4 and the following paragraph: "Hear, O Israel: The Lord our God, the Lord is One." Known as the *Sh'ma* because of the first word in Hebrew—שְׁמַע—the masculine singular *Qal* imperative of the verb "to hear or listen."
12 Hebrew: The people of Israel live!
13 Langton, *The Apostle Paul*, 9–10.

What makes a Jewish Identity?

Both anthropology and identity studies have recognized kinship as an important factor in identity formation and maintenance. Kinship ties provide a network of relationships; they form a grid locating people across time and distance as well as within communities. Who you are is a product of the family, clan, or tribe to which you belong. Kinship is a strong basis for inclusion and exclusion. Within a kinship group, kinship markers include: they are kin properties that identify with others; outside a kinship context, they exclude: they are a means of difference from others. The platform of kin, and the sense of security and belonging it generates, have produced the uniqueness of the individual.[14]

Kinship is partly based on inheritance—genes, blood, physical characteristics—partly on relationships—marriage, parent-child—and partly on shared stories and history. Kin relationships can be natural (blood or marriage), cultural (language, work, shared lives) and fictive (adoption, friendship, group, or category membership).[15] Naming is often important within kinship; traditional names are shared or inherited.[16]

Jewish identity shows a strong "kin" or family nature. These characteristics have long been recognized and studied as important principles for identity.[17] The Jewish people—*B'nei Yisrael*[18]—are not really a religion or a nation, they are a family.[19] Kinship ties hold the Jewish people together the world over, whether religious or secular, *frum*[20] or assimilated. A Jew is still a Jew;[21] he or she is part of the House of Israel. Converts tell the same stories; they are children of "Our fathers, Abraham, Isaac and Jacob"—conversion makes them part of the family.[22] The ancient rabbis teach that although the Bible makes it clear that when the Children of Israel rebel they will be punished,[23] they still remain his children (*b*. Kiddushin 12*a*). The Jewish cry today is the same as Joseph's brothers when they came to Egypt to buy food: "We are

---

14 Lawler, *Identity*, 32, 36, 39, 89.
15 Ibid., 37, 47–50.
16 Jenkins, *Social Identity*, 88.
17 Lawler, *Identity*, 37.
18 Hebrew: "the Children of Israel."
19 Steinsaltz, *We Jews*, 48.
20 From a Yiddish adjective "frim" meaning pious or devout; *frum* denotes someone who is more observant of Jewish Law than basic *halacha* requires.
21 *m*. Eduyot 1:5.
22 Steinsaltz, *We Jews*, 49, 50.
23 Deuteronomy 28:15–46.

brothers, the sons of one man" (Genesis 42:13). The telling of narratives and stories remains a key part of Jewish identity: "it is within this collective identity that narratives have been formed, reformed and continue to be performed."[24] Or, as Michael Wood put it: "We search for our roots and in the past we find ourselves."[25]

Rabbi Soloveitchik roots Jewish identity—both individual and communal—in two contracts between God and his people. The communal is expressed in the covenant at Sinai and is inherited by all those who "remain bound to the Jewish collective";[26] the individual is expressed in the covenant made by Moses on the plains of Moab: "Not with you alone . . . with whoever is here today . . . and whoever is not here today" (Deuteronomy 29:13–14). It is the tension between these two—both afforded repentance on *Yom Kippur*[27]—that keeps the Jewish people and Jewish individuals linked.

Evidence from Matthew's gospel,[28] using "fictive kinship terminology,"[29] suggests that the earliest communities of Jewish believers saw themselves as a household.[30] What many scholars describe as the Matthean Community,[31] most likely met in private homes—as indeed did many first century synagogues—possibly one private home. There, close relationships akin to family ties bound the group together; they were a Jewish community first, even though there may have been Gentile participation in the community.

"Historically, Jews have often been defined by their enemies or within the discourse of surrounding majorities."[32] Today the question, "Who is a Jew?" is vigorously contested between the different streams within Judaism and between mainstream Judaism and MJism.

---

24 Cohen, "Holocaust Testimony," 7.
25 Wood, "Tribes to Nations," 33:34.
26 Goldin, *Unlocking: Vayikra*, 131.
27 Peli, *On Repentance*, 42, 106; Maimonides, *Hilchot Teshuvah*, 2.7, in Touger, *Maimonides Mishneh Torah*, 36.
28 Such as the use of "brothers" in Matthew 23:1–12, particularly verse 8. Also see Keener, *The Gospel of Matthew*, 544-5.
29 "Fictive kin" are those kin with no biological connection; they may be adopted or included on other bases. See Lawler, *Identity*, 49–50.
30 Saldarini, *Matthew's Christian-Jewish Community*, 120.
31 For example Anthony Saldarini, Richard Ascough, J. Andrew Overman, and Ulrich Luz, among others, support the idea that Matthew's gospel was written for, or in the context of, a specific Jewish-Christian community. This idea is opposed by Richard Bauckham and others, who see the gospels as having been written for all believers; see Bauckham, "For Whom."
32 Glenn and Sokoloff, "Who and What is Jewish," 3.

The text of the *Torah* provides for patrilineal descent—a son becomes what his father was, be that by tribe—Gadite, Reuvenite, etc.—or status: Levite, *Cohen* (priest).[33] Unmarried daughters kept their father's tribe and status until marriage. Inheritance was a strictly male affair, hence the special allowance for the daughters of Tzelophehad (Numbers 27:1–11 and 36:1–12). The biblical text is clear that on marriage, the wife—even if a foreigner or a captive[34]—became a part of her husband's tribe. Only the seven Canaanite nations were forbidden to Israelites in marriage.[35] Cohen concludes that "the matrilineal principle was not yet known in Second Temple times."[36]

Orthodox Judaism insists that a Jew is the child of a Jewish mother, although the status of *Cohen* (priest) or Levite remains patrilineal.[37] Biblical examples of non-Israelite wives, such as Ruth and Tamar, were glossed with rabbinic narratives of conversion.[38] This was discussed by the early rabbis, and while Rabbi Yaakov of K'far Nuberius was prepared to rule that the son of a Jewish father and a Gentile woman is Jewish,[39] the *Mishnah* declares that the offspring of a Jewish father with a Gentile woman is Gentile.[40] The majority opinion from rabbinic times onwards can be summed up:

> Certain roles within our tradition are inherited in perpetuity. Once David becomes king, all authentic royalty descends from the Davidic dynasty. All male descendants of Moshe's brother, Aharon, are automatically *Kohanim* (Priests), while all male descendants of the tribe of Levi are, of course, Levi'im (those who serve within the Temple). Even Jewish identity itself is unalterably inherited through one's mother (*b.* Sanhedrin 44*a*). According to Jewish law, while someone can certainly convert to Judaism, a born or converted Jew cannot "convert out" (*b.* Kiddushin 66*b*).[41]

The Reform movement accept a child of one (either) Jewish parent—adopting Rabbi Yaakov's ruling from the third century CE[42]—so long as

---

33 Numbers 26:55 and 33:54.
34 Deuteronomy 21:10–14.
35 Deuteronomy 7:3.
36 Cohen, *Beginnings of Jewishness*, 273.
37 *b.* Bava Batra 109*b*, *b.* Yevamot 54*b*.
38 Cohen, *Beginnings of Jewishness*, 270.
39 Bamidbar Rabbah 19:3.
40 *m.* Kiddushin 3:12, based on an interpretation of Deuteronomy 7:3–4.
41 Goldin, *Unlocking: Bereishit*, 222.
42 Winkler, *The Way of the Boundary Crosser*, 64–67 discusses both Rabbi Yaakov's position and status in their original context.

they have been brought up and self-identify as a Jew.⁴³ The State of Israel accepts anyone with one (of four) Jewish grand-parent under the Law of Return. MJism accepts either the Orthodox or Reform position, with "their Jewish heritage being clearly traceable through grandparents and beyond."⁴⁴

Whereas in past centuries anti-Semitism has been a powerful force for unity among Jews and a compelling reason for survival, recent emancipation and rights have removed that pressure. Some commentators have asked whether Jewish identity can survive outside the land of Israel:

> Specifically, can it survive freedom and equality? The irony is that under conditions of poverty and persecution, Jews tended to stay Jews. It is only when they are affluent and integrated that, in large numbers, they assimilate and abandon their identity.⁴⁵

In response to the question: "What is most important for the future of **Jewish identity?" Professor Sam Heilman replied:**

> Jewish identity is dependent on Jews being among, living with, and sharing the destiny of Jewish people. Those who don't share this existential neighbourhood and consciousness do not play a significant role in Jewish identity. So the most important thing is creating and enlarging the Jewish street, the Jewish community.⁴⁶

In the same way as Christians are encouraged to fellowship with other Christians,⁴⁷ to build up their shared identity "in Christ," so Heilman claims that the development and maintenance of a strong and healthy Jewish identity depends on Jews spending time with, and living with Jews. Goethe famously said, "Tell me with whom you consort and I will tell you who you are."⁴⁸

Text and praxis are powerful constituents of Jewish identity. Max Weber defines ethnic groups as:

> those human groups that entertain a subjective belief in their common descent because of similarities of physical type or of

---

43 "Patrilineal and Matrilineal Descent", accessed 10:45am 18Jun15, http://ccarnet.org/responsa/carr-61-68/
44 Kollontai, "Messianic Jews," 197.
45 Sacks, *Genesis*, 285.
46 "Interview with Prof. Samuel Heilman", accessed 10:10am 20Feb15, https://kavvanah.wordpress.com/2014/09/03/interview-with-prof-sam-heilman/
47 Hebrews 10:25.
48 Von Goethe, *Maxims*, 60 § 459.

customs or both, or because of memories of colonisation and migration; this belief must be important for the propagation of group formation; conversely, it does not matter whether or not an objective blood relationship exists.[49]

Blenkinsopp emphasizes that Weber is essentially claiming that belief in descent from a common ancestor is no less effective for being subjective and artificial.[50] Characteristics such as a significant name, a shared history, language and religion, and a homeland even if not in residence, not only form the Children of Israel, but allow for the inclusion of the *gerim*, the righteous converts who come to share in the group identity, taking the name suffix "ben Avraham" or "bat Sarah" and being considered a part of "whoever is not here with us today" (Deuteronomy 29:15) that Moshe referenced in the covenant renewal ceremony on the plains of Moab.

Blenkinsopp believes that "Judaism" as such did not exist before the time of Ezra and Nehemiah. He argues that those returning from the Babylonian exile claimed to be the sole inheritors of the Land and the promises given through the prophets—they *were* Israel: "The claim to be the Israel which inherits the promises, commitments and privileges to which the traditions testify was now limited to members of the *golah*[51] who subscribed to its theology, its interpretations of the laws and its religious practices."[52] Although self-defined, their identity was anchored in their text and practice.

Identity Theory and Social Identity Theory

Erving Goffman describes the way in which performance is used as a control mechanism, designed to create an impression that will make the other participants in a situation behave in a way that aligns with the performer's wishes. With a clear distinction between front-stage and back-stage, when an individual may relax and be themselves, much depends on the level of belief in, or commitment to the part an individual is playing. Individuals may perform as teams to create a particular impression, and even the audience can knowingly participate in a ritual performance.[53] Richard Jenkins adds that interaction itself is like a controlled dance:

---

49 Weber, *Economy and Society*, 1:389.
50 Blenkinsopp, *Judaism*, 15.
51 Hebrew: exile.
52 Blenkinsopp, *Judaism*, 37, 61.
53 Goffman, *Presentation of Self*, 15, 28, 114.

Interaction is cooperative, organised, ordered, rule-governed. However, it occurs in a world of negotiation and transaction. This is a world that is created and enabled by interactional routines, a universe in which implicit and explicit rules are resources rather than determinants of behaviour.[54]

Academic theories of identity, whether individual or social, suggest that identity is both flexible and multiple; even, particularly in the case of social identity, negotiated. By this rubric, we are not necessarily who we think we are or want to imagine ourselves to be, but who we are allowed to be by the society and culture we inhabit. Social science teaches that identity—perhaps at its most basic, knowing who is who—is a combination of knowing who we are, of knowing who others are, and then, in multiple layers, knowing who they think we are and what they think of themselves. According to this mantra, identity is not, therefore, fixed—it is the result of negotiation, formed dynamically by comparing similarities and differences; often a matter of the self being distinct, or distinguished from the other.[55] A performance may be played to establish identity, and inside secrets used or held to maintain distinction or distance between identities. Groups of individuals may perform together to create or maintain a corporate identity, or the illusion of an identity as seen by others.[56]

Contrariwise, the biblical worldview offers only a single identity, given and known by God. Tommy Givens reports that "the existence, and therefore the identity, of the people is given by God,"[57] while Joel Hampton insists that "God determined for each person a destiny before they were created."[58] Jonathan Sacks points out that biblical Hebrew does not have a word that exactly matches the English word "person." Having words for a human being, mortal, man (as opposed to woman), and mankind, the idea of an individual with rights and a status in society is missing. The English word "person" comes from a Latin original meaning "mask," which enabled actors to play parts on stage. Because of the metaphor "society-as-theatre," it changed to describing the role that individual plays in society. Biblical Hebrew lacks the "person" word, Sacks maintains, because it rejects that metaphor. "We are not the masks we wear; we are the individuals whose innermost thoughts are known to God. We are what lies behind the mask . . . We are not what

---

54 Jenkins, *Social Identity*, 93.
55 Ibid., 6, 19, 21.
56 Goffman, *Presentation of Self*, 13, 84, 112–3, 142.
57 Givens, *We the People*, 280.
58 Hampton, "Equal Ultimacy Question," 104.

others perceive us to be; we are what God knows us to be."[59] Dissonance is to be expected when an assumed or contrived identity is out of alignment with the real identity, or when that true identity is not accepted in a situation or context.

The prophet Jeremiah, called as a prophet and given that identity before birth—"Before I formed you in the womb I knew you, and before you were born I consecrated you; I appointed you a prophet to the nations" (Jeremiah 1:5)—struggled when he tried not to walk in that calling: "If I say, 'I will not mention him, or speak any more in his name,' there is in my heart as it were a burning fire shut up in my bones, and I am weary with holding it in, and I cannot" (Jeremiah 20:9). Similarly, the Psalmist acknowledges God's hand and calling in his life from before birth:

> For you formed my inward parts; you knitted me together in my mother's womb. I praise you, for I am fearfully and wonderfully made. Wonderful are your works; my soul knows it very well. My frame was not hidden from you, when I was being made in secret, intricately woven in the depths of the earth. Your eyes saw my unformed substance; in your book were written, every one of them, the days that were formed for me, when as yet there was none of them (Psalm 139:13–16).

Zechariah prophesied a clear identity for his son John at his circumcision and naming ceremony, "And you, child, will be called the prophet of the Most High; for you will go before the Lord to prepare his ways, to give knowledge of salvation to his people in the forgiveness of their sins" (Luke 1:76–77), while Paul seems to visualize an exchange of identity—ours for his—when people become believers in Messiah: "I have been crucified with Christ. It is no longer I who live, but Christ who lives in me. And the life I now live in the flesh I live by faith in the Son of God, who loved me and gave himself for me" (Galatians 2:20).

Social psychology formally sees a distinction between identity theory and social identity theory; the former concerning essentially the individual, and the latter being concerned with individuals when part of, or interacting with, groups.

Identity Theory

> It is not "blood" or "descent" as such that keep a group together but the *shared consciousness* of it, the idea of common descent. The same applies even to personal identity. Even the self-image of a

---

59 Sacks, *Genesis*, 298–9.

person may be seen as an imagined identity. Identity, on all its levels, from the individual person to large groups such as nations and religious communities, is a product of imagination and of mental representation.⁶⁰

Identity theory models the self after society, as a reflection of the way actors act and react with each other. As individuals create society by their interactions, their own identity is shaped and modified by the feedback they receive from the society in which they are embedded. As society is patterned and organized, so is the self. By this reckoning, Jan Stets argues, "the self arises in social interaction and within the larger context of a complex, organised society. Since the larger context is complex, organised and differentiated, so too must we characterise the self." This posits multiple identities, of different salience or priority, including: role identities—the role we play or the position we hold in society—social identities—based upon the groups to which individuals belong—and person identities—defined by who we are and the way we behave. Stets explains that "in identity theory, researchers examine how actors identify themselves in terms of being a particular kind of person, taking on particular roles and belonging to certain groups."⁶¹

Role identities usually have a complement or a partner who play the "opposite" role to that being played by a particular actor; an example might be that of a doctor and patient. A number of possible pairings suggest themselves in this study. Asking appropriate questions can shine a light into how the relationships and identities are working:

Jew–Gentile	Are Jews and Gentiles behaving normally or are they acting out of character? Do they affect one another, altering their behavior when together? What happens when both Jew and Gentile identities are present in the same individual? Which is the dominant of the two roles?
Rabbi–disciple	Does this relationship follow the Jewish pattern or the Gentile/church pattern? How does it compare with the Pastor–congregant relationship in the church?

---

60 Assmann, "Mnemonic Device," 67.
61 Stets, "Identity Theory," 88–93.

Teacher–student	Does this look like rabbi–disciple or is it a different role? Does this model work in the Jewish world or is it predominantly a Gentile church model?

Early work on identity theory was focussed on role identities. Scholars proposed the existence of two hierarchies of identities within an individual—a prominence hierarchy and a salience hierarchy—both ordered in descending priority. The former describes how individuals like to see themselves, guided by their own priorities and desires; the latter is dependent on the situation in which the individual is located: the more often a particular identity is activated, the higher its salience. While the former is fairly stable, usually changing only gradually over time, the latter is much more fluid as the individual responds to changing situations and contexts. Dissonance occurs when the salience hierarchy is consistently out of sequence with the prominence hierarchy. Other scholars described the importance of commitment, formally defined as the number of persons one is related to through an identity. Less formally, the stronger and deeper the personal connections through a particular identity, the greater the commitment to that identity and the higher its salience. Stets reports that "research strongly supports the link between commitment, identity salience and behavior consistent with salient identities." Identities are reinforced by positive reception, while negative emotional responses will decrease commitment. Strong emotional effects are experienced when interaction partners do not behave in a way that supports the selected identity.[62]

The ranking of identities in the prominence and salience hierarchies, and subsequent dissonance, is important. Spotlight questions to understand the way that identity selection and activation is working in the context of this study might be:

Commitment	Are JBYs committed to their Jewish identity and how do they measure or assess the strength of those connections?
Prominence vs. salience	Is there a disparity between the prominence and salience hierarchies and what does that look like? How is this addressed? What emotional responses can be observed?

---

62 Ibid., 93–5.

| Reception and response | What reception is given to Jewish identity in Gentile/church circles? How do Gentiles respond to Jewish issues and concerns? |

It is known that identities can, and do, change. Two possible mechanisms for internally affected changes have been suggested: a slow change over time, as the self changes to adapt to a new situation—for example, marriage or becoming a parent; alternatively, change may be a reflection of a consistent lack of verification of one identity in favor of another. Other identity changes can be the result of external context changes: organization change or restructuring, a change in resource levels or flow, or a change in the size of an organization.[63]

One instance of identity change in Jewish believers is assimilation: the loss of Jewish identity and expression, and the adoption instead of Gentile non-Jewish church identity and expression. Is this a process of assimilation, or are JBYs simply adapting to their new situation? Is this "a matter of imposition and resistance, claim and counter-claim, rather than a consensual process of mutuality and negotiation?"[64] The attitude of leaders and the availability of resources—such as access to pastoral care, teaching and so on—may be significant factors, as may aspirations to lead, teach, or exercise some ministry role within a church. Questions to facilitate engagement with this aspect of identity theory are:

| Verification | What sort of verification of Jewish identity is given to JBYs in a Gentile/church context? Do Gentiles understand the importance of verification or non-verification and its consequent effects? |

| Rate of assimilation | Where assimilation occurs, is it a quick or a slow process? Is emotional trauma involved in the process? What support is available? |

| Change factors | Are there organizational or structural changes that affect assimilation? Is there a resource differential that is pushing or slowing assimilation? Are aspirations being blocked by resistance to assimilation? |

---

63 Ibid., 104–105.
64 Jenkins, *Social Identity*, 97.

Social Identity Theory

In the simplest terms, social identity theory proposes: that social identity is an individual's sense of who they are, based upon the groups to which they belong; that people categorize themselves and others into groups based on many different criteria; and that groups support or enhance their own self-image by denigrating, or discriminating against, other groups (to which they don't belong). Put another way, "social identity theory is a social psychological analysis of the role of self-conception in group membership, group processes and intergroup relations." Groups compete with one another for members and to be distinctive, not to mention for status and prestige. Group norms, or behavioral expectations, are constructed from appropriate in-group members and behaviors and are enacted both as part of social identity and group boundaries.[65] Creating a boundary includes those within it but, by implication, also excludes those beyond it—the out-group.[66]

It is important to distinguish between social identity, which stems from group membership—a collective "we" or "us" that is often set against "them"—and personal identity, which is a self-constructed identity based on attributes not necessarily or explicitly shared with other people. Social identity attributes may be immediately perceived from first contact: gender, age, occupation. Personal identity attributes are less obvious: taste in music, a personal history or biography.[67]

It is suggested that people have as many social identities as groups to which they belong and, like personal identities, that social identities vary in value and salience, with only one being active at any one time, depending on the context and situation. Most groups have a prototype—an amorphous collection of attributes, such as behaviors, opinions, attitudes, or understandings—that enable membership to be evaluated; the greater the "fit" between an individual and the prototype, the better "member" that individual is. Prototypes can also be compared between groups to show differentiation or similarity.[68] "People conform when they believe they have more to lose by being detected in deviance than they stand to gain from the deviant act."[69] Members who are less conformant to the prototype are often not liked or trusted by the group, so are relatively uninfluential and can be cast as deviants. Because of their position on the boundary, they can be deemed black sheep and be

---

65 Hogg, "Social Identity Theory," 111–3.
66 Jenkins, *Social Identity*, 104.
67 Ibid., 97.
68 Hogg, "Social Identity Theory," 115–8.
69 Stark, *Rise of Christianity*, 17.

Defining the Spotlights

more strongly disliked and rejected.[70] Membership of two groups that are considered incompatible generates pressure that lowers status in both groups and creates marginalization.[71]

Questions to ask at this stage concern where and why JBYs "fit" in the church prototype:

Prototype	Is there just the one "standard" church prototype against which JBYs are measured, or are there several different prototypes available?
Conformance	Are JBYs considered more or less conformant with, and so more or less accepted by, the church? Is this just a JBY perception?
Boundary	Are JBYs marginalized "on the boundary" and if so, is this a choice or something that is imposed upon an individual or JBYs as a category?
Consistency	Is the reception of JBYs and Jewish identity by the church a consistent pattern or does it depend upon the degree of assertion by each individual?

Categorizing an individual—because of the social identity they display or their adherence to a prototype—both allows us a vague idea of what to expect of them[72] and allows that person to be depersonalized; they cease to be an individual, but are instead seen as an object, a personification of the prototype. This can lead to stereotyping—where the individual becomes reduced to the negative out-group attributes[73]—and, in turn, to dehumanization: being seen as less than human. Ultimately this can lead to social exclusion and antisocial behavior or violence against groups or those thought to be members of those groups.[74] In the context of Jewish identity, popular stereotyping easily leads to anti-Judaism and anti-Semitism.[75]

---

70 Hogg, "Social Identity Theory," 125–6.
71 Stark, *Rise of Christianity*, 52.
72 Jenkins, *Social Identity*, 107.
73 Svartvik, "Introduction," 4.
74 Hogg, "Social Identity Theory," 118–9.
75 See Haaland, "Othering the Jews."

Michael Hogg identifies three motives that lead groups to be both better than and distinct from other groups: self-enhancement, uncertainty reduction, and optimal distinctiveness. Self-enhancement—the belief that "we," the in-group, is better than "them," the out-groups—is protected and promoted at great length because within the group, self is "defined and evaluated in group terms and therefore the status, prestige and social valence of the group attaches to oneself." Uncertainty reduction offers security and stability to the individual; within the group, the individual has a clear idea of who they are and how they are to behave, the group itself providing positive affirmation. Optimal distinctiveness allows for the balance between inclusion and sameness on the one hand, and distinctiveness and uniqueness on the other.[76]

These three motives may all have significance for JBYs in a church context. The degree to which JBYs are affected by self-enhancement may depend on the strength of their own individual and religious identity. JBYs do appear to suffer from much uncertainty within many church contexts and so uncertainty reduction will be a significant factor in their choice of group membership. The choice between visibility and invisibility is one that Jews have had to make throughout history; is being "seen" as Jews a viable strategy or a necessary evil when being part of church?

According to Hogg, there are a number of key components that contribute to the social identity process and the relations between different social groups. As JBYs can potentially have, or want to have, membership in two competing ecclesial contexts—church and synagogue —these components can be particularized in five questions: What is the social *status* of one group relative to the other? How *stable* is that status relationship? How *legitimate* is that relationship? How *permeable* is the boundary between the two groups and what is the possibility of dual membership? What *alternative* groups or arrangements are available? Hogg drily observes that "mobility rarely works" and explains that while the idea of mobility is convenient—especially for the dominant group, since it is a stabilizing factor that prevents pressure for change—it is actually not in the dominant group's interest since that would introduce contamination and possibly erase the other group, thus removing an object of superiority. This "leaves people with a marginal identity—they are not accepted by the dominant group, and they are rejected by their own group because they have betrayed their identity."[77]

---

76 Hogg, "Social Identity Theory," 120–121.
77 Ibid., 122–3.

Permeability	Is the boundary between Jewish and Gentile church members permeable? Are there roles and functions that JBYs find themselves unable to reach?
Alternatives	Are there alternatives available for JBYs so that they can participate—perhaps even if only in JBY events or functions—so as to be a full part of the group?
Mobility	Is mobility a practical reality within the church, or is the offer of mobility—be like us and you can do what we do—only an illusion cast by the church as the dominant group?

Although presented separately above, scholars often see similarities and overlap between identity theory and social identity theory. The categories or groups found in social identity theory may be compared to roles in identity theory; the question of salience and the way that identities are activated may indicate common ground; the processes that take place once an identity has been activated or manifested may be similar. At the same time, a role (identity) co-ordinates and negotiates with a role-partner or counter-role, emphasizing difference, while a social identity tends towards uniformity and similarity among group members. If group, role, and person identities overlap, they may affirm or reinforce the self, or they may impose constraints or limitations on one's self-perception.[78]

Participation and Identity Construction

Why do individuals participate in movements? One answer is that there is a match between the personal identity and the movement or collective identity. According to what David Snow and Doug McAdam call the Dispositional Perspective, participation in a social movement is influenced by the individual's predisposition. That is to say, individuals have pre-existing traits or states that lead them to take certain choices or actions rather than others. Perhaps they are looking for an identity; perhaps they are looking to upgrade or replace their own identity; perhaps they are hoping to find their own identity validated or affirmed. Research shows that "movement participation almost always modifies or sometimes even transforms participant identities, such that movement

---

78 Stets and Burke, "Identity Theory and Social Identity Theory," 224, 226, 234.

identities reflect experience in a movement as much as pre-existing identities," so perhaps this explanation is not sufficient. Snow and McAdam provide a second alternative, which they call the Structural Perspective; this argues that "individuals who are similarly situated structurally—that is, they are incumbents of the same or similar roles or members of the same ethnic, racial or religious groups, live in the same neighbourhood, work in a similar enterprise and so on—are also likely to have a shared collective identity." This too is insufficient, since it fails to allow for the many different motives that individuals have, making an automatic link between structure and participation unsafe. A third option, the Constructionist Perspective, recognizing the complexity of aligning personal and collective identities, focusses on the construction and maintenance of identity through "joint action, negotiation and interpretive work," but fails to account for the processes involved. Snow and McAdam ask: "How is it that prospective or actual movement adherents come to embrace the role identity associated with a movement, such that personal and collective identity are congruent?"[79]

The answer they propose lies in two processes: identity convergence and identity construction. Identity convergence brings personal identity closer to movement identity. This may be done by either one of two mechanisms. In identity seeking, the individual may adopt the position of a seeker; already having their own identity, they seek out a movement or group that shares that or a compatible identity andt will allow them room for expression. Identity construction, on the other hand, modifies the personal identity of prospective members to align more closely and bond with the group. Snow and McAdam show four ways in which identity construction occurs: amplification, consolidation, extension, and transformation.[80] These all have direct application in the case of Jewish believers and the church they attend or try to attend.

Identity Amplification

This occurs when an individual already has an existing identity that is aligned with the movement, but that is not sufficiently salient to ensure participation or membership retention. The identity needs to be amplified or made stronger; in role-identity terms, a low-order identity increases salience to motivate and ensure engagement with the movement. Snow and McAdam provide the illustration of a player moving from the bench onto the playing field. The greater the

---

79 Snow and McAdam, "Identity Work Processes," 42–7.
80 Ibid., 49–52.

salience, the stronger the commitment to the organization and the greater the blurring between the individual and corporate identities.

This might be allied to a Jewish person who has already—perhaps in childhood or earlier life—had some experience of or participation in church[81] that was not then sufficient to achieve attachment, but once that person has come to faith in Messiah, enables them to recognize, connect with and participate in church attendance or membership. Another example might be a Jewish person who had been adopted by non-Jewish parents and brought up in church but ceased attendance once they discovered their Jewish identity; when coming to faith, the "church" identity becomes salient once more and enables re-engagement.

Identity Consolidation

This occurs when two prior, and perhaps incompatible identities combine to form a new identity. These identities may be associated with different traditions or cultures, social, political, or religious. An example might be of a girl raised in a strict and well-to-do Brethren family who rejected those values for teen culture, alcohol, or drugs and becomes a single mother; later, she turns up at a local church to have her baby christened and after coming to faith starts a Christian Mother and Toddler Group in the social housing project where she lives. This is not rejection of old identities, but a creative blending of existing identities to create a new salient identity.

In the JBY context, this might apply to a Jewish person who after coming to faith is called to work as an evangelist to other Jewish people. A similar example might be a Jewish man who came to faith during rabbinic training and now teaches Jewish Studies at a church theological college.

Identity Extension

This occurs when an individual's personal identity expands or grows to have the same reach as that of the organization; they take on the vision of the movement, beyond their own personal identity. Snow and McAdam offer a number of examples, including that of members of political parties who are schooled repeatedly that in any social encounter or transaction, they are representatives or ambassadors of the political party.

---

81 Through a friend at school, singing in a choir or attending a youth club.

One example of this in the Jewish world might be a Jewish believer who, after some years of being involved with a local soup kitchen, is accepted for training as a church minister. Contrariwise, a Gentile who has always supported Israel in small ways—such as planting trees—starts attending a MJish congregation and then takes on some leadership role within the congregation.

Identity Transformation

While the previous three ways all use or are linked to a previous identity, identity transformation breaks or dissolves previous identities, resulting in a dramatic change in identity. This may involve dismantling or deconstruction of the past before reconstruction, and may result in rewriting of personal narrative. Snow and McAdam's example is of European intellectuals who converted to communism in the 1930s, and later, once its deficiencies became apparent, became disillusioned and fell from grace.

This might be seen in the case of a Jewish person who had been drawn deeply into hassidic or kabbalistic teaching, but had a dramatic "Damascus Road" conversion experience and then joined the "Jews for Jesus" organization.[82]

Snow and McAdam write: "Successful movements rarely create compelling collective identities from scratch. Rather, they redefine shared identities within established social settings as synonymous with an emerging activist identity."[83] Church history can be seen to follow that model as the followers of Yeshua started as a movement within the plurality of religious identities in Second Temple Judaism. Redefining their identity as Jews sharing the gospel with first the Jewish world—in Israel and the Diaspora—and then the surrounding Gentile nations, from a Jewish movement admitting a few Gentiles to a Gentile movement excluding Jewish identity; a movement that turned the world upside down.[84]

Social Memory Theory

You noble Diggers all, stand up now, stand up now,
   You noble Diggers all, stand up now,

---

82 One of the more militant Jewish evangelism groups.
83 Snow and McAdam, "Identity Work Processes," 56.
84 Acts 17:6.

> The waste land to maintain, seeing Cavaliers by name
> Your digging does disdaine, and persons all defame
> Stand up now, stand up now.[85]

"The Digger's Song"—probably written by Jarrard Winstanley in 1649 or 1650 during the short-lived "Diggers" commune at St. George's Hill, Surrey—is used as background music in Michael Wood's social history of Great Britain.[86] Sung by folk singer and song-writer Steve Knightley, it connects and recreates through song and music some of the social upheaval in the early years of the Commonwealth nearly four hundred years ago. Its somber backdrop to the unsuccessful efforts of the Diggers and Levellers to have land ownership adjusted in favor of the men who had so recently fought in the armies of Parliament against those of the late King, Charles I,[87] is an example of social memory at work and creates a narrated memory in the minds of its hearers. Modern listeners can hear the sense of betrayal felt by many of the men who had served in the parliamentary armies when the rhetoric of the campaign was not fulfilled as they expected. Even though "we" were not there, we are drawn into the social memory and join in "remembering" the injustice felt by those who were protesting at that time.

Memory is an essentially human property: memory exists only in the human mind, and is critical to culture and tradition. While only individuals can remember the past, "they never do so singly; they do so with and against others situated in different groups and through the knowledge and symbols that predecessors and contemporaries transmit to them."[88] This is what social memory means.

Maurice Halbwachs has been described as the father of social memory theory or, as he called it, collective memory. He sets memory in a social context, both for formation and recall, insisting that "most of the time, when I remember, it is others who spur me on; their memory comes to the aid of mine and mine relies on theirs." Going further, he suggests that it is both a collective memory—the sum of the memories of a given social group—and a social framework for memory, and that it is the individual's participation in these that enable the act of recollection.[89] Eviatar Zerubavel writes:

> It is mainly as a Jew that I "recall" the Babylonian destruction of the First Temple in Jerusalem more than twenty-five centuries before I

---

85 Clarke, *The Clarke Papers*, 222.
86 Wood, "The Age of Revolution."
87 Plowden, *In a Free Republic*, 47–55.
88 Schwartz, "Where There's Smoke," 9.
89 Halbwachs, *On Collective Memory*, 38.

was born . . . such existential fusion of our own personal biography with the history of the groups or communities to which we belong is an indispensable part of our social identity.[90]

Michael Schudson explains that collective memory can refer to "knowledge of the past based on a shared cultural stock of knowledge socially transmitted in lessons, rituals, traditions, proverbs and other forms."[91] This implies that collective memory may not always be remembered memory; it is more likely to be narrated memory—stories and ritual told and repeated by a community that create collective memory in the group. Anderson illustrates this using the illustration of passing from childhood to adulthood, when, after the tumultuous years of puberty, it may be impossible to "'remember' the consciousness of childhood." Photographs, diaries, letters and so on may preserve an illusion of continuity, but their existence reveals that the original feelings and emotion have been lost.[92] Because that personhood or identity cannot be remembered, they have to be narrated based on the physical evidence and other collective memories from the group or family.

Memories are being constantly reproduced and are a significant part of identity formation and retention,[93] but their reproduction is partly dependent on who we are now and the social contexts in which we operate. So much so, that Halbwachs believes that "the mind reconstructs its memories under the pressure of society," concluding:

> Society from time to time obligates people not just to reproduce in thought previous events of their lives, but also to touch them up, to shorten them, or to complete them so that, however convinced we are that our memories are exact, we give them a prestige that reality did not possess.[94]

Halbwachs identifies the family as a particular concentration of collective memory, where that memory forms part of the identity and position of each individual within the family. The family imposes constraints not only upon the content of the shared memories, but also their meanings and interpretations, even extending to rules on what may or may not be remembered.[95] "Remembering . . . is also regulated by

---

90 Zerubavel, *Social Memories*, 289–290.
91 Schudson, "Preservation of the Past," 5.
92 Anderson, *Imagined Communities*, 204; he gives the example of the genealogy of Yeshua at the beginning of Matthew's Gospel.
93 Halbwachs, *On Collective Memory*, 47.
94 Ibid., 51.
95 Ibid., 55–77.

unmistakably social *rules of remembrance* that tell us quite specifically what we should remember and what we can or must forget."[96] Religious groups also form a locus for collective memory, with texts, rituals, festivals, and calendars acting to reinforce and propagate the group collective memory. Halbwachs writes of "liturgy and dogma, of hierarchy and discipline" forming group boundaries and strengthening the group.[97]

The power of rite and ritual to connect both the past to the future and individuals to a group is described by Emile Durkheim. Just as groups refresh or remake their identity by assemblies, reunions and meetings where non-religious ritual reaffirms group cohesion, so in religious groups,

> Rite serves and can serve only to sustain the vitality of these beliefs, to keep them from being effaced from memory and, in sum, to revivify the most essential elements of collective consciousness ... The past is here represented for the mere sake of representing it and fixing it more firmly in mind, while no determined action over nature is expected of the rite.[98]

"Each act of commemoration reproduces a *commemorative narrative*, a story about a particular past that accounts for this ritualised remembrance."[99] When Christians celebrate the Eucharist or Jews keep Passover, this is a ritualized story—a selected narrative drawn from history, creatively interpreting a historical past to serve a present ritual. Neither claims to be perfectly accurate:[100] the narrative in the Passover Hagaddah does not exactly match the narrative account in the book of Exodus; none of the Eucharistic prayers in Common Worship exactly match Paul's account given to the Corinthians,[101] and that in turn doesn't exactly match the accounts of the Last Supper in the synoptic gospels.[102] But that doesn't matter because together they form what Yael Zerubavel calls a "master commemorative narrative,"[103] blending words, actions, responses, and participation into a form that reinforces the identity and

---

96 Zerubavel, *Social Memories*, 286.
97 Halbwachs, *On Collective Memory*, 84–97.
98 Durkheim, *Elementary Forms*, 427, 375–6.
99 Zerubavel, *Recovered Roots*, 6.
100 According to Eyerman ("Past in the Present," 166), "The issue of the historical veracity, or fit, between the narratives and real experience remains to be explored."
101 1 Corinthians 11:23–26.
102 Matthew 26:20–29; Mark 14:17–25; Luke 22:14–23.
103 Also called "master frames," Eyerman, "Past in the Present," 162.

formation of the group and normalizes the past in an order[104] to which everyone can agree.[105] In the examples above, Eucharist and Passover commemorate the Last Supper and the Exodus from Egypt for the Christian and Jewish communities respectively, defining events in each of their traditions.[106] In turn the "high commemorative density" of such events makes them interpretive keys to other events in a group's collective memory.[107] They are "actions that were meant to be efficient beyond the moment and thus to create and support memory."[108]

Commemorative acts serve as glue, a reinforcement to inhibit the ever-present possibility of fracture. If a group becomes disconnected from its past, then its identity may unravel or collapse and it may lose the ability to remember. In the ever-increasing distance between formation and the present, constant effort and vigilance is necessary to maintain the memory link.[109] This provides one explanation for Judaism's heavy emphasis on education. Maimonides held that separation from the community was separation from the world to come:

> One who separates himself from the community, even if he does not commit a transgression, but only holds aloof from the congregation of Israel, does not fulfil religious precepts in common with his people, shows himself indifferent when they are in distress, does not observe their fasts, but goes his own way as if he were one of the Gentiles and did not belong to the Jewish people—such a person has no share in the world to come.[110]

Belonging to a people, in this case the Jewish people, is more complex than simply being born Jewish. *Torah* (kosher food, *Shabbat*, etc.) may be kept, but it is known that many Greeks and Romans did just that in the early centuries of the Common Era yet were not Jewish.[111] More important is the acceptance of Jewish identity, the practical willingness to be a part of the Jewish people and history; as Jonathan Sacks writes, once again making a connection to Anderson's "imagined communities:"

---

104 The celebration of Passover is contained in a document called the "Hagaddah," a word meaning "The Telling," while the celebration itself is known as the "Seder," a word meaning "order."
105 Zerubavel, *Recovered Roots*, 7–8.
106 Notice, of course, that the Eucharist redefines and reinterprets Passover for the new community of believers in Messiah.
107 Zerubavel, *Recovered Roots*, 9.
108 Assmann, "Mnemonic Device," 71.
109 Kirk, "Social and Cultural Memory," 7.
110 Mishneh Torah, Hilkhot Teshuva, 3:11.
111 Cohen, *Beginnings of Jewishness*, 58–62.

> Destiny is what we do. Fate is what happens to us. One is a code of action, *halakha*. The other is a form of imagination, the story we tell ourselves as to who we are and where we belong.[112]

Less emphasized by Judaism, which is not a proselytizing faith[113], but strongly emphasized by Christianity in obeying Yeshua's mandate—"Go therefore and make disciples of all nations . . . teaching them to observe all that I have commanded you" (Matthew 28:19–20)—as both faiths accept and teach converts, is that commemorative acts and ritual serve to assimilate new members into the group norms, to adopt the group prototype.[114]

The idea of social memory can explain or demonstrate how a group of people maintain their corporate identity, and the processes that take place when identity is threatened by crisis and change. By jointly remembering both their own recent events (last Passover, Yo'el's *bar-mitzvah*) and shared historic events (the Exodus from Egypt, a healing that Yeshua performed), the latter particularly in the form of shared or commemorative liturgy, the corporate bonding is strengthened. By selective and strategic re-interpretation, the ritual both retains its linkage with the past and offers currency in the face of the immediate threat of persecution. One example may be the three *matzot* on the seder table at Passover, covertly representing the Trinity (Father, Son, and Spirit). The middle *matzah* is dramatically broken in two, with half being eaten before the meal, the second half hidden in a white cloth—like a shroud for burial—then re-appearing after the meal to symbolize the resurrection, and at the same time provide the elements for bread and wine after the meal according to the gospel and Pauline accounts.[115] Richard Horsley points out that a text—in this case, the Passover Hagaddah—works in a community: "the cultural tradition of a community is the key to appreciating how a text-in-performance did its work."[116]

The commemoration of individuals and events evolves; in modern time through media (art, architecture, literature, holidays, rituals, news, film, etc.), often moving away from the original "what actually happened." The techniques of "keying" and "framing"—associating a

---

112 Sacks, *Exodus*, 89.
113 At this time, although both biblical and extra-biblical evidence shows that it has been in the past.
114 Kirk, "Social and Cultural Memory," 7.
115 Cohn-Sherbok, *Messianic Judaism*, 103; Kasdan, *God's Appointed Times*, 27–28; Juster, *Jewish Roots*, 256.
116 Horsley, "A Prophet Like Moses," 168.

current practice, symbol or person as a "key" to a past action, event or person, then using the key and its context as an interpretive frame to understand or relate to the past—are mnemonic devices to facilitate connecting with and keeping the past alive.[117] The horseradish and *matzah* used in the Passover Seder memorialize the Exodus from Egypt and provide not only the link to the past, but current object lessons in interpretation (e.g., *matzah* as the "poor bread" demonstrating humility and fortitude in the face of persecution, while at the same time offering both a superiority in simplicity and purity, and a future hope).[118] Moreover, the practice of conducting the Passover as an in-group event cements Jewish identity so that Paul can teach, "Cleanse out the old leaven that you may be a new lump, as you really are unleavened. For Christ, our Passover lamb, has been sacrificed" (1 Corinthians 5:7). In the same way that the events of the Last Supper have been passed on in ritualized form to the Corinthian Church,[119] so the surrounding context of the Passover meal is used to interpret the Exodus from Egypt and cleansing from leaven, the symbol of sin. The closing words of the Seder, acclaimed in unison—Next year in Jerusalem!—point to the redemption that is still to come.

Creating Identity

Collective memory, according to Halbwachs and Durkheim, is determined by an identity—that is, a group—that is already well established. The group selects or constructs a past that is harmonious with that identity; the group collectively chooses to remember those things that agree with their identity. In more recent times, the situation has been reversed; building on Anderson's "imagined communities," social memory is used to construct identity—perhaps imagined identity.[120] If you share these memories then you must be one of this/our group.

Memory—both individual and collective—is central to the formation and maintenance of an individual and collective identity. It provides a cognitive map—directions, plans, layout, distances, elevations—that orients who they are, why they exist and where they are going.

---

117 Thatcher, *Memory and Identity*, 1, 3.
118 For the way in which the celebration of Passover draws the participants back into a Jewish context, see Klayman, "Messianic Jewish Worship and Prayer," 54–5.
119 1 Corinthians 11:23–26.
120 Megill, "History, Memory, Identity," 47–48.

From this perspective, the past is a collectively shaped, if not collectively experienced, temporal reference point, which is formative of a collective and which serves to orient those individuals within it. The past becomes present through symbolic interactions, through narrative and discourse, with memory itself being a product of both, "called upon to legitimate identity, to construct and reconstruct it."[121]

The Role of Tradition

Tradition also plays an important part in a social memory. Tradition provides answers to questions such as "What do we do?" and "How do we live?" Tradition provides both theory and praxis that tell the people of the present about the people and practices of the past on an intergenerational basis: we do this because they did this and others did it before them. It is driven by memory—we remember doing this—and, in turn, reinforces memory by repetition. It has a parallel function to social memory: if you observe these traditions then you must be one of this/our group.

Tradition needs to be distinguished from *minhag*, or custom, although custom is usually a part of traditional groups or societies. Tradition is fixed—it is the memory and practice of what has been and needs to be done; tradition provides authority and authenticity based on continuity with the past. Custom may allow variation within limits and expresses the way tradition is implemented within a particular group, society or region, and at a particular time.[122] In the same way that individual parishes choose which of several Eucharistic prayers may be used from the available set published in Common Worship, the *Authorised Daily Prayer Book* details *minhag Anglia*, the way the three daily prayer services[123] are conducted in Orthodox synagogues in the UK. MJish congregations select their own subsets of the traditional liturgy to combine with non-(Jewish)-traditional elements of ritual. Custom becomes tradition with the weight of time.

In the same way that memory can be refashioned to serve a particular identity, tradition—by dint of repetition of practice and historical claim—may also be invented to help support an identity by creating the illusion of a continuity with the past.[124] This technique is almost certainly used by the Sages to provide an authority formula for the Oral *Torah*:

---

121 Eyerman, "Past in the Present," 161–162.
122 Hobsbawm, "Introduction," 2.
123 And, of course, many others.
124 Hobsbawm, *Invention of Tradition*, 4.

> Moshe received the Torah at Sinai and transmitted it to Joshua, Joshua to the Elders, and the Elders to the Prophets, and the Prophets to the Men of the Great Assembly . . . Simeon the Righteous was one of the last of the Men of the Great Assembly . . . Antigonus of Socho received [the Oral Tradition] from Simeon the Righteous . . . Jose ben Jo'ezer of Zeredah and Jose ben Johanan of Jerusalem received [the Oral Tradition] from them . . .[125]

This created an unbroken chain of oral tradition from Moshe receiving it from God at Mt. Sinai to the time of the Great Assembly[126]—a body of scholars and elders set in the time of Ezra and Nehemiah—followed by transmission through the *zugot*, or "pairs" of men, down to Hillel and Shammai, the famous rabbis of the generation before Yeshua and founders of the two schools in their names,[127] and so on to the codification of the Oral *Torah* in the Mishnah by Rabbi Judah the Prince around 200 CE.

Scholars suggest[128] that the same technique was used for the pseudonymous writing of the *Torah* and historical books of the Hebrew Bible, and their acceptance as authoritative historical and legislative documents between the eighth and fourth centuries BCE. It is important to note that all invented traditions build on and use ancient material, using "history as a legitimator of action and cement of group cohesion."[129]

John B. Thompson identifies four aspects or functions of tradition: hermeneutic, normative, legitimation, and identity. By "hermeneutic" is meant a passed-down set of assumptions that provide a framework for understanding and interpreting the present; taken for granted in daily life, they are passed on to the next generation as they are received from past generations. The normative function acts to define behavior and practices that are considered normal and are carried out as a matter of routine on the basis that "that's what we've always done." Legitimation provides support for the exercise or justification of authority and power; tradition vests authority and requires obedience to either a person occupying a particular position, or a set of rules. The aspect of identity is

---

125 *m.* Pirkei Avot 1:1–4.
126 An almost certainly fictive body derived from the national body described in Nehemiah 8–10, in turn probably based upon the Hak'hel ritual prescribed in Deuteronomy 31:10–11; Strack and Stemberger, *Introduction to the Talmud*, 63; cf. Fonrobert and Jaffee, *Cambrdge Companion*, xvii.
127 Beit Hillel and Beit Shammai.
128 For example, Sanders, *Torah and Canon*.
129 Hobsbawm, *Invention of Tradition*, 6, 12.

active when tradition "provides some of the symbolic materials for the formation of identity" for both individuals and groups; values, beliefs and ritual from past generations shaping a person's idea of who they are and the groups to which they belong.[130]

It is important to investigate the role of tradition in the way the church and JBYs process their respective traditions—which are dominant, or which subsets of each are merged into different working frameworks—in the process of daily life. Are memories being created or maintained, and are those memories normative—affecting daily life—or ornamental? What happens when authorities clash over the meaning and value of tradition or its significance in the lives of JBYs today?

Reconstructing the Past

Is it possible for anyone to arbitrarily rewrite the past? Michael Schudson claims that the freedom to rewrite the past to serve a present need or identity is limited by three factors: the structures of available pasts, the structure of individual choices, and conflicts about the past among a multitude of mutually aware individuals or groups.[131] Firstly, there is neither an infinite supply of materials from the past, nor a full supply. History comes with holes, many documents have been lost or were never written—there is a limit to the evidence that can be summoned in a cause and, although some are able to make a little go a surprisingly long way, history can put up a struggle that makes it sometimes frustratingly unmalleable. Clashes with a majority view of "known" history make some alternative pasts unavailable or untenable.[132]

The documents describing the relationship between Jewish believers and Gentile believers are few in number. The biblical text, the rabbinic writings,[133] early philosophers and historians of the church and Jewish worlds,[134] references in the secular histories of the time[135]—all contain partial or fragmented images but are significantly contested as to their texts, reliability, and meaning. In particular, the paucity of texts describing the minority groupings of Jewish believers and the marginal or even semi-heretical position that they were ascribed is both marked and colored.

---

130 Thompson, "Tradition and Self," 91–3.
131 Schudson, "Preservation of the Past," 1–7.
132 Ibid., 6–8.
133 The Mishnah, the Tosefta, the Yerushalmi and Bavli Talmuds.
134 Such as the works of Josephus and Philo.
135 For example: Celsus, Tacitus, and Tertullian.

In the case of individual choices, there are constraints—based upon tradition and dogma, past hurts or trauma, other potentially conflicting memories and learned behavior—that impinge upon the choices that individuals or groups feel able to take or accept.[136]

In the Orthodox Jewish world, *halacha*—"the bridge over which the *Torah* moves from the written word to the living deed"[137]—(derived from the root הָלַךְ, to walk) guides the way that Jews "walk" in accordance with the *Torah*. The *halachic* process—taking decisions based upon precedent and the application of *Torah* principles into new situations—is one of consulting past wisdom to reapply the *Torah* in a specific time and situation. The past—as encapsulated in the Jewish writings such as the *Mishnah*, the *Talmuds*, the *Midrash* and centuries of responsa[138]—cannot be changed, but it can be endlessly interpreted by considering new data or opinion that was not available when a previous decision was taken. The *Mishnah* records both majority and minority opinions so that a later *Beth Din*[139] may rule in favor of them should the circumstances change.[140]

The negativity of the Jewish world to faith in Yeshua, starting from the gospel narratives themselves, to contemporary accusations of missionary activities, makes it hard for Jewish groups to accept either developments in scholarship that alter the "received" stories of past authorities, or the status of Jewish believers in Yeshua. The church outside academic circles, similarly, tends to have a rather monochrome view of church history that resists attempts to recalibrate its image and expectations of Jewish believers.

Lastly, the freedom to reconstruct the past is hampered by the efforts of others—working from the same starting point and evidence base—to do the same but in a different direction. There will be conflict over the ownership of or right to reinterpret past events and memories.[141]

Judaism itself has major differences between Liberal, Progressive, Reform and Orthodox in terms of the interpretation of, and obligation to, *halacha*. The church has numerous different denominations differing over both doctrine and praxis in many areas, not least eschatology and the gifts of the Spirit. All these movements attempt to reread the same texts to legitimize their positions and argue with each other as to the validity of their respective constructions. Some issues, such as gender

---

136 Schudson, "Preservation of the Past," 109–12.
137 Berkovits, *Not in Heaven*, 1.
138 Rabbinic opinions, which come to have legal force where the authority of a particular rabbi is recognized.
139 Literally, "house of justice/judgement;" a rabbinic court or *Sanhedrin*.
140 *m*. Eduyot 1:4–8; Berkovits, *Not in Heaven*, 8, 49.
141 Schudson, "Preservation of the Past," 10.

roles in leadership and ministry, are shared between Judaism and Christianity as activists struggle for their right to own and interpret the collective texts and memory.

Yael Zerubavel draws attention to alternative narratives—"that directly oppose the master commemorative narrative, operating under and against its hegemony"; these are known as countermemories. In the battle to suppress each other, or to find the room to be heard, there is much hostility and contested territory is created. Countermemory offers "a divergent commemorative narrative representing the views of marginalized individuals or groups within the society."[142] Are JBYs rejected by both the church and the synagogue because they bring out awkward historical truth that disturbs the narratives of both church and synagogue (self-defined opposites of a binary polarity)? Are Hebrew Roots groups and/or teaching tolerated because they don't cross that line, while JBYs go too far in pointing out that the line doesn't or shouldn't exist?

Marginality versus Liminality

Victor Turner points out the difference between marginality—someone who has no unambiguous membership in one group because they belong to "two or more groups whose social definitions and cultural norms are distinct from, and often even opposed to, one another"—and liminality: a temporary state of in-betweenness while an individual is in transition from one state to another. Liminars are "in process" and have a destination at which they will arrive, being accepted or re-aggregated back into society, usually at a higher or better status than the one they have left. Marginals, on the other hand, "have no cultural assurance of a final stable resolution of their ambiguity."[143] Turner defines *communitas* as a "communion of equal individuals who submit together to the general authority of the ritual elders" and suggests that one of the purposes of liminality is to generate *communitas* among liminars—"a transformational experience."[144] He identifies many religious movements as exhibiting "a 'liminal' character," moving their members from one state to another, experiencing *communitas* on the way.[145]

Applying Turner's insights to the context of JBYs and the question of continuing Jewish identity, it may be constructive to ask how the church views JBYs. Has a JBY left the status "Jewish," in which they

---

142 Zerubavel, *Recovered Roots*, 11.
143 Turner, *Dramas, Fields and Metaphors*, 232–3.
144 Turner, *The Ritual Process*, 95–6, 138.
145 Ibid., 133.

were at a known state in the church structure as an enquirer or a target for conversion, and, having made a confession of faith, is now passing through a time of redefinition before re-emerging into the church structure as a "Christian," something the church might view as a distinctly higher status? This would be a liminal vision, with the period of liminality perhaps expected to be fairly short. Or are JBYs seen as marginals—retaining their Jewish affiliation, culture and habits in spite of having professed faith in Messiah; are they failing or refusing, to "grow up into Him who is the head" (Ephesians 4:15), into mature (and unambiguous) Christians?

Turner observes that marginals "often look to their group of origin, the so-called inferior group" for *communitas*, for fellowship and a sense of personal identity, while they look to "the more prestigious group in which they mainly live and in which they aspire to higher status as their structural reference group." At the same time, they will often heavily criticize their "new" structural group and adopt or manifest "outsider" status.[146] This coincides significantly with anecdotal reports of JBY behavior and the personal experience of the researcher. Is such behavior tolerated as long as it can be considered liminal but becomes deprecated once the excuse of liminality has been exhausted and the JBY drops into marginality?

Repetition and Rehearsal

In "Social Memory Theory and the Johannine Festivals: A Study of Continuity and Discontinuity with the Jewish Feast of Sukkot," Mary Spaulding asserts that:

> During times of significant societal crisis and change, human beings do not readily and willingly accept the total transformation or elimination of all mnemonic associations. Instead, they cling to familiar patterns of behaviour in order to ward off threats to their corporate identity caused by the crisis.[147]

In the context of an early church, whether expelled from a Diaspora synagogue for their belief in Yeshua as the Messiah,[148] or lamenting the loss of the Temple in the 70 CE Roman destruction, the social trauma is partly ameliorated by the weekly celebration of the *Shabbat* ritual, the annual *Pesach Seder* or the building of a *sukkah* during the feast of Tabernacles. None of these are dependent on the Temple and are usually

---

146 Turner, *Dramas, Fields and Metaphors*, 233.
147 Spaulding, *Commemorative Identities*, 2.
148 As proposed by Martyn, *History and Theology*, 154–7.

Defining the Spotlights 107

conducted in a domestic or community environment. The space may have changed, but by repeating the ritual the community reminds itself of its identity. The familiar words, the comfortable dialogue of the liturgy as it sways between leader and congregation, the ancient chants and melodies—these all act as identity anchors, providing stability in identity rather than place: we are because of who we are, rather than where we are.

Jan Assmann looks at tradition through the concept of excarnation and understands it as:

> the lived knowledge that is embodied in living subjects and that is passed on in active association with others, through teaching and, above all, through a non-verbal process of showing and imitating, a form of knowledge that is largely self-evident and that has become unconscious and implicit.[149]

It is appropriate to consider the opportunities for "showing and imitating" available to JBYs within the church and so assess how familiar JBYs can be with their Jewish heritage and tradition and the correlation between the strength of identity and tradition, and number of years and generations in church.

Discussion of Identity Theory and Social Memory theory has generated lots of spotlight questions that can be focussed on the interview data to consider how the interviewees see themselves and why they and their contexts see them in that way. Another key part of communication is the question of translation.

Translation Theory

Translation—the action of translating a text, a symbol or a ritual from one language or culture to another—has its own area of rules, study and research: translation theory or translation studies. If people of different languages or cultures are to understand what others are saying and doing, translation must take place; or, as André Lefevere would have it: it must be rewritten.[150] This may be linguistic translation—the opening words of the Lord's Prayer in Latin, *Pater Noster*, or English, *Our Father*, for example—or, by explication: "When the teacher gets up and walks over to the door, this means the lesson is over."

---

149 Assmann, *Religion and Cultural Memory*, 69.
150 Lefevere, *Translation*, 1.

The Reason for Translation

Translation, according to George Steiner, is an activity that happens, whether consciously or subconsciously, in the exchange of every single speech message between human beings; when sufficiently difficult, this process becomes conscious technique rather than reflexive.[151] It should be added that this also applies to non-verbal forms of communication; a nudge or a wink needs translation in exactly the same way as a spoken exchange. Steiner asserts that translation will sometimes encounter intractable problems, both in between-language and within-one-language contexts. In the latter case, he suggests that the default action is to neglect. Borrowing terminology from the world of information technology, the inter-language situation corresponds to an Internet transmission using TCP,[152] where the default action is to hold the data stream and ask for retransmission of a garbled packet, while the intra-language corresponds to an Internet transmission using UDP,[153] where the default action is simply to silently drop or discard a garbled packet while continuing to process the data stream. Steiner concludes that the most frequent causes of misunderstanding derive from a failure to translate correctly.[154]

While some Jewish-Christian vocabulary is easily translated—for example, the names "Jesus" and "Yeshua"—if the recipient is aware of it, other issues may prove more difficult. For example, offence may be caused by a polite but consistently firm refusal to accept hospitality that involves eating pork products by a JBY who understands their Jewish identity to include observance of the kosher dietary laws. Neither party wishes to offend the other and an explanation may have been offered, but an essential translation failure has occurred between the different interpretations of certain Scriptures used by each side.

Culture also needs significant translation; possibly more so than language. A demonstration of this is the sometimes complete disconnect between the church and JBYs over Sabbath observance. Jewish tradition regards the time from sundown on Friday night until sundown on Saturday night as *Shabbat*. Some JBYs will be careful and appropriate in their observance of that day, regarding Sunday as simply the first day of the week, on which, if they are church attenders, they may go to church but are also free to work and shop. The church considers Sunday —probably from midnight to midnight—as the Lord's Day and many

---

151 Steiner, *After Babel*, 48.
152 Transmission Control Protocol.
153 User Datagram Protocol.
154 Steiner, *After Babel*, 49.

Defining the Spotlights

will, where possible, abstain from work and commercial transactions on that day. That part may be conceptually translated and, while disagreed over, understood. One less easily translatable nuance can be that, when the church and JBYs arrange a joint event, it always has to be held on Saturday because church can't or won't give up their service times or sense of Sunday; the JBYs are offended because they are always the ones to lose their day, while the church feel that they are already making a big effort by expecting their people to be available on two days of the weekend.

In some instances, JBYs may not be the best agents to effect translation, precisely because of their fluency in both languages and cultures. They are essentially bilingual. Professional translators consider that one who has acquired their second language by study and practice will produce the more consistent or reliable translation. Steiner comments that "The bilingual person does not 'see the difficulties'"; he already has his own personal equivalence table and speaks out of "his own private semantic correlation." Worse, "The polyglot mind undercuts the lines of division between languages by reaching inward."[155] The JBY is the bilingual, the one who has a foot in both the Jewish and Christian camps: the cultures, the languages, the unspoken assumptions. He may not always recognize the need to translate—because he understands, to him it is obvious and needs no explanation—or he may speak out of his internal value table that has no direct meaning or context for either audience.

Code-switching—the practice of seamlessly switching between, or in and out of, two or more languages in the same sentence or communication block—may cause confusion or concern among those not familiar with JBYs. This can be in obvious ways, such as the usage of Hebrew or Yiddish words in a stream of English—perhaps using *Erev Shabbat* for Friday evening, or *im yirtze HaShem* in place of "God willing"—or less obvious ways where the same English word has two meanings depending on the context: "law" and "cross" both have significant meaning and nuance differences in Christian and Jewish circles. The practice of code-switching may be entirely natural, flowing out of the conversation and the people involved; it may be used deliberately to make an identity statement or it may be used subversively to claim superiority or to demonstrate membership in a club to which the listener is not party.[156] These are "complex situations where in-group and out-group identity roles are expressed, judged as appropriate or

---

155 Ibid., 125.
156 Mendoza-Denton and Osborne, "Two Languages, Two Identities," 115–20.

inappropriate, and contested."[157] Voicing—reporting a third party's speech or opinions in the language of that person's context rather than the main language of the conversation—"is not a neutral phenomenon, but is loaded with value and indexical significance"; it adds opinion and cultural qualities to the reported words, which may be different for speaker and hearer.[158]

It is language that enables us to communicate with others what we have heard from God. The Bible speaks of words coming from the mouth of God;[159] the prophet Balak says, "The word that God puts in my mouth, that I shall speak" (Numbers 22:38). The connection between the divine and mankind is via the imagination, creating reality as it is voiced in and through language.[160] While speech is essentially a one-way transaction—although it can be apologized for, denied or qualified, words can never be withdrawn[161]—translation conveys the meaning from imagination to imagination via a communication link.

Spotlight questions here will be concerned with whether JBYs, and the contexts in which they are trying to live and operate, are aware that translation is occurring, whether such translation is deliberate and intentional or happening by default, and how vocabulary is being used or re-used.

Translation Options

David Bellos provides three options for deciding upon a translation strategy; all of which have been used at points in history.[162] The first is to learn the languages of all the different communities with which one wishes to communicate. The second is to adopt a single common language for communicating with other communities. The third is to simply ignore people who can't or won't adopt one's own language. The Roman Empire adopted the third option, largely ignoring the languages of the many people they conquered, with the single exception of Greek.[163] The result was that Latin remained the language of scholarship in Europe for over a thousand years after the Roman Empire ceased to exist.[164]

---

157 Thomas and Wassink, "Variation and Identity," 164.
158 Mendoza-Denton and Osborne, *Two Languages, Two Identities*, 117.
159 Deuteronomy 8:3.
160 Zornberg, *Bewilderments*, xvii.
161 Steiner, *After Babel*, 136.
162 Bellos, *Is that a Fish*, 7.
163 Adams, *Bilingualism*.
164 And continues in some areas of scholarship. For example, part of the apparatus and fore-matter for Biblica Hebraica Stuttgartentsia—the

Defining the Spotlights

The history of the Bible demonstrates that the church has subscribed to all three positions at different times. As evidenced by the Greek texts and manuscripts of the New Testament, the Early Church followed the second option, adopting Greek as the vehicular language that would provide maximum portability and coverage throughout the Roman Empire—their "known world"—until overtaken by Jerome's Vulgate translation in the late fourth century. Some scholars maintain the existence of a Hebrew *vorlage* behind the Greek gospel texts, translated into *koine* Greek;[165] the Hebrew text of Matthew mentioned by Papias[166] having been lost or, less likely, partially preserved in a single mediaeval manuscript.[167] Despite isolated attempts to translate it into "local" languages, the Vulgate itself remained the official church Bible language for over a thousand years, being declared the Catholic Church's official Bible text following the Council of Trent in the sixteenth century. In modern times, missionary organizations such as the Bible Society and Wycliffe Bible Translators are adopting the first option—translating into multiple "local" languages, even at the additional labor of having to invent a script with which to write down a previously oral language—as part of their work to fulfill the Great Commission to take the gospel to all nations.[168]

Crossing the cultural frontier between Hebrew and Greek produced valuable benefits. Exposing belief in Messiah and what that meant to the questions and intellectual tools of another culture and language system produced a broader and deeper understanding of the *Missio Dei*. As Andrew Walls observes, "the use of new materials of language and thought, and the related styles and conventions of debate led to new discoveries about Christ that could not have been made using only the Jewish categories of messiahship." Assuming that the translation itself was now a complete expression and discarding the Hebrew original, however, caused a loss of information: that "the eternally begotten Son was also the Messiah of Israel."[169]

Bellos' work inspires questions about the type of translation strategy that the church is employing—not only for JBYs but perhaps for all

---

scholarly accepted eclectic published text of the Hebrew Scriptures—is still in Latin.
165 Bivin and Blizzard, *Understanding*; Lindsey, *Hebrew Translation*, xix–xxvi; Flusser and Notley, *The Sage from Galilee*, 3; Flusser, *Jewish Sources*, 11.
166 Eusebius *Hist. Eccl.* 3.39.
167 Howard, *Hebrew Gospel of Matthew*.
168 Matthew 28:18–20.
169 Walls, *Cross-Cultural Process*, 80.

cultural groups. Does the church, or individual churches, operate on a monolithic basis? Is information being lost, and does anyone care?

Translation Studies

Anthony Pym discusses several different styles of translation. Direct equivalence, or natural equivalence, is where a word, symbol or concept from one culture has a one-to-one equivalent word, symbol or concept in another; a road speed limit might be one example in most Western cultures. With direct equivalence, translation is bidirectional. Directional equivalence, on the other hand, is "an asymmetric relation where the creation of an equivalent by translating one way does not imply that the same equivalence will be created when translating the other way."[170] From here, the question arises as to whether Jewish-Christian translation is a natural equivalence or a directed equivalence—is it non-reversible or, at least, not the same?

In the area of translating culture as well as language, Pym draws attention to where translation is sited, to which system or culture is hosting the translation and could be considered to own it and the vocabulary and symbols being used:

> The translations can become a key element in the literature (and thus "innovative" or "central"); they may be secondary or unimportant ("conservative" or "peripheral"); or they can occupy positions in between.[171]

It is, therefore, important to consider what position MJism occupies with regard to the church. Does the church see it as a translated subsystem and part of the church's polysystem? Is it being hosted by the church, or should it be hosting the church;, in which case, what translation is involved here? Who owns the vocabulary and the symbols? Is the church afraid of that?

Pym also mentions uncertainty and determinism in translation, suggesting that each language is to some degree building a worldview. As examples, he points out that death is masculine in German and feminine in Russian, while sin is feminine in German and masculine in Russian. This leads to many conflicting representations in art, where the characters of death and sin are portrayed according to the language's worldview and are puzzling to the other language group who are not aware of the language's control over worldview and characterisation.[172]

---

170 Pym, *Exploring Translation*, 24.
171 Ibid., 69.
172 Ibid., 93.

The questions here are whether Judaism and Jewishness can ever be translated beyond their own "language." Will the church ever see more than a suggestion of what it means to be Jewish? Are Judaism and Christianity close enough for there to be shared language and vocabulary so that they really do bear a family likeness?

The Challenge of Rewriting

One of the effects of translation is that people, literature and history can become rewritten. Lefevere describes the way in which rewriters create "images of a work, a period, a genre, sometimes even a whole literature." By virtue of being available in either the particular language of a culture, or in a superior or desirable communication language (such as English), these images propagate better and further than the originals. Then, because of their wider circulation, readership, and accessibility, they become the dominant versions of the sources. Lefevere points out that these rewritings are likely to have been produced under the constraints, patronage or ideology of a dominant culture that seeks advantage from the process. "Rewriters adapt, manipulate the originals they work with to some extent, usually to make them fit in with the dominant ideological and poetological currents of their time."[173]

Taking his cue from the literary world, Munday illustrates that literary transmission is controlled by two main factors: professionals within the literary system and patrons outside the literary system. Institutions and individuals exercise power through ideology, the choice of "acceptable" subjects and their presentation, through economics, how people get paid or funded for their work, and through status, how people behave and their position or standing within society.[174] These are powerful levers with which to control a society. But this is not to suggest that translators and rewriters are dishonest people. On the contrary, Lefevere asserts,

> most rewriters of literature are usually meticulous, hard-working, well-read and as honest as is humanly possible ... Translators ... have to be traitors, but most of the time they don't know it and nearly all of the time they have no other choice.[175]

Migrating that into the religious world, does the church take the place of a controlling institution, academics and clergy the place of patrons? Does an imprimatur either guarantee or block publication or discussion

---

173 Lefevere, *Translation*, 5, 8.
174 Munday, *Translation Studies*, 200–201.
175 Lefevere, *Translation*, 13.

of certain subjects? Do individual church leaders or administrators concerned for the overall well-being of their flock set the tone for local discussion, marking the acceptance or otherwise of JBYs and their discourse in a local church or fellowship? Are JBY culture and values being translated or rewritten?

Post-Colonialism

Translation in the past has been heavily dependent on the presence, either controlling or dominant, of a colonial power. Dictionaries of "foreign" languages have often been compiled by administrators (or missionaries) working in a colonized country, so that "translation has played an active role in the colonization process." The colonizer's language has become one of the ways in which the country being colonized and its inhabitants have been "rewritten" as "other."[176] Victorians saw India and the East through the language and lens of the East India Company and the missions working there to evangelize the heathen. Tejaswini Niranjana writes that:

> The *systematic* collaboration of anthropologists, missionaries and colonial administrators in the non-European world, in being independent of the willing participation of "individuals," is characteristic of the workings of hegemonic colonial discourse . . . Missionaries, therefore, functioned as colonial agents in the formation of practices of subjectification, not only in their roles as priests and teachers but also in the capacity of linguists, grammarians and translators.[177]

In their concern to fully present the gospel, missionaries had to communicate and needed to do so effectively and repeatably. Hence their focus on language. Although purportedly and, hopefully, in many cases really seeing themselves—with pure motives—as independent of the colonial power, missionaries and anthropologists were inevitably sucked into the colonial mindset and corporate mission. It was the European missionaries who compiled the Western-style dictionaries; they needed to communicate, so invested in "local" language studies, generating the tools that documented and explained the local tribal and regional languages. Intended for missionary use, for communicating the gospel accurately to the native populations, they quickly became important tools for the colonial powers. When you control the language, you control the speakers.

---

176 Munday, *Translation Studies*, 210.
177 Niranjana, *Siting Translation*, 34.

Defining the Spotlights

If history has been rewritten by a dominating "colonial" power, then how do we read the "effective text?" By asking questions such as: "Who uses or interprets the text? How is it used and for what?"[178] This addresses the problem of translation and allows a critical examination of "representation and reality" to take place. Is there evidence of a text having been rewritten by a translator's (or a translator's patron's) "colonial" discourse, so as to render the common understanding in a different way to that in which it is understood by the text's rightful owners? And what if the text is then not a written text, but a cultural tradition or a religious conviction? Agreeing with Zerubavel, Lefevere comments that, "Once a culture has arrived at a canonised image of its past, it tends to edit out those figures and features of that past that do not fit that image."[179]

Niranjana claims that:

> Translation as a practice shapes, and takes shape within, the asymmetrical relations of power that operate under colonialism. What is at stake here is the representation of the colonized, who need to be produced in such a manner as to justify colonial domination.[180]

How does this apply in the church and JBY context? How does the church "produce" or render JBYs? As the dominant "Christian" power, how are Jews in general, and JBYs in particular, represented? Are they those who have been colonized, who have been brought within the hegemony of the church power? And is there some irony attached to that, in that it was originally the Gentiles who were colonized and brought within the hegemony of the Jewish kingdom of heaven?

Language, Translation and Identity

A need for translation and the importance of language in identity is shown early in the Hebrew Scriptures. Abraham was first identified as a Hebrew in Genesis 14:13—the phrase אַבְרָם הָעִבְרִי has been translated as "Avram the Boundary Crosser,"[181] from the root עָבַר, to pass over or through, to cross—and the development of the Hebrew language from the Western Semitic language group was an important means for forming and preserving identity. Joseph's brothers needed an interpreter when

---

178 Ibid., 35.
179 Lefevere, *Translation*, 112.
180 Niranjana, *Siting Translation*, 2.
181 Winkler, *The Way of the Boundary Crosser*.

their father sent them to buy grain in Egypt[182] and although the majority of the dialogue in the rest of Genesis is conducted in direct speech, it is likely that Jacob needed an interpreter for his interview with Pharaoh.[183] Language acted to preserve family and ethnic identity by forcing a degree of separation between the families of Jacob and the Egyptians. Carmen Llamas and Dominic Watt confirm that "the connection between language and identity is a fundamental element of our experience of being human." They go on: "The variations in our dress, appearance and behaviour, and the constant variability in our language use, mark us out as belonging to a social group." Membership of a social group, they explain, "is reflected in our shared linguistic behaviour."[184] A later biblical text demonstrates this in the conflict between the Gileadites and the Ephraimites, where the pronunciation of the word "shibboleth" was used to distinguish between the two groups.[185]

Translation for Identity

Aaron Hughes argues that translating the Bible is an action that builds identity: "The translative act thus becomes one of the primary causal factors or agents that facilitates and powers the struggle for identity." More explicitly, he adds, "Translation is what enables and facilitates the creation of Jewish identities in the light of unruly social worlds."[186] Brian Stock discusses the strong and weak theses for the introduction of literacy[187] into an oral culture. In the case of the strong theses, covering the advent of literacy in a previously oral society, "changes in mentality may be the result of bringing reading and writing to a society for the first time"; conversely, the weak theses, speaking of raising the level and availability of writing in a society that has some texts, argue that "in a community that knows reading and writing, the advent of more literacy is a force for change."[188] As Israel's oral narratives were codified into a written form with the writing of the *Torah* and the Primary History (Genesis – 2 Kings), an act of translation took place and an integrative force for social cohesion and identity was created.

---

182 Genesis 42.
183 Genesis 47.
184 Llamas and Watt, "Introduction," 1.
185 Judges 12:5–6.
186 Hughes, *Invention of Jewish Identity*, x, xii.
187 Here this means specifically reading and writing, rather than the wider meaning of intelligence, level of information, and ability to debate and reason.
188 Stock, *Listening*, 5, 6.

Defining the Spotlights

Building on the concept of ideas, expressed in texts, influencing group behaviour over time, Stock proposes the term "textual community" to describe a community that holds, interprets, and is governed by, one or more accepted texts. He comments that "in textual communities, concepts appear first as they are acted out by individuals or groups in everyday life." Seeing a textual community as spontaneous and living people, he suggests that this process is iterative, so that "each community creates its culture, subjectively perceiving and objectively constructing new texts."[189] As people do, so they write, which becomes normative text that, in turn, is glossed again by the community. Moses Mendelssohn translated the Pentateuch and other parts of the Bible into German in 1783, using Hebrew script. Hughes comments that "by retaining the Hebrew of the original Mendelssohn still tried to harness the oral and aesthetic qualities of the originary Hebrew text by marking it off as a Jewish possession and as the defining element of Jewish peoplehood."[190]

Anderson points out that "much the most important thing about language is its capacity for generating imagined communities, building in effect *particular solidarities*."[191] Which community is being built or solidified by which language? Mendelssohn is attempting to build Jewish identity by using Hebrew script; the subtitle of Walter Moberly's *Old Testament Theology: Reading the Hebrew Bible as Christian Scripture*[192] makes it clear that he intends to build Christian identity by translating and appropriating the Jewish Hebrew Scriptures in Christian terms. This leaves the challenge of two faith communities using the same words, the same apparent language, but with quite different meanings. Or does that really mean that there are two synonymous languages?

Questions arising here must focus upon the way that the Bible is being translated and interpreted within the church, its denominations and individual congregations. Is there room for interpretation and flexibility to explore and accept alternative translations? What identity is being built and is the community forming around the text inclusive or exclusive?

---

189 Ibid., 13, 112.
190 Hughes, *Invention of Jewish Identity*, 120.
191 Anderson, *Imagined Communities*, 133; original emphasis.
192 Moberly, *Old Testament Theology*.

Summary

Having looked at Jewish identity, areas of sociology and translation theory, a number of searching questions have been developed to ask of the interview data. The next step is to move into the field of theology and develop a mandate for the relationship between Jews and Gentiles and a means of assessing the level of compliance being exhibited by the church today.

The Theological Framework

This chapter builds on the identity, memory, and translation questions and examples developed in the previous chapter, and lays out the theological context and some of the particular themes to develop a biblical mandate for the establishment of the church, considering a number of biblical passages. It then brings together the work of Miroslav Volf and Alex Jacob to provide a model for assessing church compliance with that mandate. This will complete setting the scene for the examination and integration of the research data against existing literature and theories, to take place in the next chapter. Notice in particular, however, that, although the following exegesis can be used to guide praxis, it should not be used as a measure of the success or failure of individuals or their personal experiences.

A Biblical Mandate

A major part of the theological context for a continuing Jewish identity among Jewish people who have come to faith in Yeshua—some would say "become Christians," but that already begs the question—is what the Bible says about Jewish identity in a post-Yeshua context. There are four specific passages that seem to have a significant relevance for this topic: Ephesians 2:11–22, Romans 9–11, particularly the Olive Tree analogy in chapter 11, Philippians 3:3–11 and Galatians 3:28–29.[1]

These four passages all come from the letters of Paul—a JBY who describes himself as "an Israelite, a descendant of Abraham, a member of the tribe of Benjamin" (Romans 11:1). Paul viewed his work—being the apostle to the Gentiles—as an extension of the tradition of the Israelite prophets, telling the Galatians, "when he who had set me apart before I was born, and who called me by his grace" (Galatians 1:15), reflecting Isaiah's words to God's servant—"The L-rd called me from the womb . . . as a light to the nations" (Isaiah 49:1,6)—and the call of Jeremiah: "Before I formed you in the womb I knew you, and before you

---

1   It is assumed for the purposes of this study that all these letters were written by Paul before the destruction of Jerusalem in 70 CE. It would make no sense for Paul to talk about destroying the wall of partition, when the post-*Hurban* church was busily rebuilding the wall in the opposite direction.

were born I consecrated you; I appointed you a prophet to the nations" (Jeremiah 1:5). His outreach to the Gentiles falls within Jewish boundaries; he sees "his faithfulness to Christ as faithfulness to God and to Israel."[2] Despite his letters being written to majority Gentile communities,[3] he maintains his own Jewish identity and encourages the new believers to do likewise.[4]

An important issue that arises in any conversation about Jewish identity in a church context is that of the "One New Man" image created by Paul in the second chapter of his letter to the Ephesians.[5] Adopting an ecclesiology based on Paul's concept of the One New Man (Ephesians 2:15) is an opportunity to restore a biblical equality where the family and the feast are not complete until both the older and younger brother are sitting together at the father's table as equals under the father's authority and united in his love. Tet-Lim Yee suggests that Paul should not be read as "a levelling and abolishing of all ethnic differences—Jews still remain Jews, and Gentiles remain Gentiles—but as a repudiation of the ethnocentric perspective which perceives the differences as grounds for estrangement and discrimination."[6] Daniel Darko argues that Ephesians

---

2   Johnson Hodge, "Apostle to the Gentiles," 276.
3   Stendahl, *Paul Among Jews and Gentiles*, 70. Gerd Theissen (*The NewTestament*, 94–101) talks of early collections of Paul's letters, perhaps as early as 100 CE, kept at Corinth or Ephesus, while Stanley Porter ("Process of Canonization," 177) notes the possibility that a collection of ten Pauline letters existed before the composition of *1 Clement* in 80–85 CE. John Miller (*How the Bible Came to Be*, 63–65) describes a canonical assembly that juxtaposed the collection of Paul's letters after the catholic letters written by the apostles to the Jews as a means of countering the Marcionite heresy and cites *Codex Vaticanus* as the exemplar. Oskar Skarsaune (*In the Shadow*, 222) sees a "background of mixed communities, in which a minority of Jewish believers acted as the teachers and theological experts from the greater Gentile majority." Some commentators suggest that the Galatian community was exclusively Gentile (e.g., Martyn, *Galatians*, 16), possibly nearly so in Philippi (O'Brien, *Epistle to the Philippians*, 5), while Rome by the mid-60s CE was probably majority Gentile.
4   See for example, 1 Corinthians 7:17–24.
5   Although the phrase "One New Man" has potential gender overtones, with the CJB and NRSV translating it as "humanity" and NLT "people," the phase is used throughout this study both due to established theological usage and Barth's particularity of argument.
6   Yee, *Ethnic Reconciliation*, 166.

uses kinship lexemes[7] "to promote the social identity of its readership as a multi-ethnic family of God."[8]

Denise Kimber Buell and Caroline Johnson Hodge report that ethnicity is a topic frequently used by scholars to explain Paul's writing: he is trying to "solve tensions" between Christians of different ethnic backgrounds. They describe a discourse where "'Jewish Christians' are the 'marked,' ethnically specific group, characterised by particularity. 'Gentile Christians,' by contrast, are treated as the unmarked or ethnically neutral group."[9] While Daniel Boyarin is clear that "Paul lived and died convinced that he was a Jew living out Judaism," he sees Paul's main thrust as creating a universal humanity—a non-differentiated, non-hierarchical humanity—merging all people into one culture, conforming to the dominant culture.[10] Conversely, Buell and Johnson Hodge see "ethnicity and religion as intertwined and mutually constituting . . . [Paul] crafts arguments that portray religious practices as creating, maintaining or transforming ethnicity."[11]

The One New Man Ecclesiology

Although in recent years it has been proposed that its language, vocabulary, and themes suggest that it is a composite letter, assembled later and published in his name, perhaps by a school of Paul's disciples, reflecting a number of his major areas of teaching and concern,[12] Paul's letter to the Ephesians has long been considered as part of the Pauline corpus.[13] For the purposes of this study, it will be assumed that the traditional dating applies, putting the letter at the end of the 50s in the first century CE[14] and that the letter was written by Rav Sha'ul, the apostle Paul. The letter is therefore being written at a time when the church still had a significant Jewish component.

Chapter 2 of the letter starts with a section about new life in Messiah (2:1–10), split into the former time of bondage (vv. 1–3), the new life (vv. 4–7) and the role of grace and works (vv. 8–10). The next section

---

7   These are lexical tokens representing family relationships–whether real or fictive–such as "father," "brother," etc.
8   Darko, "Adopted Siblings," 339.
9   Buell and Johnson Hodge, "The Politics of Interpretation," 242.
10 Boyarin, *A Radical Jew*, 2,8.
11 Buell and Johnson Hodge, "The Politics of Interpretation," 243.
12 See Mitton, *Epistle to the Ephesians*, 241–69, esp. 261–3; Martin, *Ephesians, Colossians and Philemon*, 4; Lincoln, *Ephesians*, lx–lxxiii.
13 For example, Stott, *The Message of Ephesians*, 16–21; Arnold, *Ephesians*, 46–50.
14 Robinson, *Redating the NewTestament*, 352.

(2:11–22) moves from the new life to the new community, again in three blocks: former Gentile exclusion (vv. 11–12), current Gentile inclusion (vv. 13–18), and the new status and purpose (vv. 19–22). It is possible to see chapter 2 as a plea to a church that is becoming increasingly Gentile —at least in the West[15]—to remind them of their debt to, and partnership with, Israel and the Jewish churches governed from Jerusalem.[16] Significant in the chapter is that there is no criticism or even mention of Jewish identity.[17] Focussing on making critical connections between Gentile believers and their Jewish counterparts, and with strong allusions to Romans 11, Paul paints a high picture of the inclusion of Gentiles— possibly his main audience in that letter—into the commonwealth of Israel. Jew and Gentile are now together to be God's witness to the world, together being built into a dwelling for God (vv. 21–22).

Verses 13–18 expound the mystery of the way that Gentiles, previously far off and unable to connect with the God of Israel, have been brought near. In Isaiah 56, Gentiles were promised that they might convert and become a part of the Jewish people; Gentiles and eunuchs who draw near to the L-rd, who keep *Shabbat* and the wider covenant are promised hope, a future and a place among G-d's people (vv. 5 and 7). Now, Paul says, no longer do Gentiles have to convert and become Jews. In a startling adaptation of another Isaianic passage, originally referring to those in Israel who have fallen away but are prepared to repent,[18] the cry of "Peace, peace, to the far and to the near" (Isaiah 57:19) is applied to the Gentiles: "You who once were far off have been brought near by the blood of Christ" (Ephesians 2:13)—the "far off" now being those who were previously excluded—because Messiah "came and preached peace to you who were far off and peace to those who were near" (2:17); all are now offered the chance to be made at peace (reconciled) with God.

Verses 14–16 each contain a singularity clause: "made us both one" (2:14), "create one new man in place of the two" (2:15) and "reconcile us both to God in one body" (2:16). There is a unification—a making one, a seeing as one, a relating to as one—out of what was previously two. Jew and Gentile have become one. By emphasizing a common ground

---

15 That is, west of Jerusalem. See Diarmaid MacCulloch, *A History of Christianity*, 3–4; in his treatment of the first few centuries of church history, MacCulloch labels Jerusalem, the Levant, Syria and everything to the east as "east," and everything west of that line as "west" looking to a greater or lesser extent towards Rome.
16 Witherington, *Letters to Philemon, the Colossians, and the Ephesians*, 252.
17 Campbell, "Unity and Diversity in the Church," 18.
18 Isaiah 57:15–21.

The Theological Framework

that is more important than the differences—the new identity as a believer in Yeshua as Lord and Messiah—the barrier between the two hostile groups can be dissolved to form a superordinate group. The category of "believer" is a stronger bond than "Jew" or "Gentile." However, the ongoing status of the constituent subgroups is important in overcoming resistance to the recategorization or development of a superordinate group identity. Put another way, if the subgroup identities are broken down or there is pressure to abandon the subgroup identities, then the process of forming and consolidating the superordinate group is impeded.[19] The difference between Paul and his audience is as important as their common ground in the gospel: "that difference is the condition through which, and within which, their unity in Christ is achieved."[20]

In verse fourteen, the Greek ὁ ποιήσας τὰ ἀμφότερα ἕν, literally "the one who made the both one," uses a neuter plural for "the both" followed by a neuter singular number. The neuter gender signifies that Paul is talking about classes or ethnic groups, rather than individual people.[21] Verse fifteen contains the longer phrase ἵνα τούς δύο κτίσῃ ἐν αὐτῷ εἰς ἕνα καινὸν ἄνθρωπον, literally "in order that the two he created in him[self] into one new man," turning a masculine plural "the two" into a masculine singular "one new man." By switching from the use of the neuter gender to the masculine, Paul now makes it clear that, although the classes become a new corporate entity, it is the people themselves who are involved; this is not simply an abstract construct. The word καινὸν is related to the phrase ἀκούειν τι καινότερον, "hearing something new," in Acts 17:21; the "one new man" is not just an amalgam or an homogenized blend,[22] it is something completely new—as the verb indicates: not "made" but "created." Verse sixteen's shorter ἀποκαταλλάξῃ τοὺς ἀμφοτέρους ἐν ἑνὶ σώματι τῷ θεῷ, literally "he might reconcile the both in one body to God," goes back to "the both" using a masculine plural form—people are reconciled, not a class or ethnic description—but uses a neuter singular ordinal number and noun for the locus of that reconciliation: one body.

Yee sees the One New Man against a backdrop of ethnic enmity; a "society-redefining metaphor." Suggesting a Jewish attitude that started with "we are the circumcision," via "we are the only legitimate heirs" to "only we have hope and God,"[23] he concludes that the One New Man is

---

19 Esler, *Conflict and Identity*, 30.
20 Robinson, "Distinction," 33.
21 Arnold, *Ephesians*, 158.
22 Juster, "Denominations," 103.
23 Paraphrasing Ephesians 2:12.

not "constituted by the abolition or denial of the differences between the two."[24] This is a metaphor of "warring parties, which had come to an armistice through the work of Jesus." And if a metaphor,[25] then the passage cannot be taken literally to mean that ethnic distinctions have been abolished.[26] This is not the creation of a new group without ethnic identity, but a process of transformation:[27] Greeks become transformed Greeks, while Jews become transformed Jews, both "in Christ."

In verse eighteen the word ἀμφότεροι, used in verse fourteen for the "both" becoming "one," reappears as "we both"—Jew and Gentile—having access in one Spirit to the (one) Father. Justin Hardin points out that "oneness" and "ethnic collapse" are not the same: "Paul clearly declares the former, but not the latter."[28] What is now thought—and was taught, shortly after, by those at the time[29]—to be impossible, was in fact quite possible and being lived out by Jewish believers in Messiah at the time Paul wrote his letter to the community in Ephesus.[30]

Markus Barth

Markus Barth focusses on four key points in the second half of Ephesians 2:15: making peace by means of creation, the embodiment of that act of creation in "one new man," the composite one-out-of-two nature, and the location of that "one new man" in Messiah.

Barth's first point is that the peace-making of Yeshua was an act of creation;[31] although its components already existed (the Jew and the Gentile), the result—the One New Man—was new and had not previously existed, nor could it have existed.[32] Only God can create and what he creates is always new. Throughout the Hebrew Scriptures, the verb בָּרָא is reserved exclusively for God himself; similarly, in the Greek

---

24 Yee, *Ethnic Reconciliation*, 162–4.
25 *The Oxford Dictionary of English* defines "metaphor" as "a figure of speech in which a word or phrase is applied to an object or action to which it is not literally applicable" (Stevenson, *Oxford Dictionary of English*). George Lakoff amd Mark Johnson explain that "The essence of metaphor is understanding and experiencing one kind of thing in terms of another" (Lakoff and Johnson, *Metaphors*, 5).
26 Hardin, "Equality in the Church," 231.
27 Campbell, "Unity and Diversity in the Church," 15.
28 Hardin, "Equality in the Church," 231–2.
29 Ignatius: letters to Magesians 10:3, Philadelphians 6:1.
30 Campbell, "Unity and Diversity in the Church," 17.
31 Barth, *Ephesians 1-3*, 308.
32 N. T. Wright connects the design of the church to Paul's statement in 2:10 —"we are His artwork." (*Paul and the Faithfulness of God*, 142).

Scriptures, the verb κτίζω is a divine prerogative.³³ The latter appears four times in the Ephesian letter: first, "we are His workmanship, created in Messiah Yeshua for good works" (2:10); here, "that He might create in Himself one new man" (2:15); then, "to bring to light for everyone what is the plan of the mystery hidden for ages in God who created all things" (3:9); and finally, "put on the new self, created after the likeness of God" (4:24). In 2:10 and 3:9, God is clearly signaled as the creator; in 4:24 the act of creation reflects the original creation "in His own image, in the image of God" (Genesis 1:27) so is taken as being done by God.³⁴ 2:15, however, brings Yeshua to the fore as the creator of the One New Man,³⁵ a step further than the agency in Colossians 1:16, "by Him all things were created . . . all things were created through Him and for Him" and John 1:3, "All things were made through Him, and without Him was not any thing made that was made." Once this was done—on the cross— Yeshua could then give his disciples peace: "Yeshua Himself stood among them, and said to them, 'Peace to you!'" (Luke 24:36) thus reversing his earlier assertion that he did not bring peace.³⁶ This is so remarkable that in John's account it appears twice³⁷ and is repeated a week later.³⁸ Every one of Paul's letters then wishes the believers peace with and from G-d; peace had indeed been made: "He Himself is our peace" (Ephesians 2:14). Yeshua brought peace from heaven and made peace between Jew and Gentile believers.

Creating the One New Man accomplished what could previously never have been done: bringing together in unity the chosen-ness of the Jewish people as a nation chosen by God and the chosen-ness of those from the (un-chosen) nations as individuals chosen by God, "the coming together of Jews and gentiles into a single structure."³⁹ Following Paul's analogy of wild and cultivated branches⁴⁰ being grafted into the cultivated tree, against nature, those who have been given the promises, the patriarchs and the *Torah*⁴¹ are made one with those who are without

---

33 Hoehner, *Ephesians*, 378.
34 Barth, *Ephesians 4-6*, 509.
35 Counter to N. T. Wright who seems to see God creating the One New Man in the Messiah (*Resurrection of the Son of God*, 237).
36 Matthew 10:24.
37 John 20:19, 21.
38 John 20:26.
39 Wright, *Pauline Perspectives*, 385.
40 Romans 11:24.
41 Romans 9:4–5.

the *Torah*,[42] without covenants, hope or God.[43] The hostility between the haves and the have-nots is broken down as the two, without losing their individual identities, are brought into and recategorized as a new superordinate group: the One New Man.[44] Paul's gospel priority—"to the Jew first and also to the Greek" (Romans 1:16)—is a reflection of the practical fact that redemption had to come to the Jews before the gospel could go to the Gentiles.[45] Notice that Paul does not favor either group; it is important that both groups should have approximately equal status.[46] The new entity, still recognizable as wild and cultivated branches, together and in peace, draws sap and nourishment from the same olive tree root.[47] The miracle—as Paul says, "against nature"—is not that branches can be broken off from or regrafted in to an olive tree, but that both wild and cultivated branches can exist, side by side, not competing but cooperating peaceably, and recognizable as such.[48] The miracle can only be seen when Jew and Gentile are visible and distinct; it is the paramount sign of the reconciliation God has effected between the world and himself.[49]

---

42 Romans 2:14.
43 Ephesians 2:12.
44 Gaston, *Paul and the Torah*, 148: "Paul's conviction is God's righteousness for salvation for both, without changing one into the other."
45 Robinson, "Distinction," 39; Hendriksen (1980), 61: "the divinely planned historical order." Campbell (*Unity and Diversity in Christ*, 77) observes that "The salvation of the gentiles assumes the prior realisation of the promise for Israel . . . For Paul, the option of salvation 'also for the Greek' presupposed that it is enjoyed by 'the Jew first.'"
46 Esler, *Conflict and Identity*, 31, makes this point on the grounds of social group theory. Campbell agrees (*Unity and Diversity in Christ*, 14): "Paul is usually very even-handed in relation to the main ethnic grouping of Jews and gentiles with which he chiefly operated in his mission." Morris (*Epistle to the Romans*, 68) states the theological case that, "The gospel is for all and knows no limitation by race. In the matter of salvation, God puts no difference between one nation and another." Without challenging the equality of the gospel, Nanos (*The Mystery of Romans*, 38), suggests that "Romans is a call to the newly believing Christian gentiles of Rome to recognise the pre-eminent place of Israel, the historical people of God." Gaston (*Paul and the Torah*, 118) claims that Romans 1:16 can be translated "for the Jew of course, but *also* for the Greek" and that "first" is to be understood not temporally, but of degree.
47 Romans 11:17.
48 Brewer, *Jewish Believers*, 241: "The New Testament is clear in its presentation that Jewish and Gentile believers maintain ethnic distinctions."
49 Kinzer, *Israel's Messiah*, 4.

This corresponds with the physical example of family fruit trees, created using grafting technology by horticulturists: cooking and eating apple cultivars grafted on to, and growing from, the same root stock. The varieties are chosen to flower at the same time, so that they can be easily cross-pollinated without need for an external pollen source, yet fruit at different times to phase the demands on the root stock resources and avoid a glut of fruit. The nature of the tree can only be seen when the varieties are visible and distinct: at flowering and fruiting. When the tree is only in leaf, or has no leaves, then the family nature is hidden, except from an expert's eye; it looks like one tree.

Barth's second point concerns the way the new creation happens in the One New Man.[50] He wants to make it clear that a person, not a "thing," has been created. The One New Man is not a corporate grouping; it is not like "the heavens and the earth," created together[51] or reacting together.[52] Neither is it a cooked dish, such as bread and butter pudding, made from a precise recipe, where the bread, the raisins or sultanas, and the nutmeg are cooked together yet are easily separable. The One New Man is a person, and each believer within the whole both contributes and retains their personality. It is noticeable that Paul's "you are one" text[53] uses personal terms—ὑμεῖς εἷς ἐστε—a second-person plural pronoun, "you," a masculine-singular cardinal number, "one," and a second-person plural verb, "are"; "one" is not neuter, as it might be to designate an object, a "thing." It is as one body that the two groups can be reconciled to God; there is one plan of salvation and reconciliation for both Jew and Gentile.[54]

The third point in Barth's argument discusses the way that one has been made from two[55]. Unlike the Creation, when God created everything *ex nihilo*, the Son creates the One New Man from the two constituent groups: Jews and Gentiles, the circumcised and the uncircumcised.[56] Whereas earlier in the chapter, God acts in resurrection,[57] elsewhere coupled with "calling into existence the things that do not exist" (Romans 4:17), Yeshua's act of creation is from two groups that, while dead in sin,[58] are very much alive, and hostile towards

---

50 Barth, *Ephesians 1-3*, 309.
51 Genesis 1:1.
52 Joel 3:16.
53 Galatians 3:28.
54 Witherington, *Letters to Philemon, the Colossians, and the Ephesians*, 261.
55 Barth, *Ephesians 1-3*, 310.
56 Yee, *Ethnic Reconciliation*, 162.
57 Ephesians 2:5–6.
58 Ephesians 2:1.

each other. Although some see the "new humanity" as taking over the identity of Israel,[59] Barth is very definite that:

> the incorporation of the Gentiles into Israel and the formation of one people consisting of Jews and Gentiles certainly does not mean that the Gentiles must become Jews, or the Jews Gentiles![60]

He adds that, "It is the distinctive message of Ephesians that no Gentile can have communion with Christ or with God unless he also has communion with Israel."[61] Israel must remain distinct.

Jews are not to be Gentilized, abandoning their calling and chosenness; Gentiles are not compelled to become or behave like Jews.[62] Jews may continue to observe *Torah*;[63] Gentiles are not obligated to *Torah* except in four particulars.[64] The church is not to be so homogenized that they form a third race [Roman/Jew/Christian], different from both Jew and Gentile.[65] Paul's statement that "if anyone is in Christ, he is a new creation" (2 Corinthians 5:17) cannot be taken to refer to a new species or race of person, since that would contradict his direction that "each one should remain in the condition in which he was called" (1 Corinthians 7:20). This is nothing new; Isaiah's welcome to the Gentiles who join themselves to the God of Israel depends on Gentiles remaining a distinct and identifiable grouping within the worshippers at the Temple, so that the "house of prayer for all peoples" (Isaiah 56:7) is, and can be seen to be, exactly that.[66]

As the One New Man is created from the two separate constituencies of Jew and Gentile, the traditions of each are to be remembered and brought into the union, to enrich the whole. Just as the Jewish people are

---

59 Reported in Donaldson, *Jews and Anti-Judaism*, 141.
60 Barth, *Ephesians 1-3*, 310.
61 Ibid., 337.
62 Galatians 2:14.
63 Acts 21:23–26.
64 Acts 15:19–21.
65 Harnack discusses the early use by Christians and their opponents of the *tertium genus* "third race" descriptor (*Mission and Expansion*, 266–78). Hoehner too talks of "'one new humanity,' a third entity" (*Ephesians*, 379). Lincoln claims that "the concept of the church is in fact, if not in name, that of the 'third race'" *Ephesians*, xciii), but admits that this appears to contradict Paul's teaching in Romans. Boyarin suggests that the purpose of early heresiology was "to produce the Christian as neither Jew nor Greek" and a Christianity that was not "a third race or *genus*, but something entirely new, a religion" (*Border Lines*, 4).
66 Janicki, *God-Fearers*, 80.

commanded to remember,[67] so are the Gentiles;[68] both are under a set of priorities[69] and all are blessed, enabled, and empowered by God in a unique way for the sake of each other.[70] The combination is necessary to complete the work; as Barth says, "Jews need Gentiles, Gentiles need Jews."[71]

Mark Kinzer explains that Barth's "out of the two" rather than the NRSV's "in place of the two" implies that "'the two' may remain in the midst of the 'one.'"[72] Paul is shortly to use the analogy of marriage to illustrate the relationship between Messiah and the church,[73] urging husband and wife to exhibit the role and gender-appropriate love and submission modelled by Yeshua himself. In the same way, "unity of Jew and Gentile does not imply the elimination of all distinction between the two, any more than the unity of husband and wife eliminates all gender differentiation."[74]

The fourth point that Barth makes is based on the location of the One New Man: where is he? Paul's words are theologically clear—"in Himself" (Ephesians 2:15)—but anthropologically challenging. In the same way that Yeshua's teaching and preaching ministry in Judea and Galilee was more than simply sharing information, but created a new social reality,[75] so his work on the cross was a new creation that changed the reality of relationship with God.[76] The proclamation in words—"the kingdom of Heaven is at hand" (Matthew 4:17)—became the reality of "the kingdom is in the midst of you" (Luke 17:21).

One of Barth's possible answers to his own question is that as Yeshua is the second Adam,[77] so in the same way that G-d created Eve from Adam,[78] Yeshua created his partner—his bride, the church—out of himself.[79] Paul uses a number of "formed" and "conformed" phrases[80]

---

67 Deuteronomy 8:11.
68 Ephesians 2:11.
69 Romans 3:1–2, 1:16, 2:9.
70 1 Corinthians 12; Ephesians 4:7, 11–12.
71 Barth, *Ephesians 1-3*, 311.
72 Kinzer, *Post-Missionary Messianic Judaism*, 169.
73 Ephesians 5:23–24.
74 Kinzer, *Post-Missionary Messianic Judaism*, 170.
75 Barth, *Ephesians 1-3*, 294.
76 Ephesians 2:17.
77 1 Corinthians 15:45–48.
78 Genesis 2:21–23.
79 Barth, *Ephesians 1-3*, 296.
80 Galatians 4:19; 2 Corinthians 3:18, 4:6; Philippians 3:10, 21; Colossians 3:10, and, perhaps especially Romans 8:29.

connecting the creation of the New Man to the original creation[81] in the image of G-d.

Adam Christology

The title "The Last Adam" is one of the titles given to Yeshua in the Pauline Scriptures,[82] where Paul contrasts the first man with the last Adam. In a longer passage, Paul compares death that came through one with life that comes through the other.[83] Similarly, a third text contrasts death for all in Adam, with the opportunity for all to be made alive in Yeshua.[84] If the One New Man unites Jew and Gentile in Messiah, what is the relationship between the One New Man and Adam?

N. T. Wright suggests,[85] based on his analysis of the commands given to Adam—"be fruitful and multiply, fill the earth and subdue it, take dominion over all other life forms" (Genesis 1:28)—and the way in which they are successively reapplied to Abraham, Isaac and Jacob, and the claim the Rabbis placed in the mouth of God—"I will create Adam first, so that if he sins, Abraham may come and set things right"[86]—that for the writers/redactors of Genesis, "Abraham's children are God's true humanity and their homeland is the new Eden."[87]

After the exile, the *golah* community that returned from Babylon saw themselves as the inheritors of the ritual and promises—the identity—of Israel;[88] the inter-testamental Jewish writings see Israel as Adam's heir.[89] By the time of the *Midrash*, the Rabbis will write that the world was created not for Adam but for Abraham;[90] through Abraham's descendants, Adam has become Israel, the *Torah* the way of true life for God's people, and Israel's hope the hope of the world.

Wright emphasizes the importance of seeing both continuity and discontinuity between Jewish tradition and Paul's writings. Paul has been trained in the rabbinic understandings and expectations of Second Temple Judaism and these form the backdrop for the pictures and images he uses in his letters. The key change in Paul's vision here is that "the

---

81 Genesis 1:26–27.
82 1 Corinthians 15:45.
83 Romans 5:15–21.
84 1 Corinthians 15:22.
85 Wright, *Climax of the Covenant*, 18–26.
86 Genesis Rabbah 14:6.
87 Wright, *Climax of the Covenant*, 23.
88 Blenkinsopp, *Judaism*, 37.
89 1 Enoch 90:19; Jubilees 2:23, etc.
90 Genesis Rabbah 12:9.

The Theological Framework

role traditionally assigned to Israel had devolved on to Jesus Christ."[91] No longer is Israel the exclusive inheritor of Adam's original role; this place is now taken by Yeshua; instead of Abraham putting things right, Yeshua put things right. But Abraham's children—as Paul describes in Galatians 3, the children by faith—are still involved in that process. Now Jew and Gentile, created anew as the One New Man, are the physical embodiment of Yeshua's body on the earth, called to the ministry of reconciliation[92] and discipleship.[93] That calling is on both an intra-group and an inter-group basis. The narrative of Acts is concerned with showing how Yeshua's mandate—Jerusalem, Samaria, to the ends of the earth—is fulfilled. Initially, this is Jew to Jew, then Jew to Gentile; the role of Gentile-to-Gentile or Gentile-to-Jew evangelism is only mentioned obliquely. The closing sections of Paul's letters show an increasing number of Gentiles becoming involved as leaders and workers rather than just recipients. The failure of subsequent generations to implement Paul's implicit injunction that the Gentiles were to make the Jewish people jealous[94] has resulted in a significant imbalance within the One New Man, only starting to be addressed in these days.[95]

Just Unity?

But is this passage just about unity? Can one here and in the three directly related biblical passages—Galatians 3:28, Colossians 3:11 and 1 Corinthians 12:13—see ethnic equality or ethnic collapse?[96] Paul's writings as a whole don't suggest that he sees a collapse of gender; physical gender and reciprocal roles in marriage[97] are emphasised and retained. It also appears from Acts and epistle references that Paul was not devaluing circumcision, the Jewish calendar and other Jewish practices for Jews,[98] instead keeping and observing them himself.[99] "The Ephesian letter was not about cultural homogeneity."[100]

---

91 Wright, *Climax of the Covenant*, 26.
92 2 Corinthians 5:17–19.
93 Matthew 28:19–20.
94 Romans 11:11.
95 Bernis, "Where are All the Jews," 173.
96 The phrase "ethnic collapse" is used by Justin Hardin as an opposite to what he sees Paul announcing: "equality across ethnic boundaries" ("Equality in the Church," 228–9). Ethnicity does not collapse or disappear; it is both maintained and bridged.
97 Ephesians 5; 1 Corinthians 7.
98 Hardin, "Equality in the Church," 228.
99 Acts 20:16, 21:18–26; Romans 14; Colossians 2:16.
100 Walls, *Cross-Cultural Process*, 77.

Amid suggestions that Ephesians 2 is part of a narrative of divine warfare,[101] culminating in God announcing his victory, proclaiming peace and building a Temple where his people will worship him,[102] it might appear that Jews and Gentiles are being portrayed as two opposing protagonists, one fighting for God, the other against God, at any rate "without God and without hope in the world" (Ephesians 2:12). Now brought together, the two parties are brought to peace with each other and with God. Yeshua, the agent and creator of the peace, calls Jewish and Gentile believers to partner with each other to fulfill a common God-given destiny.[103]

Believers in Messiah have been given a commission to make disciples in all the nations of the world.[104] The book of Acts records Jewish people, with a little marginal assistance from early Gentile converts, sharing the gospel with a largely Gentile audience and being wildly successful. Paul—himself an Israelite to whom was given the prerogative of sharing the gospel with Gentiles[105]—usually concludes his letters with lists of his co-workers, travelling companions, and those he has appointed as elders in the churches that he has planted. These lists usually contain a mix of Gentile and Jewish names—those from the circumcision working alongside those of the uncircumcision[106]—as the One New Man emerged and sprang into action. There is a strong interdependence that must be achieved if the target of the Great Commission is to be reached. The Jewish people will not come to faith in Yeshua without the love, intercession and support of the church;[107] the church will not be complete without the ministry and witness of the Jewish people.[108]

Unity is not the same as uniformity.[109] Unity and diversity—respecting the traditions and cultures of different peoples—is a key to building the One New Man. Distinction—difference—is not lost in creating unity; "unity implies distinctiveness and yet

---

101 See, for example, the kingship pattern proposed by Arie Leder as an outline for the book of Exodus: the occasion for conflict, the battle, the kingship, the palace (*Waiting for the Land*, 47).
102 Gombis, "Narrative of Divine Warfare."
103 Wolff, "Identity of the One New Man," 14.
104 Matthew 28:18–20.
105 Robinson, "Distinction," 33.
106 Galatians 2:7.
107 Teplinsky, "Ruth and Naomi," 137.
108 Shishkoff, *What About Us?*, 9, 132–3.
109 Juster, "Denominations," 104; Dauermann, "The One New Man."

complementarity."[110] Too often Paul's exhortation to "Be imitators of me" (1 Corinthians 11:1) has been used as an enforcement mechanism for eliminating difference[111] and, probably unintentionally, obscuring the One New Man. Becoming the One New Man is achieved through a shared and individual identity in Yeshua,[112] not through perfect mimesis or caricature of an "ideal" Christian. "The miracle of the *One New Man* is that those who are and who remain essentially different are enabled to live together reconciled, in love and mutual blessing."[113]

The Olive Tree Analogy

Paul's letter to the community in Rome—dictated to and written down by his faithful amanuensis, Tertius[114]—was written from Corinth probably between the winter of 56 CE and the spring of 57 CE.[115] Since then it has been argued over and contested by many commentators, and is described by N. T. Wright as "by common consent his masterpiece."[116] Wright divides the book into four main sections, chapters 1–4, 5–8, 9–11, and 12–16; the faithfulness of God; God's people in Christ as the true humanity; God's promises and God's faithfulness; God's call to worship, holiness and unity.[117]

There had probably been a strong connection between the churches in Rome and the church in Jerusalem, with the Roman congregations looking to Jerusalem as their mother church, following Jewish Christian liturgical rites, and observing much Mosaic law.[118] This may have been the result of Jews from Rome having been in Jerusalem at Pentecost[119] and returning home to found a community of believers in their city.[120]

Many Jews lived in Rome in the 50s CE; between fifteen and sixty thousand [121] out of a total population of perhaps a million.[122] Claudius had banished the Jews from Rome from 49 CE onwards until his death in 54 CE, which "may have left a vacuum in the early community which the

---

110 Atkinson, "Jews and Gentiles," 14.
111 Castelli, *Imitating Paul*, 128.
112 Brown, *"Celebrating our Distinctives,"* 110.
113 Dauermann, "The One New Man," original emphasis.
114 Romans 16:22.
115 Moo, *Epistle to the Romans*, 3; Thistleton, *Discovering Romans*, 2,65.
116 Wright, "Letter to the Romans," 319.
117 Ibid., 329–30.
118 Longenecker, *Epistle to the Romans*, 9.
119 Acts 2:10.
120 Schreiner, *Romans*, 11.
121 Thistleton, *Discovering Romans*, 19.
122 Keener, *The Gospel of Matthew*, 10.

Gentile believers came to fill,"[123] although they "poured back into the city with the death of Claudius and the end of his decree."[124] Shulam suggests that there were possibly many small churches that met in houses throughout the city, who would have passed Paul's letter from group to group, and that the church would have been of very heterogeneous composition, "mixed Jewish and Gentile believers,"[125] possibly including non-Yeshua-believing Jews and God-fearers as part of the Jewish synagogue community.[126] Anthony Thiselton writes about the probable conflict between the returning Jewish leaders, such as Aquila and Priscilla,[127] and the Gentile believers who had taken the reins in their absence: "How would they fare in a predominantly Gentile Christian church?" he asks.

> Some degree of friction or misunderstanding was almost inevitable. Doubtless some Jewish Christians might have pointed to their greater understanding of Scripture, and to their status as God's chosen people. Gentile Christians might have responded by pointing out that God has rejected physical Israel.[128]

It is against this background that Paul writes what many commentators consider to be his *magnum opus*, a doctrinal work that addresses the tensions between a Jewish and a Gentile view of Christianity, what Paul perhaps "hopes will heal the most serious social-theological rift in the early church."[129] Within a few verses, he proclaims that "the gospel is the power of God for salvation to everyone who believes, to the Jew first and also to the Greek" (1:16) and will go on to suggest—echoing the words of the Jewish writings[130]—that "All Israel will be saved" (Romans 11:26).

---

123 Shulam, *Jewish Roots of Romans*, 14.
124 Thistleton, *Discovering Romans*, 188.
125 Shulam, *Jewish Roots of Romans*, 14, 24.
126 Nanos, *The Mystery of Romans*, 13–14, disagreeing with N. T. Wright, who sees Romans as "a letter to a largely gentile church in Rome" (*Paul and the Faithfulness of God*, 1206).
127 Acts 18:2; Romans 16:3–4.
128 Thistleton, *Discovering Romans*, 5.
129 Moo, *Epistle to the Romans*, 3. The single-focus ministry Towards Jerusalem Council II is trying to address the same problem in the contemporary church.
130 "All Israel has a share in the world to come" *m. Sanhedrin* 10:1 and *b. Sanhedrin* 90a, based on "Your people shall all be righteous; they shall possess the land forever, the branch of My planting, the work of My hands, that I might be glorified" (Isaiah 60:21).

The Theological Framework

Chapters 9–11 address how Jewish and Gentile Christians are supposed to behave and the future of God's elective purposes for Israel.[131] Paul is concerned that the Gentile Christians in Rome may be "developing a new self-understanding that is not only distinct from, but perhaps even in opposition to, their designation as children of Abraham," thinking themselves superior to their Jewish fellow believers in Yeshua. "It is not enough that individual Jews find faith in Christ; [Paul] wants the salvation of Israel, but not simply as a small remnant attached to a predominantly Gentile church."[132]

Paul's well-known analogy of wild and cultivated olive branches being grafted into an olive tree is found in verses 11–24 of chapter 11 of the Roman letter and has already been alluded to in the illustration of family apple trees above. These verses, in turn, come almost at the end of the section recognized by most commentators from 9:1–11:36, a section about which almost everything is controversial.[133] Elizabeth Johnson sees an "overarching apocalyptic thrust" to the section,[134] C. E. B. Cranfield judges it to be "an essential element in the structure of Paul's attempted summary of the gospel as he understands it,"[135] while many scholars of the past have treated it as "a digression or even an interpolation from another context."[136] Ben Witherington notes that these chapters introduce a break in the overall rhetorical style of the letter and form "a *refutatio* of Gentile misunderstandings about Jews and Jewish Christians and God's salvation plan as it involves them."[137]

In summary, Paul describes his sorrow at the majority rejection by his own people, the Jews, of the gospel, in spite of the gifts and blessings that are—irrevocably—theirs (9:1–5, 11:26). It is not that God's word has failed, for the principle of election prevails from the earliest stories in the Hebrew Scriptures, but that faith is required to hear and respond to God which not all Israelites, in spite of their birth heritage, have done (9:6–13). Many Gentiles have come to faith and accepted God's offer of entering the kingdom precisely because they do not have that birth heritage (9:14–33). Paul longs for his people to turn from their own attempts to be righteous and recognize the Messiah, because his righteousness is the target to which the *Torah* points (10:a–b). There is no difference between Jew and Gentile in the need for faith: everyone

---

131 Wright, *Paul and the Faithfulness of God*, 1157.
132 Campbell, *Unity and Diversity in Christ*, 97, 78.
133 Wright, "Letter to the Romans," 527.
134 Johnson, *The Function of Apocalyptic*, 3.
135 Cranfield, *Critical and Exegetical Commentary*, 818.
136 Keener, *Romans*, 115.
137 Witherington, *Paul's letter to the Romans*, 17.

who speaks out by faith to claim relationship with God will receive it (10:5–13), but believers need to take the message of faith to the Jewish people, because they cannot believe what they have never heard (10:14–17). Israel's current lack of understanding is a necessary part of the process of reaching the Gentiles so that Israel themselves will eventually understand (10:18–21). So God has not rejected his ancient people—Paul himself is a fully credentialed part of the believing remnant[138]—but Israel have stumbled so that the Gentiles have an opportunity to hear and respond and fulfill prophecy by making Israel jealous (11:1–12). Israel's past provides a connection point, both for new Gentile believers and Jews who come to believe, so that they may be plugged in to, and draw current from, the power source of faith (11:11–17). The Gentiles are not to think that, because they are currently connected, they are better than the Jews, for God is perfectly capable of pushing in and pulling out any of the plugs on the plugboard (11:18–23). Although they may look different, all types of plugs can be connected and reconnected—the miracle is that they can and do work (11:24). God's plans are that there should be a short-term surplus of connection points to enable the Gentiles—who have no birth heritage—to connect easily, while, in the fullness of time, the Israelite plugs will all find a natural connection point, for their calling to connect will never be removed (11:25–32). By this method, God's wisdom and planning will be shown to be the best and he will be glorified (11:33–36).

Building on Wright's rendering of 11:11, "Granted that Israel according to the flesh has 'stumbled,' has that stumble meant a permanent 'fall?'",[139] Thistleton divides Paul's reply into three parts: that Israel's temporary failure has been for the sake of the Gentiles, of whom Israel will become jealous; the olive tree analogy; and the "mystery of God's dealings with Israel."[140] Shulam is more cautious, arguing that, while some of Israel have stumbled, this "does not substantiate the conclusion that Israel have 'fallen' and been replaced by the Gentiles as God's people."[141]

In verse 11:16, Paul introduces two parallel agrarian metaphors to carry his argument forward. The first is ἀπαρχὴ, first-fruits, the second is ἡ ῥίζα καὶ οἱ κλάδοι, the root and the branches. First-fruits are the token

---

138 Esler comments that "Paul was a 'self' with a 'self-concept' that included a number of cognitive representations available to him, and here he was making the Israelite one salient" (*Conflict and Identity*, 293).
139 Wright, "Letter to the Romans," 581.
140 Thistleton, *Discovering Romans*, 211.
141 Shulam, *Jewish Roots of Romans*, 367.

offering brought at the start of the harvest,[142] or dough after the first rising in making bread.[143] Using the analogy that both Yeshua and Paul use elsewhere of leaven working through the whole batch of dough,[144] Paul makes the point that if the first-fruits are holy—having been offered to God—then that makes the whole batch holy.[145] Similarly, he then argues, if the root (or the tree, implied at this point) is holy, the branches also will be. Here there are echoes of the commandments concerning the rules for the fruit and produce of a tree in its early years,[146] and of Yeshua's comments about the good/bad fruit of good/bad trees.[147] Although conceding that there is some debate over who is/are the referent(s) of the first-fruits and the root, Schreiner concludes that "both illustrations make the same point . . . ethnic Israel is not cast off but still remains the elect people of God."[148] The images are not simply an affirmation that Israel's acceptance of God's plan in Messiah will mean life from the dead, but "a sequence of imagery and argument . . . that will ultimately produce the result celebrated in verse 15."[149] This verse then links into the larger metaphor that Paul will build in the following verses.

In verses 17–24, Paul talks about wild and natural (or, perhaps, cultivated) branches and the way in which God did previously, and will at various times, break branches off and graft branches into the root. Branches can be grafted into the root because they all share the property "olive," albeit of different sources: Israel and the nations. They have an "intrinsic oneness," says Richard Longenecker, who identifies the natural branches as the "remnant among Israel," and the wild branches, "the engrafted branches," as the "remnant among the Gentiles,"[150] but must be mistaken as Paul says that "even they, if they do not continue in their unbelief, will be grafted in" (Romans 11:23); a remark that addresses Israel as a whole. Moreover, either a natural or a wild branch can be engrafted as a result of faith. Paul develops through chapters 9–11 the concept of the righteous remnant, assuming that God always maintains a faithful remnant by his grace, and will never cease to do so.[151] Douglas

---

142 Leviticus 23:10.
143 Numbers 15:21.
144 Matthew 13:33 and 1 Corinthians 5:6.
145 And Paul uses the same analogy to argue that a believing spouse sanctifies their partner and children (1 Corinthians 7:14).
146 Leviticus 19:23–25.
147 Matthew 7:17–19.
148 Schreiner, *Romans*, 601.
149 Esler, *Conflict and Identity*, 298–299.
150 Longenecker, *Epistle to the Romans*, 891.
151 Campbell, *Unity and Diversity in Christ*, 77.

Harink comments that Paul has a single thesis in view throughout Romans 9–11: that "God will never reject His chosen fleshly people or allow them to fail in the race of salvation."[152]

The identity of the olive tree is also subject to some debate. One option is Yeshua, who is prophetically called "the branch" or "sprout,"[153] rising from the "root" or "stem" of Jesse;[154] Paul himself is to revisit this connection later.[155] Cranfield offers the patriarchs;[156] a view supported by Keener, who says that the Gentile believers are "grafted into Israel as full members."[157] Moo suggests "the true people of God,"[158] while Barth claims it is God himself: "He is the holy root of the tree."[159] Mark Nanos covers the last base by proposing that it "appears to signify the remnant of restored Israel."[160] Wright manages to combine several of the possibilities into one:

> It is, of course, a metaphor for Israel itself . . . a family rooted in the patriarchs and the promises God made to them; a family from which, strangely, many "natural branches" have been broken off, but into which many "unnatural branches" have been grafted.[161]

The olive tree is used as an image for Israel in several places in the Hebrew Scriptures:

> I will be like the dew to Israel; he shall blossom like the lily; he shall take root like the trees of Lebanon; his shoots shall spread out; his beauty shall be like the olive, and his fragrance like Lebanon. They shall return and dwell beneath my shadow; they shall flourish like the grain; they shall blossom like the vine; their fame shall be like the wine of Lebanon (Hosea 14:5–7).

The Psalmist (attributed in this case to David) describes himself as "a green olive tree in the house of God" (Psalm 52:8), and the Sages of the Talmud affirmed the analogy, connecting other attributes of the tree and olive production to the history of Israel:

---

152 Harink, *Paul Among the Postliberals*, 174.
153 E.g., Zechariah 6:12.
154 Isaiah 11:10.
155 Romans 15:12.
156 Cranfield, *Critical and Exegetical Commentary*, 565.
157 Keener, *The Gospel of Matthew*, 134.
158 Moo, *Epistle to the Romans*, 709.
159 Barth, *Romans*, 408.
160 Nanos, *The Mystery of Romans*, 252; also see Esler, *Conflict and Identity*, 300.
161 Wright, *Paul and the Faithfulness of God*, 1213–4.

Then came forth a Heavenly Voice and said, The Lord called your name a leafy olive-tree, fair with goodly fruit (Jeremiah 11:16): as the olive-tree produces its best only at the very end, so Israel will flourish at the end of time . . . R. Joshua b. Levi said, Why is Israel likened to an olive-tree? To tell you that as the olive-tree loses not its leaves either in summer or in winter, so Israel shall never be lost either in this world or in the world to come. R. Johanan said, Why is Israel likened to an olive-tree? To tell you that just as the olive produces its oil only after pounding, so Israel returns to the right way only after suffering (*b.* Menachot 53*b*).

The connection to branches being broken off comes when Jeremiah uses the picture of Israel as a "green olive tree" whose branches are consumed by fire because of their evil deeds and idolatry[162]—a sign of God's wrath.[163] Paul speaks of branches being broken off "because of their unbelief" (Romans 11:20). Joseph Shulam tries to pass this as "pruning," an action to improve the yield of the tree, suggesting that "Israel's pruning and exile are therefore only for a temporary period and will be replaced when God forgives them and brings them redemption at the end of time."[164] Perhaps this can be connected to Yeshua's words speaking of the Father: "Every branch in Me that does not bear fruit, He takes away; and every one that bears fruit, He prunes it, that it may bear more fruit" (John 15:2).

By his use of the "olive tree" image, Paul is pointing to a common in-group identity—the tree itself—but carefully not erasing the distinctiveness of the two constituent subgroups: the natural (Israelite) and wild (Gentile) branches. As Esler observes, "efforts at social re-categorisation may fail if this strategy is not adopted by those leading the process."[165]

Picking up on the phrase "contrary to nature" (verse 24), Thistleton draws attention to the ancient aboricultural practice of grafting a wild olive onto an old olive tree to invigorate the growth of the whole.[166] While Moo says that we have no idea whether Paul is or is not familiar with olive cultivation, and suggests that Paul must be allowed to use a metaphor without being correct to the last detail, asserting that "we certainly cannot draw any theological conclusions"[167] from this aspect of

---

162 Jeremiah 11:16–17.
163 Shulam, *Jewish Roots of Romans*, 372.
164 Ibid., 372.
165 Esler, *Conflict and Identity*, 300.
166 Thistleton, *Discovering Romans*, 213–4; Longenecker, *Epistle to the Romans*, 893. Also see Wright, "Letter to the Romans," 586.
167 Moo, *Epistle to the Romans*, 703.

the argument, Esler points out that Paul could have chosen *"young cultivated olive, but chose not to,"*[168] suggesting that he was well aware of the non-edible property of wild olive branches, perhaps to provoke the jealousy he spoke of earlier.[169] Nevertheless, the unexpectedness of Jew and Gentile co-existing as believers in the body of Messiah connects well with the breaking down of the wall of partition used by Paul just before his One New Man picture.[170]

Is Paul here trying to squelch Gentile pride in thinking that they now "own" Yeshua and can do no wrong? Have the Gentiles misinterpreted their inclusion as a sign of superiority?[171] Witherington senses a put-down: "Wild olive trees never produce useful oil."[172] Not at all; if the natural branches—those who belong by nature in the tree—have been broken off, then the grafted branches—those who do not by nature belong to the tree—can just as surely be broken off. It is God's choice whom he engrafts into the root stock to draw on the rich sap. Throughout, "God's call is sovereign and is independent of human effort."[173] If God did not spare even his own Son,[174] then he will hardly shrink from cutting off branches—of whatever flavor, Jew or Gentile—who persist in unbelief, or abandon faith. "There is only one olive tree," Moo and Schreiner agree, "whose roots are firmly planted in OT soil and whose branches include both Jew and Gentiles."[175]

Messianic Jewish scholar Stuart Dauermann offers an important perspective on the natural and wild olive branches. While loved and blessed, Dauermann asserts, the nations remain "other" from Israel—the otherness of adoption:

> Gentiles remain wild olive shoots even when grafted into Israel's olive tree, while even Jews who do not believe in Yeshua remain ever and always natural branches. God's election is particularist and differentiated, expressed in enduring covenants and promises, and the seed of Jacob always retains a unique status.[176]

Overall, the olive tree analogy offers support for the idea of Jewish and Gentile believers being part of the olive tree, part of the kingdom of God

---

168 Esler, *Conflict and Identity*, 304, original emphasis.
169 Romans 11:11.
170 Ephesians 2:14–15a.
171 Schreiner, *Romans*, 607.
172 Witherington, *Paul's letter to the Romans*, 271.
173 Johnson, *The Function of Apocalyptic*, 162.
174 Romans 8:32.
175 Moo, *Epistle to the Romans*, 709 and Schreiner, *Romans*, 605.
176 Dauermann, *Converging Destinies*, 33–34.

by faith in Yeshua, and remaining distinct and identifiable as wild and natural branches grafted in to the olive tree, thus demonstrating God's calling, election and provenance in the grafting process. This is "the fulfilment of the promises made by the creator God to Israel,"[177] and extended to the world in Yeshua. Paul announces "the coming together of Jews and gentiles into a single and unified, eschatological covenant community, in which *previous social identities necessarily retain their fundamental significance.*"[178]

Counting All Things Loss

In Paul's letter to the Philippians, he challenges those who think that they have physical or inherited credentials on which to stand or of which to boast.[179] Assuring them that his personal credentials—correctly circumcised on the eighth day, so not a proselyte;[180] of the people Israel, not grafted in;[181] belonging to the tribe of Benjamin, a shrewd move given that Philippi's Roman citizenship depended on one Roman ancestral family;[182] a Hebrew speaker of Hebrew parentage, not a Greek-speaker or the son of converts;[183] a Pharisee, set apart for both the written and oral *Torah*;[184] zealous in conduct, persecuting the church with the same zeal as Pinchas;[185] and blameless in righteousness, keeping the *Torah* perfectly[186]—are as good as or better than those of others,[187] Paul nevertheless describes them as rubbish when compared to his relationship with Yeshua. These are significant attributes, all denoting a strong and genuine Jewish identity and of inestimable value if properly used.[188] Paul uses clinical accounting language to describe the way these assets have changed from a "gain" to a "loss."[189] Elsewhere Paul cites the same caliber of credentials as of significant value.[190] Markus

---

177 Wright, *Paul and the Faithfulness of God*, 368.
178 Zoccali, "Children of Abraham," 257, original emphasis.
179 Philippians 3:3–11.
180 O'Brien *Epistle to the Philippians*, 369.
181 Romans 11:17; Cook, "Philippians," 358.
182 Bockmuehl, *Philippians*, 196.
183 Stern, *Jewish New Testament Commentary*, 600.
184 O'Brien *Epistle to the Philippians*, 373–4.
185 Numbers 25:6–13; O'Brien *Epistle to the Philippians*, 375; also cf. Galatians 1:13–14.
186 Bockmuehl, *Philippians*, 202; cf. Luke 1:6.
187 O'Brien *Epistle to the Philippians*, 365.
188 Hendricksen, *Philippians, Colossians & Philemon*, 161.
189 Bockmuehl, *Philippians*, 204.
190 For example, Romans 3:1–2, 9:1–5, 11:1.

Bockmuehl notes that at no point does Paul suggest "that he has ceased to be a Pharisee,"[191] to the contrary later proclaiming in Jerusalem, "I am a Pharisee" (Acts 23:6).

On that basis, this appears to be hyperbolic language,[192] used in the same way as the gospels record Yeshua saying that anyone "who loves father or mother more than me is not worthy of me" (Matthew 10:37). Just as Yeshua recognised the responsibilities he had towards his parents,[193] in line with the fifth commandment,[194] yet spoke in such a way as to emphasize that commitment to G-d came before commitment to family,[195] so Paul recognizes the worth of his birth, abilities, education and status that G-d has given him and then uses them to advance the gospel—his Roman citizenship, after all, had saved his life in Jerusalem and got him a free, if not trouble-free, passage to Caesar in Rome[196]—but uses hyperbole to show that his relationship with Yeshua is far more valuable than they. David Stern suggests that Paul is deprecating pride in these attributes rather than the attributes themselves.[197] This can be supported by comparing Paul's "that I may know Christ Jesus my Lord" (Philippians 3:8) with Jeremiah's "let him who boasts boast in this: that he understands and knows Me" (Jeremiah 9:24).

This passage in Paul's letter to the Philippians, used incorrectly in the author's opinion by many to denigrate Jewish identity and attributes as not only of no value but a negative liability,[198] does not detract from the One New Man image in Ephesians. There is no identity collapse, simply a setting in right order and priority. Paul's overriding passion is to "know Christ and be found in Him" (Philippians 3:8–9);[199] all else, however good, is surrendered to that aim and serves that goal.

---

191 Bockmuehl, *Philippians*, 198.
192 Dauermann, *Converging Destinies*, 157.
193 Keener, *The Gospel of Matthew*, 330.
194 Exodus 20:12; Deuteronomy 5:16.
195 Gale, "Matthew," 24, notes that Jewish sources agree with regard to faith in God (e.g., *y. Kiddushin* 1.7).
196 O'Brien *Epistle to the Philippians*, 387.
197 Stern, *Jewish New Testament Commentary*, 601.
198 For example, Hendricksen, *Philippians, Colossians & Philemon*, 161–2.
199 Bockmuehl, *Philippians*, 213.

All are One

Despite some voices to the contrary,[200] it seems clear that Paul wrote all his major letters to Gentile audiences. He was, after all, the Apostle to the Gentiles, as Peter was to the Jews.[201] In a number of those letters, Paul couples the two identities "Jew" and "Greek" in order to emphasize the unity that is to be found between believers from different backgrounds, genders and status. He uses a number of binary opposites —Jew and Greek,[202] male and female,[203] circumcised and uncircumcised,[204] slave and free,[205] all categories that are distinct and cannot be blurred—to demonstrate the power of the gospel for bringing people together in unity. Paul is creating a new identity—believers in Messiah—by stressing the essentialist[206] component, the authentic and unique characteristic of the group:[207] despite their differences, crossing many lines of division in the ancient world, they are one in Messiah.[208] Caroline Johnson Hodge maintains:

> lineage, paternity and peoplehood are the salient categories for describing one's status before the God of Israel . . . notions of peoplehood and paternity are by no means rejected, played down or even metaphorised by Paul; instead they are central to his gospel and crucial to his arguments, especially in Galatians and Romans.[209]

Despite the rhetoric of levelling, the "new" community did not deliver social mobility to its members: slaves remained slaves, Jews and Greeks

---

200 See, for example, Shulam and Le Cornu, *Jewish Roots of Romans*, 35, who suggests that the Roman community was a mixed community of Jews and Gentiles.
201 Galatians 2:8.
202 Galatians 3:28; Colossians 3:11; Romans 10:12; 1 Corinthians 12:13.
203 Galatians 3:28.
204 Colossians 3:11.
205 Galatians 3:28; Colossians 3:11; 1 Corinthians 12:13.
206 essentialist: "the view that categories of people, such as women and men, or heterosexuals and homosexuals, or members of ethnic groups, have intrinsically different and characteristic natures or dispositions" (Stevenson, *Oxford Dictionary of English*, 598).
207 Johnson Hodge, *If Sons, Then Heirs*, 21–2.
208 David Stern points out (*Jewish New Testament Commentary*, 555) that the three pairs match three of the Morning Blessings said each day in the synagogue prayers by (free) Jewish men: "Blessed are You, Lord our God, King of the universe, who has not made me a Gentile/slave/woman" (Sacks, *Authorised Daily Prayer Book*, 17).
209 Johnson Hodge, *If Sons, Then Heirs*, 4–5.

retained their ethnic background and markers, gender priorities and roles are affirmed. "There seems to be an element of ongoing distinction within the boundaries of Christ-communities, as ethnic heritage is noted and expanded upon within the discourse."[210]

The Jewish world recognized a category of Gentile who could be regarded as pious by Jewish standards: God-fearers. Although the definition varied between respecting the God of Israel, respecting the Jewish community and being observant of *Torah*, they were welcomed within the Jewish community and events.[211] The New Testament records God-fearers present in synagogue *Shabbat* services.[212] Shaye Cohen observes that:

> gentiles often mingled with Jews and some gentiles even observed Jewish rituals and practices. As a result, these reasonable conclusions would lead you to label some gentiles as Jews . . . By observing Jewish practices and by associating with Jews, gentiles will have been called Jews and some will have been mistaken as Jews.[213]

Nevertheless, they remained Gentile and did not take the formal step of conversion to Judaism. They did not leave the Gentile world and their adherence to Jewish laws and customs was a matter of habit, conviction, or conscience and could be revoked at any time.

Gentiles who have come to faith in Messiah, on the other hand, have left the world of pagan Rome—their belief in Yeshua, accepting that he is Lord of all and rejecting the claims of Caesar to be lord of all,[214] have set them apart from who they were—but have not entered the world of the Jews; they have not converted to Judaism. Many of their kinship group memberships remain intact: male or female, uncircumcised, slave or free, but they are now in the liminal space between Jew and Gentile, Gentiles-in-Christ. They have a fictive genealogy derived from Abraham,[215] allowing them to be part of the family and promise to Abraham—"In you shall (πάντα τὰ ἔθνη) all the nations be blessed" (Galatians 3:8)—where Paul conflates the two blessings given to Abraham: "in you (πᾶσαι αἱ φυλαὶ) all the families of the earth shall be blessed" (Genesis 12:3, LXX), and "(πάντα τὰ ἔθνη) all the nations of the earth shall be blessed in him" (Genesis 18:18, LXX). Changes are

---

210 Shkul, "New Identity," 383, 376
211 Eisenbaum, *Paul was Not a Christian*, 111–3.
212 Acts 13:6.
213 Cohen, *Beginnings of Jewishness*, 68.
214 Acts 17:7; John 19:12; Rowe, *World Upside Down*, 106.
215 Galatians 3:29.

expected from these Gentiles-in-Christ, including complete rejection of idolatry and sexual immorality, and high levels of self-discipline and holiness.[216]

It seems that the "mixed" status of Gentiles-in-Christ is part of Paul's understanding; they are urged to retain their status at the time of coming to faith,[217] not to convert to Judaism by circumcision.[218] Johnson Hodge suggests that "God's larger plan requires gentiles to worship the God of Israel *as gentiles*, not as proselytes or something else."[219] This is in line with the prophets of Israel, who speak of the nations turning to God as nations rather than becoming Jews.[220] Post-biblical texts also reflect a vision of Jew and Gentile participating in the *Olam Haba*[221] together,[222] while the prayer known as the *Aleinu*—used at the end of each of the regular synagogue prayer services—contains the words:

> Therefore we place our hope in You, Lord our God, that we may soon see the glory of Your power, when you will remove abominations from the earth, and idols will be utterly destroyed, when the world will be perfected under the sovereignty of the Almighty, when all humanity will call on Your name, and the earth's wicked will all turn to You. All the world's inhabitants will realise and know that to You every knee must bow and every tongue swear loyalty. Before You, Lord our God, they will kneel and bow down and give honour to Your glorious name. They will all accept the yoke of Your kingdom, and You will reign over them soon and for ever.[223]

This is strongly reminiscent of the early church liturgy fragment encapsulated in the letter to the Philippians,[224] both being drawn from the book of Isaiah.[225]

Both Jew and Gentile are to achieve unity by coming together into the "in Christ" super-category; neither undergo ethnic transformation.[226]

---

216 Johnson Hodge, "Question of Identity," 157.
217 1 Corinthians 7:24.
218 1 Corinthians 7:18; Galatians 5:2–6.
219 Johnson Hodge, "Question of Identity," 168; original emphasis.
220 For example: Isaiah 2:2–4 (also Micah 4:1–3) and Zechariah 8:21–23.
221 Hebrew: the world to come.
222 Eisenbaum, *Paul was Not a Christian*, 97.
223 Sacks, *Authorised Daily Prayer Book*, 142–3.
224 Philippians 2:9–11; Ware (*Synopsis*, §22, 40) categorizes this as a "Proposed Hymn Fragment."
225 Isaiah 45:23.
226 "This does not require the obliteration of individual ethnicity" (Darko, "Adopted Siblings," 340).

There is no identity collapse; Yeshua-believing Jews and Yeshua-believing Gentiles together make up the One New Man;[227] "their separateness is necessary for God's plan for Israel, as Paul sees it."[228] The recategorization and creation of the superordinate group "will need to co-exist with whatever remains of the members' original Judean and Greek identities."[229] Unlike the Qumran sectarians, the Yeshua-believing community was not being urged to withdraw from society,[230] but instead engage with both its Jewish and Gentile parents to perform the "good works prepared beforehand" (Ephesians 2:10). This situation probably continued in Ephesus until nearly the end of the first century.[231] Campbell suggests that, despite a Gentile majority membership, there is at times, "an almost complete appropriation of Jewish identity."[232] The One New Man metaphor may have provided a corrective in this situation to rebalance the equality of role and identity.

Andrew Walls and The Ephesian Moment

The Scottish missiologist Andrew Walls wrote an influential article, "The Ephesian Moment—At a Crossroads in Christian History,"[233] about the One New Man. Arguing that the time when the Ephesian letter was written was a unique moment in the history of the church, when it was possible to create a new "Christian" identity from the two pre-existing "Jewish" and "Gentile" identities, Walls points out that:

> The Ephesian moment—the social coming together of two cultures to experience Christ—was quite brief. Circumstances—the destruction of the Jewish state in 70 CE, the scattering of the Jewish church, the sheer success of the mission to the Gentiles—soon made the church mono-cultural again; and in the eastern Mediterranean the church movement became as overwhelmingly Hellenistic as once it had been overwhelmingly Jewish.[234]

Noting the areas of the world in which church growth is taking place, where decisions and choices for the church will inevitably soon be taken for groups and in areas outside the conventional Western church's

---

227 In the same way as male and female make up "mankind." See Juster, *Jewish Roots*, 155–156.
228 Johnson Hodge, "Question of Identity," 172.
229 Esler, *Conflict and Identity*, 140.
230 Campbell, "Unity and Diversity in the Church," 19.
231 Martyn, *History and Theology*, 66.
232 Campbell, "Unity and Diversity in the Church," 22.
233 Walls, *Cross-Cultural Process*, 72–81.
234 Walls, *Cross-Cultural Process*, 78.

traditional areas of strength and influence,[235] Walls argues that the church is once again at an Ephesian moment[236] and asks whether the church has the vision and the will to bring all of its multiple cultures and peoples to the table in order to create a transcultural unity that can aspire to the "measure of the stature of the fullness of Messiah" (Ephesians 4:13).

Walls' emphasis on unity among the various national, ethnic and geographical groupings making up the church in the twenty-first century is an important objective. The Bible, however, only seems to recognize two cultures:[237] Jewish and Gentile; Israel and the nations.[238] Unity among the cultures of the nations is exactly that; however desirable, and perhaps necessary a precursor to the original blueprint, it does not address the creation of the One New Man from Jew and Gentile. Paul's fundamental call to recognize what God was doing in the first century remains on the table. Somewhat overcome by events and then suppressed by the church, it is now coming sharply back into focus and still awaits resolution.

Walls warns of two potential dangers: the first, to protect what currently exists as being the standard and trying to enforce this against all comers; the second, which he describes as the "post-modern option," is to remain distinct, accepting both expressions as valid and authentic. Either course of action denies the One New Man and, therefore, the fullness of Messiah.[239]

David Woods and "Distinction Theory"

South African theologian David Woods, based on the New Testament (NT) usage of the verb διαχρίνω, has coined the phrase "Distinction Theory" for a

> theological framework which understands Jewish and Gentile believers in Jesus as distinct in certain significant theological senses, including identity and function (role, service) in the

---

235 See also the discussion about church population growth and shift in Jenkins (*The Next Christendom*).
236 Walls is supported by some leaders within the Messianic Jewish movement, who refer to the current times as an "extraordinary hour of destiny." Shishkoff, *What About Us?*, 12
237 Accepting that the word "culture" is perhaps anachronistic here, it is the word used by Walls. The Bible recognizes a table of nations in Genesis 10, different languages, cultures, and gods. However, it maintains a strict duality between Israel and "the nations."
238 Gaston, *Paul and the Torah*, 6.
239 Walls, *Cross-Cultural Process*, 78–79, original emphasis.

economy of God's kingdom. That is, a biblical differentiation exists between Israel and the nations *within the church* similar to that which existed more visibly before Christ.[240]

Although also called "bilateral ecclesiology,"[241] "unity and diversity in the church,"[242] and *"Torah*-defined ecclesiological variegation,"[243] this term sees Jewish and Gentile identities remaining distinct but equal within the *ecclesia*. These distinctions are deliberate rather than arbitrary and the diversity is embraced for mutual blessing rather than erased in Messiah.[244] Nanos observes that Gentiles are forbidden to become Jews because doing so denies the oneness of God—if he is not the God of those not in Israel, then he cannot be the One God of all.[245] Gentile believers do not become Jews, but they are to identify with Israel, being joined to Israel's Messiah and made part of the commonwealth of Israel as co-citizens.[246]

Woods addresses two texts, Acts 11:12 and Acts 15:9, that have traditionally been taken to deny distinction between Jewish and Gentile believers, and suggests that this is both an incorrect rendering of the texts and, therefore, an incorrect application. The verb διαχρίνω has two sets of meanings: the first is "to make a distinction, to differentiate or pass judgement"; the second is "to take issue or dispute, to doubt or waver, or to hesitate."[247]

The first text—"And the Spirit told me to go with them, making no distinction" (Acts 11:12)—that is variously translated "making no distinction" (ESV), "without misgivings" (NASB) or "have no hesitation" (NIV and NJB), thus showing the range of available meanings, appears in a narrative block that starts at the beginning of chapter 11, where Peter is being questioned about his decision to go to the house of Cornelius, a Gentile. In that text, the narrative—"When Peter went up to Jerusalem, the circumcision party criticised him" (Acts 11:2)—uses the same verb, correspondingly translated "the circumcision party criticised him" (ESV), "those who were circumcised took issue with him" (NASB), "the circumcised believers criticised him" (NIV), and "the circumcised believers protested to him" (NJB). Woods argues

---

240 Woods, "Jew-Gentile Distinction," 102.
241 Kinzer, *Post-Missionary Messianic Judaism*, 151–79.
242 Campbell, "Unity and Diversity in the Church," 127–45.
243 Rudolph, "Paul's Rule."
244 Woods, "Jew-Gentile Distinction," 108.
245 Nanos *The Mystery of Romans*, 184.
246 Woods, "Jew-Gentile Distinction," 112.
247 Danker, *Greek-English Lexicon*, 231.

that the usage in 11:12 matches the usage in 10:20—of which it is a report—and should be taken to mean that Peter should not argue with or criticize the Holy Spirit's instructions.[248] This does not counter the Distinction Theory proposal.

In the second text—"He made no distinction between us and them" (Acts 15:9) where "us" and "them" are Jewish and Gentile believers in Messiah respectively—there is no significant variance between the major English translations, but Woods argues that the context of the Jerusalem Council requires a narrower interpretation: that, while there is no distinction in how they are saved, the surrounding text makes clear distinction between Jewish and Gentile praxis and obligations.[249] Read this way, this also does not counter the Distinction Theory proposal.

Woods objects to the way in which the original binary Jew/Gentile classification has been too often replaced by a new binary classification: Christian/non-Christian. This, he insists, is not biblical as the NT has many examples showing that a two-dimensional classification is now operational, adding faith in Messiah as another dimension to the original rather than supplanting it. Paul himself is an example of a Jew who believes in Messiah, while his teacher Gamaliel is a Jew who does not believe in Messiah. Similarly, Cornelius is a Gentile who believes in Messiah, while King Agrippa is a Gentile who does not. Both identities remain valid and active at the same time.[250]

Both Jewish and Gentile identity must be preserved and held in creative tension so that one does not override the other and unity can be promoted.[251] This will anticipate "the consummation when Israel and the nations, in *Torah*-defined unity and diversity, will worship ADONAI alone."[252] In fact, Woods concludes, "the intimate composition and mutual dependence of Jews and Gentiles is essential to the church."[253]

How Do Messianic Jewish scholars Interpret the Situation?

Some see the narrative of Yeshua's conversation with the two blind men[254] being played out today.[255] They suggest that the church is blind to

---

248 Woods, "Diakrino."
249 Woods, "Acts 15:9."
250 Woods, "Jew-Gentile Distinction," 114–5.
251 Atkinson, "Jews and Gentiles," 17.
252 Rudolph, "Paul's Rule," 15.
253 Woods, "Jew-Gentile Distinction," 131.
254 Matthew 2:30–34.
255 Dauermann, *Son of David*, 2.

Yeshua's Jewish identity, in part due to nearly two thousand years deliberate distancing of Yeshua from his Jewish identity,[256] and that the MJish movement is blind to Yeshua's office as Son of David, failing to pursue his agenda as the Coming King. Although healing of the former is in sight, according to Stuart Dauermann,[257] much work needs to be done to bring the One New Man to the fore.[258] Jen Rosner warns that "the way in which Israel's election and ongoing positive vocation is upheld is often at odds with a robust Christology"[259]—care needs to be taken to maintain the correct balance.

Boaz Michael has identified a number of key problems that currently mitigate against the correct formation of the One New Man.[260] The first is the forgetting that Yeshua was and is a Jew. Notice how this goes further than past historical status; this is not a statement of who the physical Yeshua was two thousand years ago. This is a reflection of God's unchanging character: Yeshua was born and raised as a Jew, he lived and taught as a Jew, he was crucified and resurrected as a Jew. He was then, remains today and always will be the Messiah of Israel and the King of the Jews. The One New Man is created "in him"[261] and so must correctly connect with who he is and his identity.

Michael's second issue is that the Gentile church has forgotten—even, today, to the point of deliberate opposition—the centrality of Israel in God's plan to redeem the world. Paul links $\pi\lambda\acute{\eta}\rho\omega\mu\alpha$, "fullness," with both Israel[262] and the Gentiles.[263] Fullness on both parts makes up the fullness of the One New Man. Much of the church's historical and modern position on the role and destiny of Israel is based upon the writings of the Church Fathers,[264] dating from the second and third centuries when anti-Semitism and anti-Judaism ran high, counter to Paul's explicit teaching in the letter to the Romans.[265] Ignatius wrote, "It is utterly absurd to profess Jesus Christ and to practice Judaism."[266] Nevertheless, Israel remains God's chosen people today;[267] not

---

256 Bockmuehl, *Seeing the Word*, 194–5.
257 Dauermann, *Son of David*, 28–46, 5.
258 Dauermann, "The One New Man."
259 Rosner, *Healing the Schism*, 235.
260 Michael, *Tent of David*, 61.
261 Ephesians 2:15.
262 Romans 11:12.
263 Romans 11:25.
264 Michael, *Tent of David*, 70.
265 Nanos, *The Mystery of Romans*, 10.
266 Magnesians 10:3 (Holmes, *Apostolic Fathers*, 209).
267 Romans 11:29.

The Theological Framework

exclusively, but in partnership with those from the nations who follow Yeshua and are part of the One New Man. God chose Israel as his people to bring reconciliation to the whole world; he chose and equipped Gentiles to complement, support and encourage Israel in that role.[268]

The third area of concern that Michael highlights is an extremely low view of *Torah* and the commandments God gave to the Jewish people.[269] By largely rejecting the Hebrew Scriptures, except for cherry-picked verses and stories that are used to construct the foregrounded Creation-Fall-Redemption narrative, as normative—recognizing, of course, that the application of the commandments is different for Jew and Gentile—the church discards the majority of G-d's teaching about holiness, obedience, compassion and faithfulness. Bibles containing just the New Testament, Psalms and Proverbs underline the low value attached by the church to the Law and the Prophets that are affirmed by Yeshua and the New Testament writers. The standard Christian canonical narrative, reducing Israel's history to a narrative of sin and rejection by God,[270] not only fails to explain the scriptural data but allows no room for the existence of Jewish believers in Yeshua. For the One New Man to reach the fullness of the stature of Messiah,[271] this imbalance must be addressed.

One New Man Ecclesiology Summary

Building on Barth's work on Paul's One New Man in Ephesians 2 and having considered—and dismissed, at least as far as this argument is concerned—a number of prominent passages commonly used to assert the contrary point of view, it has been possible to formulate a biblical mandate for inclusion and partnership between Jew and Gentile in the New Testament; a mandate that includes an equality that embraces diversity and cooperation. Consideration has also been given to how some MJish scholars see the situation today. The next section moves on to consider the work of Miroslav Volf and Alex Jacob.

Embrace and Engagement

The work of Miroslav Volf from his 1996 book, *Exclusion and Embrace*, will now be examined to summarize a process he suggests for ending exclusion and enabling true and equal reconciliation. Then the writing of

---

268 Hoyt, "The Master Plan," 148.
269 Michael, *Tent of David*, 79.
270 Kinbar, "Messianic Jews and Scripture," 63.
271 Ephesians 4:12–14.

Alex Jacob in his 2007 paper, "Root and Branch," will be considered, where he describes four possible models for engagement between JBYs and the church. The two schemes will then be combined to construct a measure that can be used to assess the experiences reported by the interview respondents.

Volf's "Drama of Embrace"

Written from his experience in the 1990s Balkan conflict, Miroslav Volf talks about a four-stage process to bring an end to exclusion: what he calls "The Drama of Embrace." He lists four sequential steps: "opening the arms, waiting, closing the arms and then opening them again."[272] His argument is that all four must be present and must happen in that sequence for embrace to be embrace and not oppression or exclusion.

As Volf describes it, the first stage of opening the arms is an invitation—to engage, to participate, to embrace—an expression of desire for the other and a sign that space has been created within the self for the other to enter. It must also include a measure of humility, recognizing that the self is not complete in some way without the other and being prepared to allow the other to come sufficiently close that hurt could occur. The second stage, waiting, without imposing upon the other or attempting to force the pace, allows the other the freedom to respond. The wait is necessary to allow the other to see and assess the risk in coming close, for a desire to respond to arise and be noticed; this may take time when the hurt has been prolonged or severe, to overcome fear or rejection. Volf's third stage, closing the arms, must be reciprocal: the two parties embrace each other, while maintaining boundaries of touch, strength, and identity. The other may not be crushed or squeezed; identity and integrity must be preserved while, at the same time, sharing and experiencing each other's space. The fourth and last stage, reopening the arms, demonstrates freedom, guarantees identity and invites trust for a further cycle of embrace.[273] The two have not become one; the mutuality of embrace respects the freedom of both parties and underlines that neither is controlling nor coercing the other into relationship.

In a relationship that has been so abusive over such an extended period, where such hurts and accusations of coercion have built up, how is the church to go about embracing Jewish believers in Yeshua without suffocating them or stripping their identity? How can the church rebuild trust and woo the Jewish identity into embrace? Western modernity—a

---

272 Volf, *Exclusion and Embrace*, 141.
273 Volf, *Exclusion and Embrace*, 141–5.

The Theological Framework

dominating force in the last two hundred years—has stressed "the universal rather than the particular or vernacular, the anonymous or disengaged rather than the personal."[274] Stressing the universal favors the dominant majority identity over the competing minority identities. Whether feeling threatened by mimesis[275]—be like us—or fear of exclusion,[276] Jewish identity in the church is often ill-equipped to compete with the dominant and historically suppressive Gentile identity.[277] Even though Jewish believers are one of the God-ordained components of the One New Man,[278] the church is reluctant to acknowledge the possibility of the older brother and what that might entail.[279] Many MJs do not believe that JBYs are ever fully accepted within the church.[280] Church in the UK, for a JBY, can be a minefield: "standing to sing, sitting to pray, hugging, men and women sitting together"[281] are only some of the cultural contradictions that may need to be overcome.

Volf goes on to offer "four notable features of a successful embrace:"[282] fluidity of identities, nonsymmetricity, underdetermination of outcome, and risk of embrace. Volf suggests that these flow from God's own embrace of humanity at the cross and should—although this is a tougher call for humans in a context of exclusion—be part of one's motivation even in a state of enmity.

To understand the first—fluidity of identities—one must recognize that all people live in a number of overlapping contexts and communities; people are never totally part of one, and only one, group.[283] They hold different values, principles and identities, however large the degree of overlap may appear to be. As they journey, they pick up mementoes and souvenirs that become part of their "home" for a season. There must be flexibility in identities, recognizing that both parties are on their respective journeys and that change in the selves, the identities—that may or may not increase the common ground—will and must occur.

---

274 Sheldrake, *Spaces for the Sacred*, 22.
275 Castelli, *Imitating Paul*, 17.
276 Exclusion may be by elimination, assimilation, domination or abandonment. Volf, *Exclusion and Embrace*, 74–75.
277 Kollontai "Between Judaism and Christianity," 4, §10; Hocken, "The Present," 2.
278 Ephesians 2:15.
279 Hocken, "The Present," 7.
280 Kollontai "Between Judaism and Christianity," 4 §11.
281 Glasspole, *One Size*, 10.
282 Volf, *Exclusion and Embrace*, 145.
283 Hogg, "Social Identity Theory," 115.

Nonsymmetricity is a recognition that the two parties are not equal, and presupposes recognition of the other as a recipient of the self's self-sacrifice. However much they may belong together or need each other, they are not identical. They are not to merge, but are simply taking one more step towards the other, towards the enemy. In the power of the cross, Volf asserts, "embrace includes not just the other who is a friend but also the other who is an enemy."[284]

The third feature stems from the strict avoidance of force or coercion: underdetermination of outcome. If the embrace itself is voluntary, either party may refuse the embrace or a further embrace. No particular outcome can be guaranteed, although some change will have happened to both selves as a result of the offer being made.

Volf's last feature—risk of embrace—follows from the previous features. Both the self and the other may be taking a serious risk of not being understood, of rejection or of being further hurt or damaged in some way. Nevertheless, the willingness to take that risk, to open the arms and be prepared to offer the possibility of embrace, may be the only way to move forward in the relationship, to achieve understanding or a measure of unity and historical reconciliation.

Alex Jacob's "Models of Engagement"

Alex Jacob writes with concern about the way the church has responded to Jewish identity in recent years. Noting that a frequently expressed objective of the MJish movement is to establish MJish congregations in which authentic Jewish identity can grow, he contrasts that with the older dominant position of expecting Jewish believers in Yeshua to be fully absorbed into church congregations. He laments that, while this may not be understood as assimilation, that is the reality that follows with Jewish identity being lost "if not within the first generation then certainly in subsequent generations."[285] Jacob proposes four possible models for Jewish believers in Yeshua.

The first is "Church Absorption."[286] In this model, JBYs can choose which mainstream church, denomination or fresh expression to join, and are encouraged to participate in and enrich the local congregation of their choice in carrying out the vision and calling of that church. This is the closest to the Gentile church vision of unity: there is no "wall of partition" (Ephesians 2:14) and "all one in Christ Jesus" (Galatians 3:28) is observed. While this is the classic missionary position, it results in the

---

284 Volf, *Exclusion and Embrace*, 146.
285 Jacob, "Root and Branch," 3.
286 Ibid., 4–5.

The Theological Framework

highest attrition rate of Jewish identity, generally offering no opportunity for any outward sign or observance. Heilman's observations are appropriate here. This resembles Volf's embrace being stopped in the third act—arms closed—with the JBY having been welcomed in and then locked into assimilation. Paul's One New Man vision is broken because there are no distinct and visible Jewish participants. The vast majority of UK churches follow this model.

Jacob's second model is "Church Integration."[287] Based on a conviction that Paul's writings and the New Testament in general do not indicate that JBYs should abandon their Jewish identity, this proposes that JBYs should join local churches who should reciprocate by encouraging the JBYs to retain their Jewish identity and extend their ritual practice in a variety of ways, such as a Jewish worship style or liturgy, celebrating the feasts in the Jewish calendar, and standing against anti-Semitism and replacement theology. Although attractive in some ways, offering nearly the same benefits to the church and appearing to fit within the multiple identities of a good church, it is highly dependent on the vision and goodwill of local ministers and is likely to be resisted by more traditional church congregations amidst accusations of Judaising. JBYs feel a lack of appreciation and recognition of their Jewish roots either denominationally or at grass roots.[288] It, too, resembles Volf's third act freeze, although, in this case, the embrace is just loose enough to allow some wriggle room within the locked arms. The One New Man may be partially visible on occasion. There are very few working instances of this model in the UK.

Jacob's third model—"Separate but Open"[289]—allows for the formation of separate and distinct MJish congregations that welcome full Gentile participation and share events with local churches. This allows development of Jewish identity in Messiah in a Jewish context and setting, but is criticized for rebuilding the wall of partition,[290] even though that is a misunderstood phrase that has high emotional content. Advocates of this position argue that it still creates unity within the church by allowing all to participate in "Jewish" church. Perhaps it could be seen as the ultimate destination of the accommodations offered in Jacob's second model. Two main criticisms are offered: that significant Gentile participation distorts the vision of building Jewish communities for Yeshua and blurs the distinction between Jew and Gentile that is necessary for the One New Man to be seen; and that,

---

287 Ibid., 5–6.
288 Kollontai "Between Judaism and Christianity," 5 §12.
289 Jacob, "Root and Branch," 6–8.
290 Gibson, "Supersessionism," 264.

instead of retaining a strong but participating Gentile identity, many enthusiastic Gentiles adopt a *faux*-Jewish identity.[291] Combining both Jewish expression and Gentile participation is a difficult balancing act that not many congregations achieve, generally slipping towards the church and so losing their connection at a serious level with the Jewish world. Perhaps this model resembles Volf's full embrace cycle including nominal release, while slipping a tether on the Jewish wrist so that they cannot go too far away.

Jacob's last model—"Separate"[292]—establishes separate MJish congregations that welcome Gentile visitors, but discourage long-term Gentile participation in a deliberate stance to create and maintain Jewish space and identity, and preserve links with the wider Jewish world. Heilman would approve. Arguing that this places them in a strong position to influence and attract the mainstream Jewish community to participation and evangelism—although this has yet to be proven—this firmly sees JBYs as a Judaism rather than a Christianity. This situation would allow one embrace cycle from Volf's "Drama of Embrace," but would probably discourage further embrace for the sake of facing and offering embrace to the wider Jewish world.

Jacob's Model	Volf's Drama of Embrace	Difficulty	Result	Frequency[293]
Church Absorption	Stopped at the end of the third act—arms tightly closed	Easy; default position	Guaranteed assimilation; One New Man broken—no Jews	Vast majority of UK churches
Church Integration	Stopped at the end of the third act—arms loosely closed	Difficult; prejudice and tradition to overcome	Guaranteed assimilation; One New Man partially visible sometimes	Very few in the UK

---

291 Perhaps an equal and opposite error to that of the church assimilating JBYs to its standard prototype. On the other hand, it is different in that the assimilation pressure comes from Gentiles who want to be Jewish.
292 Jacob, "Root and Branch," 9.
293 Thee estimates are based upon the author's personal experience, several interviews of respondents who visit churches and congregations as part of their ministry occupations, and anecdotal reports from a number of other JBYs. They are necessarily estimates rather than precise figures.

The Theological Framework

Separate but Open	Release at end of fourth act, with tether	Easy to set up, difficult to maintain balance	Steady threat of assimilation; One New Man usually visible	Some examples in the UK
Separate	Full release, no further engagement encouraged	Medium, but numbers will always be an issue	Risk of exclusivism or schism; One New Man often visible	Few examples in the UK

This now forms a four-position matrix spanning the continuum between fully Gentile church and fully Jewish Messianic synagogue that classifies the possible attitudes and positions of JBYs in relation to church scenarios. Language has already been mentioned as a possible issue, but cultural issues also play a big part in decisions about identity. It is important not to forget the role that translation plays in the matter.

This study proposes that the alignment between Volf's four-act Drama of Embrace and Jacob's four models for Jewish Engagement with the church can be extended to include the level of translation that is taking place between the parties to the embrace or engagement. This can enrich the understanding of the level of engagement or accommodation that is taking place in the scenarios and experiences described by the interview respondents, as well as acting as a lens to analyze the theories arising from the GTM data.

The Sanders Four Step Process

James A. Sanders proposes a four-step process for the historical adaptation and reuse of outside material into the text of the Bible (the two left-hand columns in the table below): de-polytheizing, monotheizing, Yahwizing and Israelitizing—not all steps being fully worked out in each example.[294] This study suggests that it is possible to see a similar four-step process at work in the treatment of Jewish identity

---

294 Sanders, *Canon and Community*, 56. Sanders is writing within the context of canonical criticism of the Hebrew Scriptures and his work is not without criticism (see, for example, Childs, "The Canon in Recent Biblical Studies," 41–2). However, the parallel between his proposed four step process of absorption and assimilation of external (i.e., non-Israelite) material into the Israelite Scriptures, and the process of absorbing and assimilating external (i.e., non-Gentile-Christian) Jews into the Gentile Church, seems remarkably clear.

by the church: de-Judaizing, exclusivizing, Christifying and churchifying (the two right-hand columns in the table below).

De-polytheizing	Removal of the polytheistic background, context and detail	De-Judaizing	Removal of the Jewish background, context and detail
Monotheizing	Attributing the event and/or result to one God alone	Exclusivizing	Attributing the event and/or result to one savior alone
Yahwizing	Identifying that one God as YHVH, the God of Israel	Christifying	Identifying that one savior as Jesus Christ, the Savior of the World
Israelitizing	Resiting the original narrative in an Israelite context and culture, vocabulary and celebrations	Churchifying	Resiting the original narrative in a church context and culture, vocabulary and celebrations

Sanders offers the flood narrative as his prime example of Ancient Near East material being adapted and re-signified in the Bible. First, all mention of Enlil, Marduk, or other gods is removed from the story, then the story is retold with only one God—the Creator and Redeemer—in sole charge; next that God is identified, perhaps a little clumsily, variously as YHVH and Elohim. Sanders admits that this particular story is not resited in an Israelite culture—the ark comes to ground on Mt. Ararat rather than the obvious Mt. Zion—although the motifs of the vineyard, Gods promise and the family line of Shem do come into view.

A similar process, however, can be seen in the conversion of a Jew into a Christian. Firstly, Jewish culture and tradition is removed, defined as redundant, unnecessary or even harmful; it is replaced by a tight focus upon the Christ event—the crucifixion and resurrection in particular—as the exclusive means of relationship with God. Christ is then shown to be all-sufficient and the lens through which the Scriptures are to be read and interpreted. The process is completed by resiting the convert firmly in a church context with its vocabulary, festivals and life-cycle traditions.

The Theological Framework 159

Summary

The argumentation presented above seems clear that Paul gives the church a mandate both for unity and diversity in Ephesians 2 and Romans 11. History would suggest that this mandate has been ignored and abused since the sub-apostolic era but, with the emergence of MJism and the resurgence of Jewish identity among people of Jewish heritage in the church, perhaps it is being reconsidered in these days. In the next chapter, Woods' theory, and the Volf-Jacob and extended Sanders models, provide another set of ways to assess the research data to evaluate how the church is living up to that mandate and what the situation looks like on the ground.

The Data Revisited

Having defined a number of spotlights—sociological, translational, and theological—the time has come to take a detailed look at the interview data to see how Jewish identity is faring in at least some of the churches in the UK. The respondents are considered in six groups (Younger JBYs, Older JBYs, Para-church Groups, Dysfunction and Deliverance, Church Leaders Who are Jewish, Church Leaders Who are Gentile), allowing the respondents' voices to be heard in more detail and reviewing their comments against the spotlight questions, the theological mandate and the assessment criteria developed in the last two chapters. This gives priority to the data: it is data-led. Some specific issues will then also be examined against the spotlights and, before closing, the chapter will revisit the spotlight questions in order to see what answers seem to be available. Finally, the issue of training will be covered, before moving on to draw conclusions in the last chapter.

Many of the Jewish respondents in this study reported a degree of discomfort and dissonance in church. Whether "fish out of water" or not feeling "at home," many JBYs retain a sense of distance or disconnection from church. While some JBYs seem to settle down and simply "belong," with some being only too keen to lose their Jewishness, others —even those who have become or are training to become, clergy—report a lingering lack of ease, a feeling that this isn't quite right. A number became believers in the early part of their lives, joined a church and were fairly comfortable, but have then awoken to their Jewish identity when a bit older and have felt a growing discomfort from that point onwards. Some JBYs feel that the church as a whole is endemically locked in replacement theology; although denied by ministers and elders, the threads and assumptions of replacement theology run through and underpin liturgy (or equivalent ritual in non-liturgical churches and chapels), sermons, songs, attitudes and language.

Respondent Vignettes

The original detailed interview scripts are summarized below and turned into fairly black-and-white cameos or vignettes by describing the respondents in terms of the spotlight questions from the theoretical chapters. The vignettes are also grouped by age and across the Jew-Gentile divide to form similar categories of individuals.

Seeing the grouping of similar respondents and comparing their vignettes will show the way the similarities and differences paint a picture of the situation as experienced and processed by JBYs in the churches today.

Younger Jewish Believers in Yeshua

The three voices in this section are Shana, Carl, and Serena. All three are in their late twenties, are Jewish, and share a degree of ministry experience.

Spotlight on Shana

Shana is a younger, professional, and cosmopolitan MJ, living in London. Having known MJism all her life, she has a distinct opinion about church and her church experiences. She hasn't been in church now for three and a half years but is very insistent on being a full JBY. She keeps her faith alive and active by contact with family, friends and other JBYs through the Internet.

Shana has encountered a number of instances of the traditional Gentile church model: the church leadership know that they are right and that it is their job to coerce Shana into abandoning her Jewish ways by switching her religious authority from home/*Torah* to the church leadership. Shana is very committed to her Jewish identity, lifestyle and observance—her prominence hierarchy is well-defined and stable; she experiences dissonance when the salience hierarchy the church suggests she should have does not match; her response is to leave the identity-hostile environment and she is reluctant to re-engage with another church without some safeguard against the same challenge occurring again. Church offered no verification of her Jewish identity, instead questioning it in an effort to bring about change; attempted identity transformation. Shana's report suggests that the church viewed her as outside the parameters of their "normal" social identity prototype; in spite of her confession of faith as a JBY, she feels that the church continued to keep her on the margins, refusing membership or permission to play in the worship band—denying belonging and participation—as a lever to persuade her to change. For Shana, the church boundary was not permeable; dual (social group) allegiance was not something the church could tolerate.

It is not clear whether the church viewed Shana as liminal—in the process of change—or not yet started on change. On the one hand, they accepted her statement of faith in Yeshua and considered that they had the right to ask for allegiance to their leadership team; on the other hand, they drew the boundary of membership, forcing Shana to remain marginalized and retain outsider status. Full translation was refused by the leadership, who made no attempt to understand or relate to Shana's position—adopting the Roman model described by David Bellos—although her peers were interested and accepting. The church had their particular interpretation of the text and would not tolerate an alternative interpretation or implementation.

The church that Shana had been attending was making no attempt to implement the biblical mandate and would probably not have recognized its validity, rejecting David Woods' call for distinction. It seems to be operating in Jacob's "Church Absorption" model—that any JBYs are welcome to join the church, but only as Gentile members, thus guaranteeing assimilation and denying the One New Man—and cannot see that there is anything to reconcile with anyone. Steps one and four of the extended Sanders process, de-Judaizing and churchifying, are at work to convert a Jew into a Christian.

Although Shana's Jewish identity continued and, if anything, strengthened after coming to faith in Yeshua, she has so far been unable to exercise or deploy it to any extent within a UK church context because the churches she has been in refused to recognize it as part of their world.

Spotlight on Carl

Carl self-identifies as a MJ. He is married and has one child. At the time of the interview, he was training for ordination as a church leader after university and some years trying to discover what it meant for him to be living as a Jew in a charismatic church.

Carl's experience of church has been positive although limited to a few places. He clearly sees a number of partnership roles: with God, the church, and his putative congregations. Although Carl is very committed to his Jewish identity, this comes below his identity in Messiah in his prominence hierarchy and he, therefore, only experiences a low level of dissonance between Jewish and Christian life in his salience hierarchy. When dissonance does occur, he seeks contact with other JBYs to regain balance. While he recognizes that church is not always an easy place for JBYs, he feels a strong call to be involved in improving that situation which overrides his concern for Jewish identity. Church offers no validation of Carl's Jewish identity, which he suppressed during selection for ordination training, and he is well assimilated to the standard church model while intending—from inside—to help others retain their Jewish identity. His certainty of calling is promoting the assimilation process. He is aware both that the church has only one prototype for ministers, with very little flexibility, and of the need to conform to that prototype. Mobility and permeability of the Jew-Gentile boundary for Carl is a one-way street: becoming less Jewish and adopting a Gentile persona. Although he has aspirations for serving in a higher Jewish population area in the future, he acknowledges that this has only a low probability of happening and he is resigned to doing what he can for individual JBYs and in educating the church.

By applying for ministerial training and acquiring proficiency in the rituals and language of ministry, Carl demonstrates that he is no longer liminal. While he may retain personal Jewish identity, he has left the status "Jewish" and transitioned to "mainstream Christian." He still shows some marginal behavior by seeking support from the inferior group. His identity construction shows signs of amplification, consolidation, and extension.

Carl does not code-switch, although he recognizes JBY and Jewish terms in conversation. He has learned the language of the group with whom he feels called to communicate and belong. He offers translation of the Jewish world into church contexts through his own internal value table and some rewriting based upon the identity priorities in his prominence hierarchy. While he is not openly opposing the church's master commemorative narrative, Carl acknowledges the church's history of bad behaviour towards Jewish people and has aspirations for the JBY voice to be heard even if only in a church that he leads.

The church that Carl inhabits is generally uncomfortable with the biblical mandate, mostly opposing David Woods' call for distinction. The denomination almost entirely functions in Jacob's "Church Absorption" model and operates a simple, straightforward and all-inclusive form of the extended four-step process in all its steps: the conventional gospel/conversion narrative.

Although Carl retains a lively personal Jewish identity and is currently able to exercise that role in academic argument and social activity while completing training, he is aware that, once in-post as a minister, his options for bringing that role to prominence will be much more limited as he will have specific responsibilities to represent the church and the church's chosen image of God to his congregations.

Spotlight on Serena

Serena's mother is Jewish. Strongly identifying as a life-long Christian and a daughter of the parsonage, Serena has been attending the same church in a national Pentecostal denomination for the last ten years and has recently been ordained as a minister of that denomination after attending their Bible college's BA course and serving as a probationer minister for a year. The church has a number of ethnic groupings, including eastern European and black.

Serena's Jewish identity is almost entirely suppressed: she has no experience of practiced or cultural Judaism; her Jewishness is anecdotal, family history, and is not salient in her life and work in the church. Her active Gentile identity is dominant and she behaves and responds like a normal Gentile. Serena has no commitment to her Jewish identity; it is not a part of her prominence hierarchy and she, therefore, experiences no dissonance with her high-salience Gentile Christian identity. Having been brought up as a Christian in a ministry family, assimilation is complete; all identity verification has been as a Christian.

Serena has some difficulty with social group prototypes. While her church denomination has a very non-ambiguous evangelic Protestant prototype, she was prepared to concede that she was uncertain about the salvation status of Jews who do not believe in Yeshua. The denomination's strong teaching on covenant, God's sovereignty and consistency combines with biblical promises made to the Jewish people to generate conflict with the narrow evangelical insistence on "Jesus only." Similarly, although there was no hint that her own Jewishness was an influence, Serena deprecated the stripping of Jewish identity from JBYs in the church.

In one way, Serena's identity has not changed, she has always been a Christian, with her Jewish identity just a genetic curiosity. Equally, as she has moved into adulthood, her identity has been conformed more closely to that of the denomination she serves, a form of identity extension.

Neither marginality nor liminality apply to Serena. With no practical Jewish background and dependent on others for knowledge of the Jewish world, she is unable to translate or build bridges. However, counter to her denomination, Serena is concerned about information loss. The denomination, moreover, while very informal, has little flexibility on biblical translation and interpretation—particularly in the area of its Pentecostal distinctives.

Serena and her denomination would probably claim compliance with the biblical mandate, although their interpretation of it would be more mimetic than Barth might suggest. They would probably not endorse David Woods' call for distinction. The denomination has a canonized image of its past and its strong prototyping will tend to "produce" JBYs in their prototype image. In Volf's terms, while the embrace remains closed, frozen at the end of the third act, there is room to breathe within the embrace!

Summary – Shana, Carl, and Serena

Although all of Jewish descent and of a very similar age, and all firm and committed followers of Yeshua, Shana, Carl, and Serena offer three very different approaches to life as a JBY in church. Shana is sufficiently firmly committed to her Jewish identity and practice to resist church encroachment and assimilation. This, in turn, causes rejection and marginalization by the church because she doesn't fit, and also resists fitting, the standard church prototype for Gentile Christians. The church loses out by not having her musical and theological input as she probably has a lot that she could share and help the church to understand. At the same time, Shana misses out on fellowship and opportunities to minister and grow as a believer. In her current trajectory, Shana is likely to stay out of church and retain her Jewish identity. Shana's children will probably inherit both a Jewish and a Christian identity as MJs.

Carl places his call to be an ordained minister above his call to Jewish identity and practice, so is prepared to negotiate in many areas. He assumes that God knows what he is doing and adjusts his requirements and expectations accordingly, so Carl has traveled some distance down the road towards assimilation while retaining a significant measure of personal Jewish commitment and identity. He has a number of specific topics about which he feels particularly Jewishly strongly, but more usually he accommodates the church prototype with more or less grace. Whereas Shana grew up with a strong Jewish identity, Carl's—though present—has always been background, and he has had very little opportunity to practice and reinforce it in Jewish life. The church partly benefits by being able to call upon Carl's background knowledge and ability to lead a church Passover meal, but partly loses because Carl's Jewish identity is weak and compromised/assimilated. In his current trajectory, Carl will remain in church and gradually lose more of his Jewish identity. He may succeed in passing some Jewish identity to his children.

Serena has almost no Jewish identity and has been assimilated to the Gentile church from birth. Although she is Jewish according to *halacha*, she doesn't consider herself Jewish and sees life, faith and practice from a Gentile Christian point of view. She has sympathy and tolerance for some JBY positions, but would not dream of following them herself—her calling to work and mission within the Christian church is her first and only priority. The church benefits by having a totally committed and dedicated minister and is—to all intents and purposes—unaware of Serena's Jewishness. Unless circumstances dramatically change, Serena will remain in the church and her anecdotal Jewishness will probably be lost by the next generation.

Shana, Carl and Serena make a credible example of Steven Fraade's point: "We should not ignore the role of visualisation, alongside orality and aurality in collective memory."[1] Shana participates strongly in the Jewish collective memory, Carl at a peripheral level, and Serena does not participate; this is a result of both upbringing and current practice. Where a person has not been told—there is no communications medium for tradition.[2] Many of the ten points made by Kleim and Jones[3] can be seen at play.

Older Jewish Believers in Yeshua

The three voices in this section are Bethany, Grant and Pip. All three are in their early sixties and Jewish. Some have been involved in leading ministry, but they share a lot of life experience.

Spotlight on Bethany

---

1   Fraade, "Memory and Loss," 118.
2   Kirk, "The Memory-Tradition Nexus," 142.
3   Kleim and Jones, "Neural Plasticity," 227.

Bethany comes from a Holocaust survivor family who deliberately hid their Jewishness "for fear that it could all happen again." She was brought up as a Christian and made a confession of faith and was baptized when she was twenty-one. She now attends a church with a healing and deliverance ministry that has encouraged her to keep *Shabbat* and celebrate the feasts as well as to help and encourage other JBYs.

In previous churches, Bethany lacked an appropriate role partner, so her "Jew" and their "Gentile" behaved badly towards each other. In her current church, she has a matching role partner and the Jew-Gentile relationship has stabilized allowing her to participate normally and take an active role in the mission of the church. Bethany has a strong Jewish identity at the top of her prominence hierarchy and, therefore, experienced significant dissonance between "who she really is" and the identity that she was forced to accept—between her prominence and salience hierarchies—until this was resolved. In previous church, verification was entirely negative; her churches did not understand the importance of validating her Jewish identity, resulting in emotional trauma and a decision to leave. Now, with positive validation, she is able to identify with, support, and encourage the church vision.

Bethany's experience of church suggested that church had only one prototype, that did not include Jewish identity. As she did not conform, she was not only no longer accepted; both she and her husband were marginalized and pushed over the boundary—they no longer belonged, they were only allowed to visit. Previous church offered no alternatives and there was no mobility. The church were looking for identity amplification and opposed identity consolidation. New church enabled identity extension. Previous church had an inflexible hermeneutic, a normative function that excluded Jewish identity, legitimation only of their prototype, vision and leadership, and a rigid Gentile Christian identity. New church has a hermeneutic that favors Jewish identity, a normative function that positively encourages Jewish practice and legitimates the One New Man Jew-Gentile partnership model. The new church identity is formed around different stories and allows Jewish memories to be created and maintained.

In previous church, Bethany was accused of promoting an alternative narrative, subverting the church's majority master narrative; hostility and contested space ensued. Bethany appeared, to them, to be going backwards through liminality: from Christian back to Jewish, despite her protests that she retained faith in Yeshua as

Messiah. Current church encourages Jewish observance and identity manifestations, so that Bethany has emerged from a liminal state and been accepted in her JBY identity.

Bethany is now in an affirming "One New Man" environment, a context where David Woods' Distinction Theory is practiced. Her current church is close to Jacob's "Church Integration" model, in that it is Gentile-led and meets on Sundays, but has characteristics of both "Separate but Open" and "Separate" models: there is a majority Gentile participation, but they aim to display the One New Man at all times. Steps one and four—De-Judaizing and Churchifying—from the extended Sander's process are being reversed to encourage Jewish identity in the church.

Spotlight on Grant

Like Bethany, Grant comes from a Holocaust survivor family. He had no religious upbringing at all and "was born again from absolutely nowhere when I was forty." He knew of his Jewish identity, but it was completely latent until he first visited Israel four years ago. He was a worship leader within a charismatic house-church movement for twenty-two years until he and his wife felt the Lord move them to a large reformed tradition church that he describes as "a large fellowship made up mostly of white middle-class professionals, very Bible-based and evangelical but not at all charismatic—with no interest in Israel." Now retired, he volunteers with CMJ and another UK mission.

Grant seems to be in quite a combative position with regard to potential role partners. He sees himself possessing knowledge that others lack, which it is his calling to share with them, even if they are unaware of or hostile to it. This subverts the normal leader/disciple relationship by attempting to "trump" the standard church position with a "better" biblical interpretation that comes by revelation. By acting out the rabbi/student role he antagonizes church leaders and members. His strength of feeling about his "missionary" role colored the whole interview and made it difficult to see other points.

Grant is very committed to his Jewish identity, weak and largely non-practicing though it is. He is robust in defending his position against attack and discouragement on the grounds of divine appointment. He has had good identity verification in his previous church context, which reinforces his rejection of the non-verification in his current church context. At the same time, he is not sufficiently motivated by his Jewish identity to engage with Jewish practice on more than an occasional social basis.[4]

Grant has himself experienced identity amplification, in the same way as Snow and McAdam's example of a player moving from the bench onto the playing field, but seeks to impose identity transformation upon the church leaders and members, mentioning a "Damascus Road" experience. Grant is attempting to rewrite the past—as far as his church is concerned, subverting their master narrative by inserting countermemories and linking them to biblical texts and eschatological interpretations. This is highly contested territory and may result in rejection or even expulsion from church.

Translation of past and current Jewish culture and interpretation is being offered, but currently being refused. The church may be displaying fear, or even hatred, of the original source[5]—so a kind of anti-Semitism—due to Grant's efforts to redefine vocabulary and symbols. His church is employing Bellos' third translation strategy: ignoring people who can't or won't adopt their language; translating Grant's words, they are not aware of, or do not care about, information loss. The church leadership are controlling the discourse in the interest of protecting the flock and hold to an inflexible position about biblical interpretation: no alternatives considered.

Grant's church would not consider the mandate for the One New Man, nor would they accept or understand David Woods' Distinction Theory. The steps of Sanders' extended process—De-Judaizing, Exclusivising, Christifying and Churchifying—are complete and non-negotiable. By Jacob's model, "Church Absorption" is the only option, although Volf's four-act drama of reconciliation has not started—there is nothing to reconcile.

Spotlight on Pip

Brought up in a strongly atheist home with minimal contact with Judaism except for family contact with Jewish relatives, Pip is well-educated, professionally qualified, totally cosmopolitan and well-travelled—having lived abroad for a number of years—and a mother of three. She attends what she describes as a "large, friendly

---

4 The researcher has received many anecdotal reports from both Jews and Gentiles of the negative impact that can be caused by JBYs who proclaim the importance of Jewish identity but don't act on that importance in their own lives. Grant seems unaware of or is ignoring this inconsistency and how it may affect others.

5 Pym, *Exploring Translation*, 108.

conservative evangelical church" and has a wide circle of Jewish and non-Jewish friends. She identifies strongly as Jewish, but openly describes herself as a Christian.

Pip sees herself behaving normally as a JBY in church. Although her Jewish identity is important and frequently displayed in her salience hierarchy, her identity as a Christian is dominant in her prominence hierarchy and so she experiences no dissonance in church. Her strong presentation of Jewish identity—at a cultural level—in a middle-class professional church context is well received and validated because it is paired with a strong Christian identity. Pip is almost completely assimilated and finds Judaism—her old-if-ever culture—primitive and uninspiring. Her Jewish identity is very context-dependent: strong when the only Jew in a given environment, non-existent when with other Jews.

Pip has conformed to the standard church prototype, passing her Jewishness off as an interesting cultural attribute. Well accepted as an equal by church leaders—at an intellectual, cultural, class, and faith level—she is not at risk of being marginalized or kept at the boundary of church life. She displays identity consolidation—blending her Jewish and Christian identities with education, class, and status to create a stable salient identity.

While Pip has memories of the past—her grandmother, family events—these have been rewritten at a cultural level to support her consolidated identity. She accepts and affirms the church's master narrative. She is well placed to offer translation between the Jewish and church worlds at an anecdotal level, although her personal equivalence table is colored by her own faith, degree of assimilation, and rewritten view of Judaism. She uses her Jewish heritage and life experiences as bridge-building tools for translating into different age and faith contexts.

Her concern for evangelism in general, Jewish evangelism in particular, leads her to insert ideas and concepts into the "textual community" of her church, in the hope that they will become accepted and normative. She blends and compares her family anecdotes and stories with those of church leaders and members as ways of broadening the scope of the church's imagined community. At the same time, both intentionally and unintentionally, these efforts reduce both the value and the salience of her own Jewish identity to bring it in line with other ethnic or cultural markers, to deny the specialness of being Jewish.

Pip sees no mandate for the One New Man as a joint and visible expression of Jewish and Gentile particularity, being closer to

Andrew Walls' perception of today's "Ephesian Moment" as a blending of many ethnic, racial, and cultural identities. Her preferred position on Alec Jacob's "Models of Engagement" is "Church Absorption," seeing no need for church-JBY reconciliation because they are all one. The One New Man appears to be audible at a verbal level, but Pip's fully assimilated status means that in practice there is no Jewish presence.

Summary – Bethany, Grant and Pip

Although all of Jewish descent and of a very similar age—and all firm and committed followers of Yeshua—Bethany, Grant, and Pip offer three very different approaches to life as a JBY in church. Bethany is living and growing a Jewish identity in an unusually supportive church; Grant is on a mission to subvert a hostile Gentile church to a more favorable position on Jewishness in general and Israel in particular; Pip wants to level Jewishness with other ethnic, racial, and class status to bring JBYs into a normative church expression.

Whereas Bethany and Grant both want Gentiles to take on some measure of Jewish observance, Pip would be horrified at the suggestion. Bethany and Grant want to develop and encourage a Jewish social memory, with varying degrees of commemorative acts and participation; Pip finds Jewish ritual, practice and dress uncomfortable and primitive.

While all three are concerned about Jewish evangelism, their aims are rather different. Bethany's active Jewish expression sets her apart from Grant and Pip; she wants both JBYs and non-believing Jews to come to a fully Jewish understanding of the gospel and express it in Jewish ritual and lifestyle terms. Grant's main focus is on Israel and an imminent eschatology: he is more concerned to use Jewishness and Jewish ritual as a tool for outreach and evangelism than to experience or value it for himself. Pip is simply looking for more Jews to become Christians and find a home in the church; her own memory and experience of Judaism would not lead her into any level of Jewish observance, nor to encourage any other JBYs or converts in that direction.

Para-church Groups

Para-church groups are those groups who work alongside and around churches—they are not affiliated to any one church or denomination.

There are a number of mission agencies that specifically target Jewish people in the UK—arguably the source of many of the JBYs currently in the UK church. Three voices—each from a different agency—of varying ages, categories, and positions share their thoughts about Jewish believers in church.

Spotlight on Jasper

Jasper is in his late forties and works full-time as a missionary for one of the more aggressive Jewish mission agencies. Coming from a Holocaust survivor family, he describes his upbringing as "secular." He attends a large, independent, conservative evangelical church and because of his work has spoken and taught in hundreds of other churches around the country.

Jasper's work as a missionary means that he has two strong role identities: as an evangelist and teacher, doing outreach to Jewish people; and doing development work for the mission, speaking and teaching in churches. Those roles give him a level of immunity in church, where he can be openly Jewish because he "needs" that for his missionary work. His "missionary" role also provides a good fit with the standard church prototype, decreasing pressure to assimilate further. While his home church consider his Jewish identity as "irrelevant" and "baggage," they and the wider church nevertheless offer significant verification in approving his professional calling. Church is, however, unable to nurture his Jewish identity as they don't want him to become more Jewish (and therefore less Christian) and, being generally afraid or fearful of Jews and Israel, will not encourage anyone else to become involved. The issue of trust is important here as his lack of conformance would otherwise be likely to generate dislike or marginalization.[6]

In many ways, Jasper's Jewish identity is quite dominant, giving a short, slightly aggressive, slightly impatient style of speaking, typical of Jewish people, and Israelis in particular. His professional role inevitably creates a barrier between himself and church members in general; while not clergy or an elder, he will be perceived by many as having that status. Both identity consolidation and identity extension are visible in Jasper: he has consolidated his Jewish identity with the evangelist calling to become involved in specifically Jewish mission; since working with the mission he has taken on the vision and attitudes of the organization.

---

6   Hogg, *Social Identity Theory*, 125-126.

Like many Jewish people, Jasper has built a working framework of tradition and memories. He uses non-normative rewritings of Jewish tradition to gain acceptance for conversation with Jewish people and subvert the anti-JBY rabbinic thrust. He won't allow rabbinic authority to validate or define his own Jewish identity, while incorporating rabbinic Jewish practice and tradition in some areas of his life. He is amused by rabbinic attempts to challenge the authority of the church and his own authority as a JBY. He openly trespasses on mainstream Jewish space in his mission-branded clothing and uses confrontation as a tool for evangelism.

Jasper is an effective bilingual. He presses the right buttons within the church vocabulary to communicate, teach, and raise funds; he speaks the right language and deftly negotiates difficult issues. Despite his secular upbringing, he shares enough vocabulary and *Yiddishkeit*[7] with Jewish people to mingle anonymously (when not in uniform) and sound like a Jew; his confidence and *chutzpah* make him a successful evangelist. He code-switches with ease. On the other hand, his translation is directed, non-reversible; he shares Christian values into the Jewish world but cannot translate, or is not interested in translating, Jewish values and issues into the Christian world: mission is his imperative. He offers a high level of accommodation to his church.

Jasper recognizes the significance of both Jewish and Gentile identities being present in the One New Man, but sees the urgency of mission as an overriding priority that excuses churches continuing to teach replacement theology providing they are constantly involved in mission—bringing people to faith in Christ. He similarly agrees with David Woods' Distinction Theory, recognising that God loves Jew and Gentile equally but has different requirements of them. In terms of Volf's "Drama of Embrace," Jasper's priority on mission will override concern about stripping JBYs of their Jewish identity; what matters is that they are saved—the universal takes precedence over the particular. The mission for which Jasper works favors full completion of the extended Sanders process.

---

7 *Yiddishkeit*: *Yiddish* word meaning, "the quality of being Jewish; the Jewish way of life or its customs and practices" (Stevenson, *Oxford Dictionary of English*, 2058). More colloquially: a level of ease and familiarity with Jewish customs, vocabulary and, in some cases, liturgy, to be able to "play the part" and appear as a "normal" Jew.

Spotlight on Eric

Eric is in his mid fifties and an ordained church leader. He identifies as Gentile with a Jewish heritage. He works full-time in senior leadership with a large UK-based Jewish mission agency, and is married with a grown-up family. He has many years' experience working with churches and JBYs in a variety of different contexts and countries.

Eric sees the Jew and Gentile roles as partners and holds a high view of the value and importance of Jewish identity in the church today. Although he admits that the Gentile role is currently dominant, his aspiration is that the Jewish role becomes more equal and that the Jewish voice should be more heard. He expresses concern that the relationship between JBYs and the church is heavily stacked towards assimilation and that Jewish identity is under significant pressure in a number of ways—that the church (in general) offers little or no verification of Jewish identity, promoting a mimetic standard prototype to which JBYs have to conform to gain acceptance. On the other hand, unlike most other respondents, Eric reports ways in which some churches have helped JBYs to discover and develop something of their Jewish identity. He sees JBYs as translators, with potential for bringing an awareness of *Torah*, the feasts and other important Jewish lifestyle and life-cycle issues into the church in an enriching way.

While Eric would prefer identity convergence between JBYs and the church—compatibility allowing room for expression[8] with some identity consolidation, creatively blending Jewish and Gentile identities to form a new JBY identity—his experience suggests that identity transformation is most likely. Eric is looking for a constructive rewriting of the church's master narrative to include some of the Jewish memories and tradition so that JBYs would be less marginalized with less contested territory.

Eric reports some limited church engagement with *Shabbat* and the Jewish feasts, allowing JBYs a few opportunities to "show and imitate" within a church context. At the same time, he also reports some instances of churches disengaging with Jewish roots teaching, which he regrets as a backward step: this is information loss due to translation being denied in favor of one common language and vocabulary. Eric acknowledges Jewish ownership of some vocabulary and symbols and would like more of that translated and brought into the church.

---

8 Snow and McAdam, "Identity Work Processes," 48.

Eric is very aware of, and promotes, the biblical mandate for the One New Man, agreeing with David Woods' Distinction Theory. Having visited most Messianic groups in the UK, he is aware of the risks and dangers of both totally distinct or isolated MJish groups and groups where Gentile numbers overwhelm the JBYs and risk swamping their Jewish vision. He stresses the need for communication; for the church and MJish synagogues to stay in active relationship. He would want to see Volf's "Drama of Embrace" brought to full conclusion: reconciliation, embrace and release leading to partnership and shared working in the mission of the kingdom.

Spotlight on Adam

Adam is Jewish, in his late fifties, an ordained clergyman and working in senior leadership in a Jewish mission agency. He attends church but no longer serves in a church context, having been involved in mission for over twenty years. He was brought up in a Reform Jewish home and is married to a Jewish wife.

Adam is pretty relaxed about Jewish identity, but holds to the idea that identity is a given and difficult to hide, while expression is a matter of choice. He is concerned that conventional forms of orthodox expression—*tzitzit, kipa*—are stereotypes and can be caricatured, rather than genuine. He sees Jewish identity strengthening on coming to faith and points back to scriptural references for what he thinks JBY identity ought to look like. He is confident in his own Jewish identity, and while not always comfortable in church, doesn't feel threatened in identity terms.

Adam is unhappy about the way that JBYs are received in church. Based on how he sees his own work as a clergyman, he thinks that the church has a problem with institutional anti-Semitism, and that being overtly Jewish will damage a ministerial career or the opportunity to do ministry. He thinks that JBYs will move church while maintaining their Jewish identity rather than assimilate where they are not given positive verification. This implies that the boundary between Jewish and Gentile church members is not permeable—some roles or status either cannot or cannot easily be reached by JBYs—and that mobility within the church is limited based on a mistrust of Jewish people.

In Adam's case, identity construction appears to have been by temporary identity extension. He felt the call to ministry and was ordained, but has since withdrawn to some degree. His problem is with church rather than with faith in Yeshua; he remains very active in mission generally, mission to Jewish people particularly, but doesn't participate in church leadership or ministry outside his mission context. This looks very like marginality: Adam retains his connections and identity in his original group for personal identity, while living and working in the church world.

Brought up Reform, Adam's position on Jewish ritual is that observance is optional. He recognizes the value of repeated liturgical ritual within the Jewish tradition for building and maintaining memory, of learning about God. He would support Jewish people for whom he had pastoral responsibility in exploring and living in Jewish time. Echoing Spaulding, the festivals remind the community of its identity.

Adam is essentially bilingual. His family background means that his level of *Yiddishkeit* is more academic than habitual and his everyday language and context is Christian, but his Jewish identity and way of thinking remain strong so that he is well placed to be an effective translator. Passionate about mission, his translation is generally directed, though he seeks to bring some Jewish values and teaching back into the church world to benefit the church and change the church's anti-Jewish narrative.

Adam would support the biblical mandate for visible Jew and Gentile in the One New Man and would support David Woods' Distinction Theory, although he would stress that expression of that must be by choice.

Summary – Jasper, Eric, and Adam

All three respondents are committed to mission among Jews—bringing Jewish people to faith—but their attitudes to that task and to Jewish identity vary significantly. Jasper places top priority on Jews becoming Christian and maintaining a Christian life in church, using his Jewish identity as a tool in the process. Eric takes a gentler approach, seeing church as a place where Jewish people can discover their Jewish identity and be in partnership with churches and Gentile mission. Adam strongly defends his Jewish identity, admitting his discomfort in church, while continuing to press for Jewish people to come to faith, but prepared to help them retain their Jewish identity.

While Jasper and Adam are both bilingual, Jasper's translation is strictly non-reversible, whereas Adam wants to see the church learn and benefit from Jewish practice and ritual. Eric, too, thinks it is important for the church to acquire some Jewish ideas about time, learning/study and rest.

Jasper, despite his own difficulties with church—for which he is prepared to accept responsibility because of his poor articulation of distress—feels that JBYs belong in church. Eric is ambivalent: JBYs may be in church or in a Messianic congregation depending on availability and geography. Adam admits to personal discomfort with church and suspects that the church has an institutional problem with Jewish people.

Dysfunction and Delivery

These respondents are involved with diagnosing some of the more extreme problems of dysfunction that JBYs have in church and helping them to find a way of reaching a workable situation. Having all themselves experienced some of this dysfunction or being involved in helping others recover from such dysfunction, they bring three very different perspectives on the damage that can be done to JBYs in church.

Spotlight on Juliana

Juliana is in her fifties, fiercely and proudly Jewish; she expresses herself with firmness and conviction, displaying a high degree of coherence.

Juliana's own Jewish identity is very strong and despite being ordained as a church minister, she has resisted assimilation beyond her church duties, maintaining an active practice of Jewish ritual and study. As a leader, she operates in both the rabbi-disciple and teacher-student models. Her Jewish identity is at the top of her prominence hierarchy and, because she has been unable to negotiate verification with successive churches, she has experienced significant dissonance and emotional hurt. In general, she has had very poor reception in Gentile church; the level of trauma and hostility has probably prevented assimilation occurring. Juliana has encountered a very inflexible standard church prototype, with which she was unable to conform and was, therefore, rejected and marginalized. Stereotyping and social exclusion have been involved. Her experience of church was of negligible permeability with complete denial of her Jewish identity, no alternatives and—despite being accepted as a leadership candidate—only a promise of mobility that never materialized. The churches and denomination in which Juliana was primarily involved were insisting on identity transformation, whereas she practices identity consolidation.

Juliana and her family have retained and cultivated their Jewish social memory, preserving and maintaining those memories through Jewish ritual, liturgy, and lifestyle. This has generated significant stress with a church that has denied its significance and value in her life. She has refused the church permission to rewrite the past. As she articulates a coherent set of countermemories that challenge and subvert the church's master narrative, she has experienced significant personal conflict as she has fought and, continues to fight to be heard. On Victor Turner's scale, she is no longer considered liminal —in progress—but seen as having jeopardized her Christian salvation for the sake of continuing Jewish identity. Not only does she continue to preserve links with her group of origin, but she refuses to acknowledge the higher prestige and status of the church, seeing it as an equal rather than a superior.

Juliana is naturally bilingual and although she is concerned to share Yeshua with Jewish people, she is not "driven" by mission. Her translation style is natural equivalence, fully bidirectional as she studies and teaches in and between both cultures. She is aware of the sensitivities of each culture and is both deliberate and intentional in using vocabulary and symbols correctly. Until her (more recent) ordination and calling as a church minister, church nevertheless rejected her translation, denying her choice and use of vocabulary, insisting that it alone had the right to own and control the vocabulary and symbols. Juliana's old church denomination rendered Jews and, by extension, JBYs, according to their model, only offering salvation and good standing in their terms—a colonial attitude.

Juliana sees Jew and Gentile as natural role partners in the Body of Messiah. She, therefore, supports both the biblical mandate for the two participating in the One New Man and David Woods' Distinction Theory. Her church operated in the "Church Assimilation" model on Jacob's scale; on Volf's Drama, although embrace is offered, the arms remain tightly and firmly closed—there is no reconciliation or recognition of the "other" except as a target for conversion and assimilation. Juliana's faith in Yeshua means that she has accepted the two middle stages of the modified Sanders process, Exclusiving and Christifying, but she firmly rejects the first and fourth stages, De-Judaising and Churchifying.

Spotlight on Sherry

Sherry is in her mid seventies, married with children, has a degree in theology, and attended Baptist churches for many years as well as serving in other denominations. She has worked with at least two Jewish missionary agencies and has led a local Messianic fellowship (that deliberately meets only "several times a year at the major Jewish feasts") for over twenty years. She has paternal Jewish identity that she denies, describing herself as Gentile. She regularly attends church and the "occasional" Messianic fellowship.

In many ways, Sherry reflects the earlier Hebrew-Christian stance—allowing "Jews who 'converted' to Christianity to retain some measure of Jewish (Hebraic) culture and identity"—rather than the contemporary emphasis on MJism, "Jewish believers in Jesus who not only assert their Jewish identity but also actively engage in the formation of Messianic Fellowships, Congregations and Synagogues."[9] Younger JBYs, such as Shana, Micah, and Ryan, along with others at all ages struggle because their Jewish vision is for more than just being a consultant on Hebrew name pronunciation.

Sherry declines to acknowledge her Jewish heritage or identity, describing herself as Gentile. Her education, long church attendance and, work in Jewish mission agencies have given her a more typical "church" outlook than other respondents. The Hebrew-Christian stance, and the Messianic fellowship that she led, see regular participation in Gentile church to be more important than fostering or encouraging Jewish identity. This is the Gentile church model. Sherry sees the commitment to Jewish identity being mainly for the purpose of evangelism, particularly close family, and is wary of Jewish identity being welcomed in church—almost as if she would prefer it not to be. Jewish identity is low in her prominence hierarchy, possibly because it has always been low in her salience hierarchy, so she tolerates church and teaches other JBYs to do likewise. She reports poor JBY accommodation in church with side remarks about JBYs "buried alive in church" or being in a hostile environment, "rebuffed from all quarters."

Sherry seems to feel that there is only one standard church prototype, into which JBYs must try to fit, with Messianic fellowships—which must not meet too often in case they distract JBYs from church or cause the church to distrust their JBY members —as a safe environment where JBYs can commiserate with and pray for each other, while maintaining some Jewish identity by

---

9   Harvey, *Mapping Messianic Jewish Theology*, 10.

participating in some memorial events around the major Jewish feasts. She feels that it is important that JBYs do conform to the church model to build sufficient trust for them to be accepted and allowed to make small contributions to local church knowledge. She encourages consistency in church to avoid JBYs being marginalized or kept on the boundary. Merging into and identifying with the in-group is safer than being seen and isolated as the out-group.

Sherry's description of discipleship sounds like identity transformation. She encourages small-scale retention and rehearsal of Jewish memorial events, rather in the mold of Durkheim—for the sake of the memory without expecting it to make any difference—and making sure that it does not interfere with the church master narrative. Sherry's discipleship process moves a JBY quickly through the liminal state: leaving Judaism, joining Christianity, then back-linking to use Jewish identity and connections only as tools for evangelism of family and friends.

Sherry sees no opportunity for Assmann's "showing and imitating" for JBYs in church. The passing of Jewish identity to the next generation will be minimal due to no active engagement in Jewish activities or practice. Sherry proposes that JBYs offer minimal translation: Hebrew name pronunciation, explanations of biblical Jewish customs, when asked. She would see JBYs as a translated subsystem, part of the church's polysystem, hosted by the church, with the church owning and controlling the vocabulary and symbols. She clearly sees JBYs as clients to the church's patron, with the local church being in a position to block or allow publication or discussion.

Sherry would probably agree with the biblical mandate for the One New Man—interpreting it to say that both Jew and Gentile should be included in the One New Man but are not supposed to be visible—but disagree with David Woods' Distinction Theory, preferring JBYs to be largely indistinguishable from their Gentile fellows. Her position of church on Jacob's model is "Church Assimilation," although she would probably allow a little room for maneuver within the closed embrace. Sherry would complete the last three of the four steps on the modified Sanders process, allowing the first step—De-Judaizing—to remain incomplete.

Spotlight on Carol

Carol is in her late sixties and leads a deliverance and healing ministry in the UK. She has no Jewish heritage or family, but has a number of JBYs in her church and has been involved in helping many others discover and activate their Jewish identities.

Carol and her church are unique among the respondents interviewed in this research. Although in many ways they follow the traditional charismatic/Pentecostal church model, Carol sees the Jew being Jewish as normal behavior and a natural role partner for the Gentile Christian, bringing needed balance and a sense of holiness. While Carol's own identity is firmly Gentile, she tries hard to raise the salience and value of Jewish identity in any JBYs who visit or fellowship in their church. The church emphasizes and appreciates traditional manifestations of Jewish identity and practice to reinforce Jewish identity in JBYs. By promoting Jewish identity, she is trying to reverse the assimilation of JBYs into the church by releasing them into what she would see as normal expressions of Jewishness. Carol and her church also exercise a ministry rescuing JBYs from oppressive or abusive church situations, either by joining their church or by deliverance from the oppression so that they can survive in their own context.

Carol deprecates the image she has of the standard church prototype and is using an alternative JBY prototype to move her whole church towards what she considers a more biblical position. She is redefining in-group behaviors and attitudes to substitute positive inclusion for negative exclusion. This offers security and stability for JBYs due to uncertainty reduction, and at the same time enables self-enhancement for the in-group by having more "biblical" status and prestige than other churches. The church promotes a high permeability between Gentile and JBY members—there are no barriers other than ability and calling—and mobility in roles and functions is apparent. Carol seeks to construct identity by identity amplification.

By promoting traditional Jewish feasts and celebrations, the use of Hebrew, and other signs of Jewish identity, Carol tries to create or amplify Jewish traditions and memories. This provides "show and imitate" opportunities to identity and pass on JBY Jewish identity. She is attempting to rewrite the past for a second time—back to something of its original state, allowing for faith in Messiah. In a sense, the church is acting as a *Bet Din* to overturn the traditional rabbinic "no" to Yeshua, so allowing the JBY to find acceptance in the traditional sources and documents—principally, the Bible. The "awkward truths" of past church behavior are acknowledged and apologies made.

Carol sees a JBY in traditional church as being stuck in a liminal state: they have left their Jewish identity but are unable to accept a Christian identity on the standard terms; standard church will not accept them as fully equal believers without a renunciation of their Jewishness, so they have become marginalized. By accepting them —or announcing acceptance on behalf of the church—as JBYs, she enables them to exit the liminal state as full members of both the church and their Jewish identity.

Translation is generally good, if lacking a depth in Jewish identity. Other respondents might criticize Carol as providing only caricatured Jewish identity and components, but that may offer enough acceptance and reinforcement for JBYs to recover and maintain their Jewish identity successfully. Carol's church offers shared vocabulary and symbols that will resonate with a JBY's internal equivalence table. The church sees JBYs in the "older brother" mode and proclaims that it wants to learn from, and walk in, Jewish practice. The translation, however, is mainly non-reversible and quite shallow, being limited to common expressions and vocabulary and not—currently—attempting to bring a serious engagement with Jewish learning into the church context. Possible reasons for this are the relatively strong and dominant Gentile leadership, almost ownership, of the church, and the lack of any well-qualified Jewish teachers or leaders with a good immersion in traditional Jewish learning who are part of the church.

Carol firmly accepts the biblical mandate for the One New Man and is trying to implement David Woods' Distinction Theory. The thrust of the deliverance ministry is to move from the third to the fourth act of Miroslav Volf's Drama: from the closed embrace to release and ongoing relationship on terms of equality. On Jacob's church model scale, Carol's church falls between "Church Integration" and "Separate but Open"—released but under Gentile leadership, One New Man often visible. Carol is working to reverse steps one, De-Judaizing, and four, Churchifying, of the modified Sanders process, almost to the point of reintroducing the third and fourth steps—Yahwizing and Israelitizing—of Sanders' original proposal.

Summary – Juliana, Sherry, and Carol

In some respects, while all three of these respondents are offering a recovery path for JBYs who are losing their Jewish identity or are feeling oppressed in the church, each offers a very different approach. Juliana is unashamedly Jewish and offers a clear road back to significant Jewish identity and practice that would suit those from a more religious background. Sherry offers a clear assimilationist approach based, instead of ignoring or suppressing Jewish identity, on a reasoned acceptance for letting that identity take a very low profile while providing a safety valve or shoulder to cry on while in process. Carol offers the most radical proposal: attempting to merge Jewish identity and practice into the church world, changing church to become more Jewish-friendly and more accepting of and participating in Jewish practice and celebrations.

Juliana's work is likely to produce two strong strands—the church of the circumcision (being Jewish in practice) and the church of the uncircumcision (being Gentile in practice)[10]—related and cooperating while meeting in different space and time. Sherry's process will result in slightly better adjusted or less traumatised JBYs in church, losing more of their Jewish identity over time and being unable to pass it on to the next generation. Carol's activities could produce a truly balanced Jew-Gentile partnership in one congregation—celebrating and observing both Jewish and church practice with a genuine unity and shared identity.

Church Leaders Who are Jewish

These respondents are current church leaders or church leaders in training who come from a Jewish background. It is interesting to observe how they reconcile their Jewish identity with leading a predominantly Gentile church.

Spotlight on George

George is a full-time ordained clergyman in his fifties, working in a busy inner-city church context. He has a strong Jewish identity and his family have been in the UK since the 1930s. He leads a *Beit Midrash* group one weekday morning most weeks, drawing attendees —mostly of an older age group—from a wide geographic area. While not everyone in the group is Jewish, "everyone who comes has a strong Jewish interest."

George's own Jewish identity is very strong and he sees his church congregation as his role partner. He code-switches between "rabbi" and "teacher" about his position. He feels a strong

---

10 Drawn from the gospel to the circumcision and the gospel to the uncircumcision spoken of by Paul in Galatians 2:7.

responsibility for the spiritual health of his congregation, as the shepherd or guardian of the flock. While he is very committed to his own Jewish identity, so that it is near the top of his prominence hierarchy, his sense of calling to the "ministry" overrides that, and he exhibits little dissonance with the negotiated salience hierarchy of his normal life. He sees the church's favorable reception of Jewish identity as a temporary situation, the novelty value of having a convert feeding the church's long-established supersessionist ideas.

While his faith in Yeshua as a JBY is very solid, George gives the impression of playing out a role—the Christian clergyman doing his best for the congregation—while maintaining a separate Jewish home life. On the surface he appears very assimilated, but in discussion he reveals a strongly subversive connection with what Turner called the "inferior group" for vocabulary and informal ritual. His Christian profile receives a high level of verification from his church denomination and congregation; his Jewish identity receives verification through the study group. George's congregation would be hostile to, and confused by, his Jewish identity so it plays only a minimal role in his public identity. George's identity construction takes the form of identity consolidation.

George avoids a clash between his two identities by keeping them apart. He maintains Jewish memory by participating in Jewish ritual and events with his family, by leading the study group, and by contact with his wider family. He lives with the tension between the two different stories of tradition but wishes they could be harmonized. He refuses to allow the church to rewrite his Jewish past, while honoring the church's master narrative in his official capacity. The church context allows no opportunity for any Jewish practice.

By keeping his two major identities separate, George avoids translation issues. His level of Jewish knowledge allows him to be bilingual—but he chooses not to translate into the church world, which operates in the model of the Roman Empire. Information is being lost in that context, but is being preserved in the study group context. While George does have a few JBYs in his congregation, they are all fully assimilated and are not interested in Jewish identity.

George would agree with the biblical mandate for the One New Man, seeing himself as part of the Jewish component within the church, but effectively hidden. He might accept David Woods' Distinction Theory, but his calling as a clergyman would not allow him personally to observe it.

Spotlight on Avi

Avi is in his mid sixties, has been an ordained clergyman for nearly forty years, and still serves in active local church leadership. Born and raised Jewish, his Jewish identity is firm but culturally adjusted. He has spent some years working with missionary agencies.

Avi tells probably the most positive story of all the interviews. As a current working church leader, he has been able to maintain his Jewish identity at a high level—though not without a certain level of inner conflict—and bring that into his ministry and as a blessing to the church.

Avi sees the Gentile church as his natural role partner. He sees himself with both JBY and Gentile clergyman identities, with his context determining which is dominant. Both are placed high in his prominence hierarchy and both are similarly high in his salience hierarchy, so although he visualizes one identity asking the other what it is doing, he experiences little identity dissonance. Apart from a few specific instances, his force of character has enabled him to negotiate a high acceptance level for his Jewish identity in the Gentile church world, so he gains verification for both identity components. His work for mission agencies has made his nonconformance with the standard church prototype acceptable and he reports never having been marginalized. He has served in leadership in both MJish and Gentile church congregations and alternates between the rabbi/teacher roles comfortably. Avi shows good understanding that many people with Jewish heritage have—accidentally or deliberately—been completely assimilated into the Gentile church/Christian model and cannot, or do not want to explore any Jewish identity in their lives.

Avi's identity construction has followed Snow and McAdam's identity consolidation path.[11] His identity remains that of an activist —for both Jewish and Christian causes—with a consistent redefinition of the shared and opposed identities from both constituencies.[12] His Jewish upbringing and the cultural and social memories remain fresh, while his years of service in the church world mean that he functions well within the church framework. These memories and experiences show no significant clash in meaning or significance, apart from Avi's robust condemnation of replacement theology. Avi is not in a liminal state; the church have

---

11 Snow and McAdam, *Identity Work Processes*, 50.
12 Ibid., 56.

accepted him as a member and clergy-person fully emerged from the Jew-Gentile transition: almost as if a Jewish Gentile.

Avi is comfortably bilingual and translates fluently. He code-switches occasionally, for major items such as Jewish feast names, but relates well in both the JBY and church worlds. His translation appears to be mainly directed—unidirectional. Apart from using the Jewish festivals as vehicles for education in the church and evangelism towards Jewish people, Avi demonstrates no interest in or importance for wider Jewish values and teaching.

Avi considers himself a walking example of the One New Man and would support the biblical mandate for both Jewish and Gentile identities being present and visible. It is unclear whether he would support David Woods' Distinction Theory. His working life has been mainly in Jacob's "Church Assimilation" model, with some years in "Separate but Open." While he shows some signs of resisting the first step, De-Judaizing, in the modified Sanders process, he seems comfortable with the other three steps.

Spotlight on Stephan

Stephan is in his mid fifties and has been a believer in Yeshua for around fifteen years. Married, from a career as a management consultant, he is now training for ordination. He attends a busy, evangelical and charismatic church in the London area. His completely Jewish family immigrated to the UK at the start of the twentieth century from Eastern Europe.

While Stephan proclaims a strong Jewish identity, he is much more assimilated to the Gentile church than he may be aware. Coming to Christianity after more than half of his life away from religion (except for family occasions) and a Reform upbringing that didn't inspire him or make a strong social memory connection, his Judaism was—and is—social and cultural. That said, he shows good awareness of the ways in which politics can both polarize and deter Gentile and church engagement with the Jewish continuity he seeks to promote.

Stephan projects a normal Gentile Christian identity with the benefit of specialized background knowledge and experience. He is an integrated part of the church he regularly attends, and will train to serve as a minister. As a Christian he is acting entirely in character; as a Jew, out of character. His adopted Gentile identity is dominant. He doesn't think of himself as Gentile, but his Christian identity behaves exactly like a Gentile. He is committed to his Jewish identity only as social and cultural: he is Jewish, but he is a mainstream church-going Christian. His prominence hierarchy includes his Jewish identity, but at a lower priority than his Christian identity, and his salience hierarchy has negotiated Gentile Christian behavior. There is no dissonance and Stephan seems happy with his position. His identity is verified in his church context; the background knowledge that his Jewish identity supplies is accepted and affirmed as interesting and relevant. He is substantially assimilated into the standard church prototype and shows high conformance with the typical church-leader model. Identity extension is probably the best way to describe Stephan's identity construction.

Stephan maintains weak links with the Jewish world, attending Jewish family events, such as seders or *bar-mitzvah* celebrations. As the Reform Jewish movement is very relaxed, he can participate freely without challenging his Christian identity. These links confirm his social and cultural identity. He is aware of the history of church-Jewish relations, but chooses not to raise this as a counter-narrative; he shares memories based on the biblical narrative and current cultural expression. This matches the expectations of the dominant church group, so is welcomed and appreciated. Stephan is not in a liminal condition; he has been accepted as a full church member, with only minimal concern during his ministerial selection process. Stephan considers the MJish world to be unsafe and doctrinally questionable. He sees no need for a separate MJish expression of faith in Yeshua.

Stephan has good translation facilities. He communicates well and fluently, but on a selective basis. He translates what he considers relevant Jewish history and practice into the church world, assuming Christian ownership and control of vocabulary and symbols. He is concerned for evangelism and mission towards Jewish people, so will translate the gospel into the Jewish world, but is not concerned about or interested in Jewish learning or a wider sharing of Jewish values and teaching. While this represents information loss, Stephan's own background has not equipped him to be aware of, or to value, this information.

Stephan would certainly agree with the biblical mandate for the One New Man, but his ideas of Jewish identity would not produce a distinctly recognizable Jewish component. He would not accept David Woods' Distinction Theory. His church model is Jacob's first alternative: "Church Assimilation" and he is very unenthusiastic about the more Jewishly expressive models. On the extended

The Data Revisited 189

Sanders process, Stephan is complete on the last three stages, retaining only a cultural memory of Jewish background, context and detail from a low starting point.

Summary – George, Avi, and Stephan

While all three Jews currently in church leadership proclaim unchanged Jewish identity and varying degrees of desire for Jewish expression, in practice all three are significantly assimilated to the Gentile Christian church world in which they live and work. Cultural and historical Jewish knowledge is accepted and welcomed by their churches; current practice or identity display is not and—to a marked degree—it is not desired by the individuals. George is perhaps the most open to helping a JBY retain their Jewish identity; Stephan the least. Jewish continuity is almost nonexistent; there will be no next generation.

Church Leaders Who are Gentile

The last group of respondents are current church leaders—leading a local church or responsible for groups of churches—or church leaders in training who are Gentile. Their perspectives vary widely from no understanding to significant awareness and engagement. A slightly larger group is included to cover the range of voices sampled.

Spotlight on Jeffrey

Jeffrey is in his early fifties and the full-time leader of a small-to-medium-sized independent non-denominational city church. He has no formal theological training and has been a part of the church for over thirty years, the last ten on the senior management team. Jeffrey's church has a wide range of ages—children, families and older folk—in what he describes as a "predominantly white, British background" cultural make-up. They would welcome a greater diversity.

Jeffrey sees no particular or essential value in Jewish identity as compared with other ethnic or national identities, beyond some educational benefits in understanding the Bible. He holds the supersessionist position that identity "in Christ" subsumes all other identities. Many of the identity theory questions are, therefore, unanswerable. His church would not encourage the maintenance and observance of Jewish identity and practice; although they have had some Passover demonstrations, these have been done by interested Gentiles. He guesses that Jewish identity would be received with interest, but has little or no practical experience of what that is, means, or would look like. Past church members with a strong interest in Israel have not been encouraged and now worship elsewhere. Essentially, Jeffrey has one standard church prototype—the strongly mimetic modern evangelical Christian—anything else has only anecdotal or educational interest.

Jeffrey's church maintains only one set of memories—the standard Christian set—and any subversion or counter-narrative would be discouraged. They have a "normal" set of meanings for narrative and any attempts at rewriting would be denied. Similarly, the biblical text is held to have only one meaning—that of instruction—and alternative meaning or translation is refused. Jeffrey's ideas about Judaism come from limited exposure to a nineteenth century cleric.[13] There is no shared language and vocabulary with a Jewish world. Church leadership controls the discourse within the church.

Jeffrey sees no Jewish significance to Paul's "One New Man" image and rejects David Woods' Distinction Theory. He is working entirely within Alex Jacob's "Church Assimilation" model and all four stages of the extended Sanders process are complete.

Spotlight on Quentin

Quentin is in his early sixties and leads a large and fairly busy Anglican church in the Home Counties. He has worked for a Jewish mission agency in the past, both in the UK and for a number of years in Israel. Although supportive of much that is Jewish and Messianic Jewish, he is not uncritically pro-Israel. His Gentile identity is stable, generous and non-envious of Jewish identity. He is well connected in the world of Christian-Jewish relations.

Quentin is very enthusiastic about Jewish identity and sees Jewish and Gentile identity as being natural partners in the church. He would support JBYs who wanted to express their Jewish identity, offering positive verification to JBYs in a church context. On the other hand, he thinks that the church is wrong to have a standard prototype that excludes Jewish identity and encourages conformity and assimilation. He thinks that there should be no barrier between

---

13 Jeffrey has read some of the books written by Alfred Edersheim, an Anglican clergyman, written in the later part of the 1800s for a Gentile Christian audience to provide some explanation of biblical culture and expression.

Jew and Gentile in church roles and functions and would work with any form of identity construction that did not deny Jewish identity, while accepting that there are some JBYs who don't want to identify as Jewish.

Quentin supports grounding Christian memories and rituals in their Jewish parallels and antecedents. Essentially, he wants to rewrite the past to its original Jewish setting and context. He actively teaches a countermemory to the standard church master narrative—telling the stories of bad behavior by the church towards Jewish people. He would see a JBY who has come to faith and not continued with Jewish identity and expression as still in a liminal state, until this is restored and developed. Although his church does not celebrate the Jewish feasts, Quentin has done so with Jewish friends and MJish groups. He would be open to bringing more Jewish consciousness and festival awareness into his church. He is personally *Shabbat* aware and occasionally takes *Shabbat* as his day off, celebrating it with friends according to Jewish practice.

Quentin encourages translation between the Christian and MJish worlds. He wants that to be a fully bilateral exchange, exploring equivalence and shared vocabulary and symbols to gain understanding and communication. He thinks it is critical for the church to understand much more than a suggestion of what it means to be Jewish so that the family likeness between Judaism and Christianity can be seen, recognized and embraced.

Quentin fully supports the biblical mandate for the One New Man and teaches the importance of David Woods' Distinction Theory. While his church has a little way to go to catch up with his vision, Quentin wants the church to be in at least Jacob's second model, "Church Integration," and supports the third, "Separate but Open." The extended Sanders' process would be largely rejected; while accepting the key role of Yeshua, Quentin's vision is for Jew and Gentile to partner together in a context much closer to the Jewish model.

Spotlight on Edward

Edward is a Gentile Christian in his late thirties, married with children and, at the time of the interview, a minister in training. He has worked in church youth ministry for a number of years and is a qualified social worker. His experience of Jewish issues is very slight and he has only ever met a couple of Jewish people.

Edward is very open to the inclusion of Jewish identity and practice into the life of the church, so long as it can be done in a way that doesn't confuse or upset others. He sees JBYs as exactly equal to Gentile Christians, but values the Jewish background, particularly in the explanation of culture and context for understanding the Bible. He would want to enter into dialogue with JBYs to learn about time conflicts and would offer positive verification based on relationship and activities that draw people closer to God. He thinks the church should have enough flexibility to evaluate Jewish identity and JBY practice to see the benefits they can bring to the church. His own high view of Scripture leads him to honor and value JBYs who are living a different life out of obedience to Scripture.

Edward would be open to translation—hearing alternative meanings and interpretations of Scripture that enable more people to understand about God. He is interested in the ideas of shared vocabulary and symbols, to gain depth of understanding and see things in more detail and scope.

Edward's lack of experience with JBYs and Jewish issues leaves him in Jacob's "Church Assimilation" model, though with significant interest in the "Church Integration" model. His own position is that of fully completing all four steps of the modified Sanders' process, but the interview suggests that he would be prepared to partially reverse the first and last steps, De-Judaizing and Churchifying.

Spotlight on Amanda

Amanda is in her late fifties and leads a church in a large and relatively high-concentration area of Jewish population. She is married and has lived and worked in Israel for some years in the past. Like Quentin, she has a clear and unambiguous Gentile identity in which she is content. Both her own background and the Jewishness of the area in which she lives and works generate a rather different perspective.

Amanda is very clear and positive about the importance and distinction of Jewish identity, which she sees as a necessary role partner with Gentile identity. She promotes and encourages Jewish identity among JBYs in her congregations, offering positive verification, discouraging assimilation and, on occasion, recommending synagogue rather than church attendance. She insists that the standard church prototype needs to include JBY identity, seeks to draw JBYs into mainstream church, and chides the church for its inconsistent reception and welcome of JBYs. Her outlook most closely resembles identity consolidation: the bringing together of two formerly incompatible identities (Christian, Jew) to form a new salient identity (JBY).

Amanda tries to preserve Jewish social identity and memory by encouraging forms of Jewish ritual and festival observance in her church. This provides opportunities for "showing and imitating,"[14] albeit it in a non-Jewish context. She teaches the unity of the two memory traditions without glossing over the church's bad behavior, suggesting that the church's master narrative is not always correct or faithful to the Scriptures. Amanda sees a new JBY as very liminal and vulnerable to pressures from both their "old" community—family, synagogue, and life—and the "new" community: the church world. She works for maturity and a firm JBY identity, able to participate in and, where possible, to be reconciled to both communities with a foot and presence in each. The strong and dominant Jewish community within which Amanda lives and works is highly intolerant of JBYs and Amanda is aware of the tensions and conflicts that surface whenever a Jewish person comes to faith in Yeshua.

Amanda is very involved in translation. She has regular meetings with the rabbinic leadership in her area to discuss matters of security, nonreligious interworking and matters of community interest and support. Her church is hosting Modern Hebrew classes for both communities as a neighborhood and community building project; these are funded by and hosted in the church, taught by a member of the Jewish community and attended by significant numbers of both communities. She and her church are adopting the first of Bellos' translation strategies: learning the language of the community with whom they want to communicate.[15] While her translation target is full equivalence, the working context restricts the level of communication and range of subjects that can be discussed until trust is built up to enable a fuller exchange. While recognizing that some of the vocabulary and symbols are owned by the church, Amanda is keen to acknowledge Jewish ownership and control of much shared territory. Her years of working in Israel and subsequent study have made her aware of the churchs past colonial behavior and the need to find ways of expressing practical love and appreciation in a non-colonial way that doesn't depend on or reinforce church power or control.

---

14 Assmann, *Religion and Cultural Memory*, 69.
15 Bellos, *Is that a Fish*, 7.

Amanda fully supports the biblical mandate for Jewish and Gentile identities in the One New Man and recognises and where possible implements David Woods' Distinction Theory. Amanda's own church is trying to implement Jacob's second church model: "Church Integration"—including Jewish ritual, symbols and vocabulary into a relaxed denominational church structure. While recognizing that the church in which she serves has embraced all four steps of the modified Sanders process, she is personally involved in mitigation and reversal of the first and fourth steps: De-Judaizing and Churchifying.

Spotlight on Iain

Iain has been a clergyman for more than half his life, now living and working in a senior church position in London. He has always been involved in interfaith relations, the Jewish-Christian relationship in particular. His current position includes involvement in the commissioning and monitoring of both initial and ongoing ministerial training for his denomination. He has a firm and generous Gentile identity.

Iain puts understanding and resolving the Jew/Gentile relationship at the core of all other interfaith and diversity issues and relationships. He is governed by the principle of self-definition, to allow JBYs to remain Jewish even if the mainstream community disagrees. He wants to protect a place in the church for JBYs who do not consider themselves Jewish, while allowing JBYs who do consider themselves Jewish to determine their own role and place in the church. He stresses the importance of visible participation of Jews and Gentiles in the church. Being prepared to disciple JBYs towards their Jewish identity, and allow display of Jewish identity in church as well as forms of Jewish ritual and worship, he would offer positive verification of Jewish identity and resist assimilation. Iain feels that there should not be a "standard" church prototype, but that many identities should be welcomed and celebrated within the church and does not want to see groups marginalized or having their voice or concerns ignored.

Iain voices the need for ministerial training to cover more of the Jewish perspective, but is also aware of the pressure on training to cover everything. He feels that ongoing ministerial training and development is just as important. Iain is also something of a polyvalent translator, listening to many voices in order to identify common ground and find a way forward to increase understanding.

Iain supports the biblical mandate for the One New Man, but would be cautious about implementation of David Woods' Distinction Theory, being concerned about the development of independent JBY groups not connected to the wider church family. Iain would be prepared to support the formation of Jewish-identity-based congregations within the churches in his jurisdiction, sharing premises, leadership, and facilities, provided that they remained in close communion. This somewhat loosely looks like Jacob's third model: "Separate but Open," working with the dual expression model.[16] Against the extended Sanders process, Iain deprecates the De-Judaizing step and is negotiable on some of the Churchifying step.

Summary – Jeffrey, Quentin, Edward, Amanda, and Iain

Gentile church leaders cover a large spectrum from those who really have no idea that JBYs have problems in church or why, to those who are acutely aware of the issues and are trying to change the system from the inside to accommodate JBYs in church.

Jeffrey falls in the first category; for him Jewish identity is little more than any other ethnic identity, with no particular need for accommodation or preservation and little to offer the church except mild educational benefits that could be obtained from a book. Edward, in training and with no practical experience of JBYs, is open and wants to listen to and learn about Jewish people in church, expecting—optimistically and perhaps rather naïvely—that he can negotiate a change in church tradition and worship patterns to accommodate JBY church members. His major concern is that a biblical lifestyle and pattern should not be lost to the church. Quentin promotes and teaches about Jewish identity, but has little to play with in his context. He is critical of church leaders who just "go with the flow" or "follow the crowd," taking an easy way out to avoid grasping the nettle of changing church attitudes and practice. Amanda, on the other hand, while retaining her church context, is encouraging Jewish identity and practice in her church, celebrating Jewish festivals and events. In that respect, she is helped by working in a Jewish population area, which makes everything Jewish more "normal." Iain, from a supervisory and managerial level, sees the importance of Jewish identity as a key part of church identity and would allow considerable scope for JBY activity, service styles, and ritual within his domain of churches, provided it was properly

---

16 Juster, *Jewish Roots*, 203.

explained and connected, and didn't disenfranchise JBYs who didn't want to identity as Jewish within the church.

Vignette Summary

The vignettes show a variety of differences. Some respondents are happy in their current positions, some are trying to improve them; others are unhappy and making the best of what they can get. There are some incredibly bright spots, while a few are quite dark. The common thread of all the Jewish respondents and most of the Gentile respondents is that, although their opinions of what Jewish identity is and how it should be manifest vary considerably, they are all proud of Jewish identity and want to at least preserve it at its current level. Many of the Jewish respondents want to be able to share their identity, learning, and experience with the wider church, even if that has a personal cost. The clergy respondents are generally enthusiastic, but limited by their contexts and denominational structures. The non-clergy respondents are generally frustrated by the way the church doesn't understand, won't investigate and consider their position, and is generally dismissive of Jewish identity and its importance to JBYs. In two cases, clergy and non-clergy respondents belong to the same church: one set have quite differing views of the same context and environment; the other very similar.

Specific Issues

Two specific issues warranted a cross-community comment: the level of training that is, or could be, provided for church ministers; and the question of Jewish continuity—passing Jewish identity on to the next generation.

Ministerial Training

The training of clergy in Jewish concerns was an issue consistently raised by the majority of the respondents. Current clergy wished that they had had training; clergy in training wanted to have training and non-clergy both wished their clergy had had it and would like to have some themselves. The need for training was identified in several different areas:

a. background knowledge of Jewish methods of hermeneutics and exegesis; knowing how the Jewish community approach and

read the Scriptures to provide a parallel track of interpretation alongside the standard Christian views
b. knowledge of life and religious practice in Second Temple times, to inform the reading of the gospels, and to understand what Yeshua and the disciples said and did
c. experience of Jewish ritual and worship, on *Shabbat* and at the festivals, to inform and enrich Christian worship and teaching
d. understanding the significance of Israel and Jewish people today, the case for and against engaging in mission to Jewish people, knowing how to relate to Christian Zionism
e. helping Jewish people who come to faith in Yeshua

Much of the knowledge currently held by clergy is self-taught, from reading books, research on the Internet, and attending meetings. Some clergy have been on official church tours of Israel but are concerned that they had little contact with Jewish people and their expressions of faith in Messiah, instead being given a politically correct—but, in some cases, anti-Jewish—tour involving other narratives.

The response of the denominational colleges was that, while they try to expose their students to scholarship of all kinds, including Jewish commentators and writers where appropriate, they feel that their hands are essentially tied by their denominations and the need to train clergy according to appropriate standards and expectations. Timescales are already very tight, curricula are very full, and, although some of the colleges try to include material or contact with Jewish practice and people, this is often only at the professional clergy level—that is, working relationships with clergy of other faiths in contexts such as multi-faith chaplaincy teams—and treats Judaism and Jewish people simply as one among a number of other non-Christian faiths rather than a serious partner for dialogue and mutual learning and relationship.

Only the non-denominational college demonstrated a significant understanding of Jewish issues and provides a nominal pathway through its training courses that includes Jewish-Christian[17] and Messianic Jewish study modules at undergraduate and postgraduate levels. This is, however, still cast in a predominantly Christian frame,[18] and it remains to be seen if they can successfully maintain sufficient interest to keep the course options viable.

---

17 Counting "Introduction to Biblical Hebrew," "Lands of the Bible," "The Church and Israel," an independent study project, and a dissertation as Jewish-Christian study modules.

Most ministerial training does not recognize the difference between Jewish and Gentile identities and roles as believers in Messiah and, therefore, refuses the pairing of Jewish and Gentile identities within the body of Messiah. It offers no verification of Jewish identity and essentially promotes assimilation by offering only a limited number of standard denominational church profiles, thus consistently marginalizing JBYs unless they are protected by sympathetic clergy. JBY and Gentile ministry candidates are trained in the same way to produce the same Gentile product. Identity construction, or ministerial formation, follows whichever route produces the desired result. Training redefines partially shared identities within the collegiate training context to produce Christian activists.[19] Only Gentile Christian memories are taught and experienced; by definition training teaches the standard answer and interpretation to promote the views of the organization. Clergy in training and in ministry face constant pressure to conform, for the sake of their career and position; countermemories of their own or others are difficult to process. Similarly, translation is generally discouraged, as each denomination has, and defends, a monochrome view of doctrine and Scripture. Church leaders and training colleges set the tone of conversations and control the discourse within their denominations, rewriting those who disagree with them as "other."

Jewish Continuity

Jewish continuity—being able to pass Jewish identity on to the next generation—is a key issue for many JBYs in church. Both the interview data and published works show that Jewish identity fades quickly across generations. Unless strongly constrained by parents, children grow up in the church, adopting the majority Gentile culture. Parents are pressured by church leaders and programs to compromise on children's activities and other ministry commitments that take place on *Shabbat* and other key formational Jewish times. At the same time, constraint can make Jewish identity and practice a "parent" thing and, therefore, rejected by children particularly if it makes them different from their peers. Most of the respondents with a strong Jewish identity and who are concerned about continuity would prefer not to raise children in church, and only do so reluctantly in the absence of a viable alternative.

---

18 When compared, for example, with the range of modules offered by Messianic Jewish Theological Institute, http://www.mjti.org
19 A loose adaptation from Snow and Adams, "Identity Work Processes," 56.

A number of respondents have indicated that the church hinders Jewish continuity by denying its value and importance, and in many practical ways. They feel that church encourages intermarriage between JBYs and Gentile believers, thus creating blended families where there is no consistent identity and religious practice.[20] David Rudolph comments:

> The Gentile Christian lifestyle is distinct from the Jewish lifestyle and churches typically do not have the vision, leadership training or resources to support the goal of raising Jewish children. Christian theology may even run counter to this purpose. Loss of Jewish identity is almost certain in the local church.[21]

However good church may be, it is a Gentile Christian environment and, as Rudolph comments, "without Jewish communal involvement, it is extremely difficult to impart a clear and unambiguous Jewish identity to children."[22] Church non-participation in Jewish customs, feasts, and ritual makes external or home fulfilment difficult and different; it sets children apart from their peer group in church and creates pressure to assimilate, to be like everyone else. The memories created will be uncomfortable and compare unfavorably against group activities in church so that children complain.[23] The unconscious and implicit knowledge formed by the non-verbal "show and imitate"[24] of the JBY-church relationship will be of conflict and rejection.

Answering the Questions

Now it is time to re-present the questions and the models generated in the previous chapters—which have been used as spotlights in the respondent vignettes—and consider what answers have been generated among the respondent interviews.

---

20 King, *If I'm Jewish*, 2–3; Glaser, *Strangers to the Tribe*, 17; Rudolph, *Growing Your Olive Tree Marriage*, 5–11.
21 Rudolph, *Growing Your Olive Tree Marriage*, 48–49.
22 Ibid., 51.
23 King, *If I'm Jewish*, 128.
24 Assmann, *Religion and Cultural Memory*, 69.

Role Identities

Stets points out that almost all identities perform correctly when partnered with a corresponding identity or counter-identity; for example, doctor–patient, clerk–customer.[25] Most respondents report that churches do not recognize the Gentile and Jewish identity as different, seeing only "Christian," so they cannot relate to their natural counter-identity. Most churches represented in the interviews offer no serious ongoing teaching other than sermons and light midweek house-group meetings that usually focus more around relationship and practical life issues. Church leaders work naturally in the pastor-congregant mode rather than a teacher-student identity pairing, and a long way from the Jewish rabbi-disciple model.

Commitment and Identity Hierarchies

The respondents showed a range of commitment to their Jewish identities and a range of understanding of what Jewish identity meant to them. There is no standard by which to measure the strength of their Jewish connections. Some are, and remain, closely connected, both to family and to practice, while others are almost completely disconnected. In the case of those who exhibit a strong Jewish identity, this is high in their prominence hierarchy[26] and may cause dissonance with their salience hierarchy[27] in church situations where Jewish identity is not accepted or received. While churches are usually fairly quick to recognize and understand identity disparity between Christian and non-Christian identities, they are less aware of the Gentile–Jewish believer identity differences and have much less understanding of them. In general, most churches appear to greet Jewish niceties either with a blank look of incomprehension or a horrified look of disbelief.

Identity Verification

Church appears to offer little or no verification of Jewish identity to its JBYs, who are left to get what support they can from other JBYs

---

25 Stets, "Identity Theory," 89–90.
26 The prominence hierarchy arranges identities in the order in which the subject values them. See Stets, "Identity Theory," 91.
27 The salience hierarchy arranges identities according to the environments in which the subject operates and the level of each identity allowed by, or negotiated with. the other actors in those environments. See Stets, "Identity Theory," 92.

and mission agencies. Gentile Christians as a whole have no understanding of the importance of verification and its consequences. According to the respondents, unless the JBY has a strong Jewish identity and is prepared to fight and—if necessary—stand alone or outside the conventional church membership groupings, assimilation is usually a foregone conclusion, often proceeding rapidly under the pressure for social acceptance and the universal mantra that Jewish identity and practice ends when becoming a Christian. In practice, this is the position urged by both mission agencies and the MJish support groups who press their members into church membership and participation.

Identity Prototypes

While churches have different identity prototypes matching both their denominational distinctives and their larger type groupings,[28] most respondents report that the churches they attend or have visited have a very standard non-Jewish identity prototype based around the full "replacement" conversion model: "You were a Jew, now you're a Christian." JBYs report being considered fairly nonconformant by these sorts of churches, which appear to be intolerant of JBY identities that do not agree with their "standard." Gentile correspondents, although generally JBY sympathetic, confirm these reports. JBYs also report varying levels of marginalization: in the better examples, they are fairly well integrated into their churches; in the worst, they were asked to leave or refused access to some groups or activities. Since the correspondent reports offer a range of positions, it is difficult to show a consistent pattern, although within each church the pattern seems consistent.

Boundaries and Permeability

At one level, this question is difficult to address, given that most churches don't seem to recognize the JBY identity as significant—in general, church leaders only see Christians, and they don't understand or appreciate the difference between a Jewish and Gentile identity. Given that, the majority of respondents report that at a church level there is considerable permeability of the boundary between Jewish and Gentile members. Most roles and functions are available to both categories of believer. Some respondents reported the opposite: that there was little permeability and that they were

---

28 Such as "Pentecostal" or "Conservative Evangelical."

excluded from certain roles or functions, or—once their Jewish identity became known—that they were asked to relinquish those positions or were deselected. No respondent mentioned any alternatives allowing JBYs to participate on an equal footing, nor did any church leader speak of any groups or events specifically for JBYs, apart from separate congregations or fellowships. Mobility is real, provided that a JBY conforms to the dominant Gentile Christian identity and makes no mention of their Jewish identity. Some respondents report that a known Jewish identity definitely blocked mobility.

Identity Construction

All four of Snow and McAdams' types of identity construction were manifested by the respondent base. According to many respondents, the church wanted, or saw, identity transformation: from Jewish to Christian. Some respondents indicated that this had been their initial position as believers, but that they had later withdrawn from total transformation by reasserting their Jewish identity. Those respondents who were aware of the issues felt that amplification or consolidation was the most appropriate: producing a JBY identity from the constituent Jewish and Gentile identities. A number of constructed identities were very firm, to the extent of almost obliterating any underlying Jewish identity.

Tradition and Memories

Most of the respondents agree that the churches maintain a master commemorative narrative, in which the church controls both the tradition and the collective social memory. Few new memories are created, although existing memories are strongly maintained, fiercely so in some cases when JBYs or Jewish-sympathetic Gentile Christians offered a countermemory that challenged the dominant tradition. In general, the church has a standard operating framework and is intolerant of discourse that might call that into question. Where respondents have persisted in raising historical or theological issues that compete with the church's master commemorative narrative, the church has moved either to stop the discussion or to expel the parties involved from membership.

Although many church leaders, either as direct respondents or reported by non-leader respondents, are negative about Christian Zionism, Prayer for Israel groups or other pro-Jewish movements, a number of churches have welcomed Hebrew Roots groups because their teachings provide historically sensitive educational reinforcement material that supports and broadens the standard narrative. Mission agencies are likewise tolerated because their mission role allows deviation from the norm for their mission activities without suggesting or requiring change in the church.

Liminal Status

Many of the respondents report their feelings that the churches see them as in a liminal state, although they would not use that term. There seems to be a certain tolerance extended to new JBYs combined with an expectation that they will soon grow up and get over it: they will lose their Jewish particularity and behave like everyone else. JBYs who retain their Jewish ideas are then marginalized, their confessions of faith are placed in doubt and they become un-trusted members of the community.

Opportunities to "Show and Imitate"

Only two of the several churches either directly experienced or described in the interviews provided any opportunities for participating in Jewish heritage. In general, the church provides no experience of Jewish tradition or ritual for its JBY members. This actively discourages JBY familiarity and engagement with their heritage and also sends a clear message about the value the church places, or would allow to be placed, on such heritage.

Code-switching

Several of the respondents employed code-switching during their interviews, demonstrating that this was a habit they normally practiced. The interviews indicated, however, that the church environment is not comfortable with Jewish "loan words" being included in normal conversation, teaching, or questions. Using Hebrew words or names suggests superior knowledge or privilege, which is resisted by clergy and other church members.

Translation

Most of the church contexts in which the respondents live and operate are unaware that translation is occurring when talking to JBYs. On the whole, they assume that they own the language, vocabulary and symbols of "church" without considering where they came from or that others have an interest, or prior ownership claim.

Where translation does occur, this is done by the JBY either by default or to avoid confusion.

On the whole, the churches seem to have adopted Bellos' third translation strategy: ignoring those who can't or won't adopt their own language. Mission agencies translate outwards as part of their mission outreach, but translation is generally unidirectional and does not bring Jewish learning and culture into the church. It is inevitable that information—experience, culture, education, interpretation—is being lost as JBYs come into the church and lose their Jewish identity and practice. Only the JBYs seem to mind.

Messianic Judaism

Until recently, MJism has been regarded as something of a nuisance by the churches. The presence of JBYs, claiming to be both Jewish and believers in Messiah, has muddied the waters of Jewish-Christian relations in a way that many of those engaged in this interfaith work find difficult. Claims of ongoing Jewish identity blur the one clear line upon which both the church and the synagogue are agreed: that a person is either a Jew or a Christian but cannot be both. Church leaders are reluctant to accept JBYs as anything more than Christians with a Jewish heritage; synagogue leaders insist on it. The step of allowing JBYs to formally have a foot in each camp and be recognized as Jews and followers of Yeshua seems to be too large for either the church or the synagogue to countenance.

Church Control

Several of the respondents reported that the church that they attend or to which they belong takes a controlling role with regard to the general discourse that takes place within its circle of influence.[29] Some church leaders actively discourage conversation about or participation in Jewish or Israel-related events among their membership—they won't allow their premises to be used by groups or organizations that cross that line, thus making membership or even attending services, uncomfortable for many JBYs. JBY culture and values are ignored or rewritten in the standard old church "Pharisee" model, accusing the JBYs of trying to Judaize the church members.

JBYs can be seen as religious trophies in church, those who have seen the light, who have converted to Christianity, who have

---

29 Covey, *Seven Habits*, 82.

abandoned the wrongs and evils of Judaism—to quote one of the respondents: "playing for the right side now." This perpetuates the Jewish–Christian divide: Jewish being bad, wrong, in rebellion; Christians being good, right, and obedient. This renders JBYs as in need of salvation, as being a particularly valuable catch due to their previous sins and errors in Judaism. This is a difficult place for a JBY to be —particularly one who wants to retain their Jewish identity and culture!

The Biblical Mandate

Many of the respondents, including a majority of the church leaders interviewed, agree with the biblical mandate for the One New Man. Several—and, by report, the majority of the church, its leaders and colleges—do not, seeing either a new "third race" that is neither Jew nor Gentile, or following Andrew Walls' theory that Paul's picture in Ephesians is simply figural and should be replaced in each age by those people groups and identities that come to the table. Others agree in name only, offering such different definitions that the mandate's meaning is obscured or avoided.

Distinction Theory

David Woods' "Distinction Theory," that Jew and Gentile are supposed to remain distinct but equal within the *ekklesia*, and that that very distinction is part of the vision and design of the kingdom of God, has less support. Generations of church teaching in replacement theology have taught the church that there is no value in Jewish identity and no distinctive Jewish calling, that all having been taken over by the church.

Volf's Four Act Drama

Almost all of the interviews and respondents portray the church's relationship with JBYs as stuck at the end of the third act, with the fourth act—release—not accomplished. Either the church remains with its arms tightly locked, having captured the Jewish believers and holding on tight to make sure that they don't go back to Judaism; or the church arms are relaxed a little to allow some room for movement and so as not to suffocate the Jewish believers, while keeping them on a short rein. Apart from one or two encouraging bright spots, there seems to be little trust of JBYs by the church, who are not generally inclined to allow them to reach higher church or mission agency positions.

Jacob's Models

The majority of churches attended or described by the respondents fall into Jacobs first model: "Church Absorption." Most JBYs are simply absorbed (or assimilated) into the church and their Jewish identity gradually eroded. One inspiring example is working at Jacob's second model: "Church Integration," adapting the church to incorporate measures of Jewish liturgy, celebration and practice; at least a significant acceptance of Jewish identity. A small number of MJish congregations, both leaders and attendees, were also included in the survey: all followed Jacob's third model: "Separate but Open." With heavy Gentile participation and varying levels of connection with local churches, these represent an attempt to define a distinct Jewish identity and expression of worship and faith that is not "church." This option was reluctantly accepted by some as necessary, but the majority response was that some way ought to be found to incorporate JBYs into the church and that separation represented not only a loss but also a failure.

The Extended Sanders Process

The four steps of treating Jewish identity proposed by this study paralleling James Sanders' process for adapting and re-using outside material in the Bible are heavily in evidence throughout the interviews. The first step, De-Judaizing, has been standard church practice since at least the fourth century. It remains the majority practice apart from a few churches and leaders who are trying to roll it back and preserve Jewish identity. The second step, Exclusivizing, could be argued to be a basic tenet of the gospel and is universal in its application, as is the third step: Christifying. Only again in the fourth step, Churchifying, are there areas where the historical position is being pushed back to break up church monoculture and allow Jewish vocabulary, culture, and celebrations to be used and enjoyed by the whole church as well as JBYs.

Training

Michael W. Macy speaks of the way in which learning[30]—education and training—could bring changes to the situation of JBYs in church.

> Learning can alter the probability distribution of beliefs and behavioural responses competing for attention within each individual. Positive outcomes increase the probability that the associated behaviour will be repeated, while negative outcomes reduce it. The process closely parallels evolutionary selection, in which positive outcomes increase a strategy's chances for survival and reproduction, while negative outcomes reduce it. In evolution, strategies compete *between* the individuals that carry them, not *within*. Evolution thus alters the frequency distribution of behavioural responses competing for reproduction within a population. In biological evolution, these responses are genetically encoded in DNA; in cultural evolution, they are encoded in norms, rituals, routines, traditions, mores, protocols and the like.[31]

If one generation can be persuaded—through education, positive experience, and patience—to offer a more hospitable reception to JBYs, then inheritance or iteration should take over to produce greater levels of change. The rituals and traditions of the Jewish people—religious, cultural and social—have encoded lessons that have been learned in the past and now act as a teaching mechanism to inform choices today. This is learned behavior: church behaves like "this," so JBYs respond in "that" way and the cycle continues. JBYs trying to engage with church and share from their heritage receive negative feedback and are discouraged from trying again. Taken to the natural conclusion: they either assimilate—that is, essentially become Gentile in all but name—or they try to find a more affirming environment. Appropriate ministerial (and lay leadership) training offers a realistic way to break the cycles of learned behavior and improve the church environment for JBYs.

The academic interviews showed two distinct positions on behalf of training institutions. While the denominational colleges pay lip service to the idea of including and valuing Jewish input to their courses—for example, including Jewish commentators in biblical

---

30 This is a typical Hebrew wordplay. The root למד means both "to learn" (*Qal*) and "to teach" (*Pi'el*) depending on which stem is being used, which can only be seen in a pointed text. In a normal, unpointed, text, the meaning must be determined by context.
31 Macy, "Rational Choice," 72, original emphasis.

classes—in practice, there is no interest in bridging the gap between the standard Christian templates and a JBY or Jewish template. Driven by the demands of costs, timing, and the denominational templates for trainee ministers, the colleges simply do not have time, resources or suitably qualified and experienced staff to provide the training, to build bridges into the Jewish world at anything other than a relatively sterile, professional, ministerial contact level.

The non-denominational college both sees the need and understands some of the requirements but is delicately positioned for survival in a commercial world. Not supported by a denomination, it must achieve solvency by selling its courses and providing what the customer wants (and is prepared to buy). While a number of more Jewish-friendly modules are offered, the courses do not lead to any formal ordination or approval for MJish leadership or congregational positions. Neither are they substantively Jewish in content; they do not provide exposure to mainstream Jewish material,[32] ritual practice,[33] and placement experience. Perhaps this is a chicken-and-egg situation: there would be more individual and congregation demand for MJish clergy training and ordination if there were more full-time MJish congregations or MJish groups with a vision to plant congregations either independently or in a dual expression context. Mutual recognition between denominational and non-denominational clergy ordination and qualifications would pave the way for ongoing professional development and clergy-to-clergy learning.

Summary

This chapter has spotlighted a significant but smaller sample of the respondent interviews. This has been a presentation of a number of the respondents—younger JBYs, older JBYs, missionary groups, and recovery groups who sometimes have to pick up the pieces and sort out the casualties caused by the missionaries, JBYs in church leadership, and Gentile church leaders—to explore their data in the light of the spotlight questions from previous chapters. There has also been a more detailed look at some areas of particular concern, followed by a linear examination of how the questions might be answered by the respondent

---

32 For example, Rabbinic Studies, Reading Jewish Texts (such as the Mishnah and the Talmud), Jewish History, and Ethics.
33 Such as life-cycle events, familiarity with the Siddur and the Torah reading cycle, the festival liturgy—essentially how to lead and train others to lead services and less formal events.

data. The next chapter will draw conclusions, propose some theoretical points and make recommendations for further research.

Putting It All Together

The field research behind this book involved conducting over fifty interviews with Jewish and Gentile people in the UK who have active experience of Jewish believers in church: JBYs currently in church; JBYs who have been in church but are currently not; church leaders—both Jewish and Gentile—with and without JBYs in their churches; mission agencies responsible for bringing Jews to faith and encouraging them to join churches; and Gentiles who are or have been in churches with JBYs or JBY-friendly clergy. A mixture of voices—old and young, male and female, Jewish and Gentile—have painted a picture of Jewish life in church and the struggle to maintain Jewish identity that, in spite of several bright and optimistic spots, does not often make comfortable reading. "Non-Jewish believers typically have a very limited understanding of JBYs."[1] The church's low regard for, and hostility towards, continuing Jewish identity, combined with an identity-transforming paradigm and expectation for discipleship, the absence of any constructive support or networking for maintaining Jewish identity, and the denial of opportunities to share or practice Jewish culture within the local church, lead to identity assimilation and the inability to pass Jewish identity meaningfully on to subsequent generations.

Given the variance of Chain-Referral Sampling[2] and both the time-limited and non-statistical nature of the research, it is not possible to generalize the findings of this program to the whole population of either JBYs or churches in the UK. Nevertheless, the findings are sufficient to suggest that the existential phenomenon of JBYs in UK churches is real, that JBYs in church do have significant difficulty maintaining their Jewish identity, and that the church as a whole is failing both by omission and commission to obey the mandate given by Paul. The feelings and behavior of the respondents closely match what the social science and translation theories would have suggested had church attitudes and behavior been used as criteria for predicting JBY behavior. The "Data Revisited" chapter has assessed the self-perception of JBYs in the church as to the reception of their identity, and seen it contrasted with the One New Man ecclesiological ideal in "The Theological Mandate."

---

1 Brewer, "Jewish Believers," 238.
2 Goel and Salganik, "Assessing Respondent-Driven Sampling," 6746.

The research data suggests that the One New Man is rarely, if ever, seen within the UK church.

This project has brought interview data from JBYs and those engaged with JBYs in churches to interact with three areas of social science: identity theory, social memory theory, and translation theory. To take one example, Michael Hogg writes that:

> Social identity theory addresses phenomena such as prejudice, discrimination, ethnocentricism, stereotyping, intergroup conflict, conformity, normative behaviour, group polarisation, crowd behaviour, organisational behaviour, leadership, deviance and group cohesiveness.[3]

Many of these behaviors can be identified both in the church and JBY positions in the interview data. Understanding how and why people may behave—in this case a CRS sample of JBYs and Gentile Christians interacting in different church contexts—helps to provide an explanation for some ways in which a closer adherence to the biblical mandate may be realized.

Conclusions from Interview Data

The following series of conclusions drawn from the interview data describes the ways in which continuing Jewish identity is typically treated by churches in the UK. Notice that this applies to the church as a whole; there are a few exceptions where Jewish identity is preserved and encouraged, but the majority position—as informed by the respondents in this project—is that:

1. The church as a whole does not accept the biblical mandate laid out by Barth and supported by Woods' Distinction Theory for both Jew and Gentile to be distinctively present and visible within the Body of Messiah.

    This is the first and foundational step in the process. The biblical mandate from Paul's letter to the Ephesians, suggested by Markus Barth and extended in this book, supported by Woods' Distinction Theory, requires that the One New Man be present and distinctively visible within the Body of Messiah. The biblical record shows that it was already in question when Paul wrote to the Romans;[4] the historical record that the formal Jewish voice had been effectively

---

3 Hogg, "Social Identity Theory," 111.
4 Urging the Gentiles in the Roman church not to be arrogant towards the Jewish believers (Romans 11:18).

removed from the church by the Council at Nicea in 325 CE and that JBYs ceased to be a recognizable part of the church even as individuals by the end of the fourth century.[5]

The vast majority of churches in the UK, at least as reported by the interviewees and the literature, see only a "Christian Church" that is neither Jew nor Gentile, and resist attempts to draw that distinction amidst accusations of rebuilding the partition wall.[6]

2. If the church can be said to have engaged in Volf's four-step Drama, it freezes at the end of the third act; having welcomed JBYs, it does not easily let them go or allow for Jewish expression in worship or lifestyle.

   Volf's "Drama of Embrace" has four acts: opening the arms, waiting, closing the arms, and opening them again. Volf describes the first opening of arms as, "a gesture . . . reaching for the other." Without recognition of JBYs as the "other" in a Jew-Gentile distinction, but seeing them only as "Christian," no reconciliation is necessary, and the embrace need not take place. Seeing JBYs as "other" but an other that needs saving and bringing into the fold, rescuing them from Judaism, means that the embrace itself, visualized by Volf as requiring reciprocity and mutuality as well as "a soft touch" so as not to crush and assimilate the other,[7] is often held and too tight, lest the JBYs get away. The fourth act, opening the arms for release, never comes because the church does not trust that the JBY may not slip away back into Judaism.

3. The church as a whole has adopted identity transformation as its strategy for Christian identity construction, scrapping or discarding all that went before and building a standard (denominational) template identity prototype.

   Following the texts "Once I was blind, but now I see"[8] and "if anyone is in Christ, he is a new creation. The old has passed away; behold, the new has come,"[9] the church follows the identity transformation model as a means for constructing identity in its members: "discarding past or current identities to produce a dramatic change in identity, such that one now sees oneself as strikingly

---

5 Goldberg, "Rise, Disappearance and Resurgence," 17–19.
6 Cohn-Sherbok, *Messianic Judaism*, 68–70; Varner, "Messianic Congregations," 39; see also Telchin, *Messianic Judaism*.
7 Volf, *Exclusion and Embrace*, 141–5.
8 John 9:25.
9 2 Corinthians 5:17.

different than before."¹⁰ Each church denomination identity model, although with many similarities and shared vocabulary, is unique to the denomination and excludes others by assimilation: "you can survive, even thrive among us, if you become like us; you can keep your life, if you give up your identity."¹¹

4. The church as a whole is inclined to lapse into varying levels of anti-Semitism, either from individual ministers and congregations or institutionally. This is "'confessional anti-Semitism' that has been, from ancient to modern times, a persistent element of Christian theology."¹² Both laity and clergy who overstep the limit of allowed expression may be deselected or denied further opportunities to read, preach or lead.

    The church, either as an organization or a local congregation imposes discipline upon those it sees as disturbing its established views and positions on Israel, Jewish matters, people, and converts and how they should behave.

5. The church as a whole sees as normative and wants to complete all four steps of the modified Sanders process, particularly the first (De-Judaizing) and the last (Churchifying), for each of its members.

    Sanders identifies "the hermeneutic process by which the wisdom of others was adapted and resignified."¹³ The church neutralizes the "otherness" of JBYs; adapting their knowledge of Hebrew, the Old Testament and Jewish culture and religion by making JBYs experts on how to pronounce Hebrew names and provide background pictures for gospel stories. They become resignified following the "these things happened to them as an example, but they were written down for our instruction" (1 Corinthians 10:11) paradigm, and so absorbed into the church culture without cost to the church.

6. The church as a whole works in Jacob's "Church Absorption" model, assimilating believers of every kind into its standard model for Gentile Christians. No Jewish expression of ritual or practice is encouraged or allowed within a strongly determined set of denominational prototypes.

    Although JBYs can choose which church or denomination to join, once there they are expected to conform to the norms for that

---

10 Snow and McAdam, "Identity Work Processes," 51–2.
11 Volf, *Exclusion and Embrace*, 75.
12 Davis, "Teaching the Bible Confessionally," 24.
13 Sanders, *Canon and Community*, 56.

Putting it All Together 215

church, to carry out the vision of that church, which—being predominantly Gentile—will not include any Jewish ritual or practice; they are not expected to try to change it. This is modeled on the standard Gentile interpretation of "neither Jew nor Gentile . . . all are one in Christ Jesus" (Galatians 3:28). The only significant variation between prototypes is for denominational distinctives.

7. The church as a whole does not recognize that it is a Gentile church; this is not a word that it would use of itself, nor a description that it would readily accept.

   This is a further consequence of not recognizing the distinction between Jew and Gentile: the church is simply full of Christians. The description "Gentile" has little or no meaning to churchgoers and would be taken as offensive or discriminatory because of Bible translations offering pagan, barbarian or Greek in that place.

8. As part of its general "replacement theology" position that sees no enduring role or place for Israel in God's economy—as opposed to any other nation—the church as a whole does not recognize any particular significance in Jewish identity, "not only within the church but also outside it."[14]

   Following Paul's statement that he considered his Jewish status and identity as "loss,"[15] the level of anti-Jewish invective from some of the Early Church Fathers, and the common "replacement theology" view that the church is the new Israel,[16] Jewish identity is simply one cultural identity or set of baggage that people may have on becoming believers.

9. Nevertheless, a significant part of the church feels a need to render Jews (in general) and JBYs (in particular) in a certain colonial way in order to justify its own past misbehavior and portray them as especially needful of evangelism.

   This need can often be driven from a dispensational perspective, whose vision of the Last Days[17] predicts a Third Temple being built in Jerusalem followed by a pre-tribulation rapture and seven years of tribulation[18] during which time the Jewish people will be the

---

14 Soulen, *The God of Israel*, 2.
15 Philippians 3:8.
16 Based on a mistaken understanding of Galatians 6:16.
17 This vision is constructed from passages in Daniel, Revelation, and several of Paul's letters.
18 Referred to as "Jacob's Troubles" from Jeremiah 30:7.

surviving witness to Messiah.[19] In this and similar visions, Jewish evangelism is seen as hastening the day of the Lord's return.[20] While such a dispensational perspective may no longer be taught in mainstream colleges and seminaries, it remains a persistent thread in popular and less scholarly writing.

10. Therefore the church as a whole does not see any significance or value in continuing Jewish identity, other than that which it would recognize in a Chinese, Korean, or Ghanaian social and cultural identity, in a church context.

    As Jewish identity has no particular value or significance, why should it continue in a privileged position? The church is happy to see cultural expressions of "church" in many other ethnic or national groups because, although a particular dress style may be observed and a particular language spoken or food eaten, these are all essentially "church." Maintenance of Israeli cultural identity would be similarly tolerated—speaking Modern Hebrew and eating falafel and hummus. But Jewish identity that embraces religious difference from "church" is not expected to continue.

11. From a theological point of view, the church as a whole doesn't recognize Jewish identity as continuing past the point of coming to faith in Messiah: someone who was Jewish (following some definition of Judaism, however strongly or weakly) is now a Christian.

    The church treats Judaism as if it were any other religion: mutually exclusive with following Jesus. The convert passes "from death to life" (John 5:24) and is now expected to live in that new life and not the dead past.

12. On that basis, the church as a whole takes no measures to protect or foster Jewish identity; to the contrary, it is generally discouraged. There is no room for bringing any Jewish ritual or practice into a church context apart from historical background information that may "enrich" understanding of the Scriptures or the context/world of the New Testament and its writers.

    Continuance of Jewish practice is seen as a sign that conversion might not be genuine. Maintaining Jewish identity—and hence particularity—is seen as divisive or trying to be superior.

---

19 See, for example, Hal Lindsey's *Late, Great Planet Earth* and the *Left Behind* series by Tim LaHaye and Jerry B. Jenkins.
20 2 Peter 3:12.

13. The majority of church leaders who are Jewish are zealous for their congregations and so play down or ignore their own Jewish identity so that their people should not be disturbed or confused. Conversely, the church leaders who are most positive and encouraging about Jewish identity are themselves Gentile.

    What could have been a bridge for sharing Jewish identity and values and broadening exposure to a wider audience from a "safe" source is, therefore, being denied. This will not only not help their particular congregations to grow in understanding, but will deny these clergy the opportunity to maintain their own Jewish identity.

14. Many, but not all, church leaders are wary of, and resistant to, pro-Israel movements; the various Christian Zionist organizations are regarded with suspicion. It is difficult for JBYs to disassociate themselves from these organisations to be heard in their own right.

    Whether pro-Jewish, One Law or Israel-advocacy, these movements are often regarded as a distraction to the vision of the church and its leader. Pro-Israel people are seen as very obsessive and are regarded by some church leaders as a nuisance, disturbing their congregation. JBYs are often thought to be associated—whether they like it or not—with these groups and so are tarred with the same brush.

15. Consequently, JBYs struggle to maintain their own Jewish identity in the face of denial, negative verification, social and peer-group pressures, and leadership disapproval. All of the social identity and social memory mechanisms for maintaining a significant or coherent self-Jewish identity are denied.

    Without any positive identity reinforcement mechanisms, it proves impossible to maintain a strong Jewish identity and be able to pass it on to the next generation. JBYs come into church, but their children do not identify as Jews and Jewish continuity is broken. As the Sages said, "The deeds of the fathers are a sign for the children."[21]

16. A few church leaders do hold a different view and in various degrees recognize continuing Jewish identity and encourage its maintenance. A subset of those few go as far as to positively encourage, look for, and promote Jewish identity among their congregants.[22] In these churches, JBYs can grow and flourish as Jews as well as believers in

---

21 Midrash Tanchuma *Lech L'cha*, 9.
22 Sometimes rather more than their congregants, Jewish and otherwise, wish!

Yeshua, the One New Man is often visible, and the church—both Jewish and Gentile members—is blessed.

By all accounts these churches are few and far between. The level of Jewish continuity and identity is quite variable and very dependent upon the church leader involved. It remains to be seen how or if these churches change when their leadership changes.

17. Due to location, distance, and time—not to mention that while some JBYs are quite extrovert, others are typically introvert, so don't want their Jewishness noticed—most JBYs cannot attend churches that would support their Jewish identity. In the majority of cases, the typical assimilation profile will occur: the JBY will retain some fading cultural Jewish identity, which they will not be able to pass on to their children in anything but name, and their grandchildren will be fully assimilated Gentile Christians.

At least through the eyes of the some of the informants, the framing of the multiculturalism debate seems manifestly unfair. Todd Endelman reports that, while everyone appears to agree that there should be room for diversity at the table and that "those who wish to be included must embrace some of the behavioural and attitudinal norms of the dominant group," the debate is about how far the newcomers have to divest themselves of themselves: "What is at stake in the multiculturalism debate, then, is the price to be paid for inclusion rather than the right to be included."[23] If the Gentile Christian church is the dominant group, how high a price are they demanding for inclusion and acceptance?

Richard Gibson outlines the stark choices available to JBYs:

> to hide or limit their identity in order to fit in at a local church congregation, find a Messianic Jewish fellowship where they can exist naturally and not feel the need to deny their heritage, stay at home and avoid the conflict or simply stay in the Jewish community.[24]

Why Do JBYs Attend Church?

One of the respondents spoke of "isolated Jewish believers buried alive in churches," needing to keep their heads down to avoid unwelcome attention, including suppressing or denying their Jewishness. They mentioned anti-Semitic and discriminatory sermons, stressing the need for JBYs to be able to meet and fellowship with each other outside a

---

23 Endelman, *Leaving the Jewish Fold*, 1.
24 Gibson, "Supersessionism," 276.

church context, where "group members would grow in the Messiah to the stage where they really can teach and support one another; and remember they exist in a hostile political climate, and are rebuffed from all quarters."

If this is so, why is it that so many JBYs—and they can be found in many churches throughout the land—put up with church? Why do they continue to attend church services in such negative circumstances?

One possible answer is that, for them (each in particular) there is no viable alternative, either due to location, distance, or safety. MJish congregations are few, and thin on the ground. They tend to be located close to areas of more concentrated Jewish population, such as North London, Brighton and Hove, Manchester, and Gateshead. Travelling on *Shabbat* is tiring and inconvenient, apart from technically contravening biblical injunction[25] and rabbinic rulings.[26] Most of the BMJA groups only meet monthly or less frequently, making them an unattractive option for the only source of fellowship.[27]

Another possible answer is that church is usually well defined: each denomination does what it does; there is a consistency and a hierarchy. Services are generally quite predictable, following standard and recognized patterns. Denominational clergy and many non-denominational leaders have theological and pastoral training and a denominational structure offers accountability and safety.

A third possibility hinted at in the data is that some JBYs are comfortable in church. Often from weak or suppressed Jewish backgrounds, their Jewish identity is already only cultural or nominal and church presents no particular threat. They integrate easily, as other Gentile believers coming to faith; and the liturgy and rhythm of church, while not Jewish, is close enough to what experience they have of Judaism (if any) that they feel a familiarity.

David Rudolph offers a fourth possibility: community and fellowship. "Most JBYs," he writes,

> . . . join a local church because they value Christian community. They can raise their children as believers in Jesus and participate in Christian worship. They can contribute to the work of God through their church. However, the majority do not give much thought to the question of Jewish continuity or covenant faithfulness. Some

---

25 Exodus 16:29.
26 *b. Eruvin* 15*a*.
27 "Fellowships," accessed 4:20pm 26Aug16, http://www.bmja.net/?page_id=20

are even taught that it is counter to New Testament teaching for Jewish Christians to live as Jews or raise their children as Jews.[28]

Why Might Messianic Jewish Congregations in the UK be Unsafe?

A number of the respondents mentioned that they didn't consider MJish congregations in the UK to be safe. Why should this be? Other respondents are past leaders of BMJA fellowships and would dispute this suggestion.

One reason may be the leadership, constituents, and vision of a number of groups that position themselves in this category. For example, one of the respondents, themselves Gentile, currently leads a "Messianic" congregation, rather than "Messianic Jewish" congregation, in which there are only one or two Jewish people—sometimes none—in a congregation of a hundred or more Gentiles. A number of MJish congregations in the UK promote the "One Law" position, teaching that Gentile as well as Jewish believers are obligated to follow *Torah* law in areas such as worship, festivals, and diet—with the sole exception of circumcision. A very small number of congregations are conversionist, teaching that Gentile believers must convert to MJism in every respect, including full *Torah* observance and circumcision.

A second answer is that there is no recognized training, or training requirement, in either theology or pastoral care. Everyone does "what is right in their own eyes"[29] and there is no consistency[30]—everything is done from an amateur, self-taught basis. People start or lead congregations on the basis that they have been called by God to lead and a previous leader (if there was one) or the congregation affirm their calling to that position. There is no approved or accredited ordination process for MJish leaders within the UK. Most leaders are essentially unaccountable.[31]

A third answer is that there are no support or denomination structures. With the exception of mission agencies—Chosen People Ministries, for example, supervises a congregation in North London—all the congregations are autonomous, independent, and self-governing. The BMJA, to which a dozen or so fellowships or congregations belong, is

---

28 Rudolph, *Growing Your Olive Tree Marriage*, 51.
29 Echoing Judges 21:25.
30 Foreman, "Messianic Judaism," 80.
31 To be fair, it is true that there are a number of churches that operate in the same way: they are essentially stand-alone independent church units. They are, nevertheless, a very small fraction of the total church population.

only an umbrella, and provides minimal fellowship and an annual conference.[32] There is noone to call on, no authority to invoke, no safety net, no appeal process.

A fourth possible answer is that there is no collective vision or definition. Every leader has their own vision, driven in part by their own bad experiences in church or other congregations. There is no common liturgy or rules, no agreed pattern of services or service components.

A fifth, and more speculative reason, based on practical experience and anecdotal reports, is that MJish congregations tend to attract the "nutters"[33] and church "rejects"[34]—those who have strange ideas, mental and behavioral issues, who have been hurt or offended by the local churches. Inexperienced and untrained leaders struggle to keep such people in check and to maintain the congregation as a safe place, particularly if the vision of the congregation is towards the charismatic end of the spectrum where much is excused or at least not stopped soon enough in order to allow freedom for the Spirit.

Connecting with Messianic Jewish Scholarship

Comparison and connection with MJish scholarship shows just how different the situation for JBYs in the UK church is from the wider MJish world.

Richard Harvey – Mapping Messianic Jewish Theology

Richard Harvey's *Mapping Messianic Jewish Theology* considers the theological positions of a number of scholars, practical theologians, and leaders who are currently active within Messianic Judaism and involved with JBYs—in America and Israel.[35] While this book investigates the status and feelings of JBYs in the UK church, it will be constructive to compare the behavior of JBYs and the UK church against the streams and concerns that Harvey identifies and to assess the degree to which those concerns play a part in the UK church context.

---

32 "Fellowships," accessed 16:20 26Aug16, http://www.bmja.net/?page_id=20
33 A colloquial term much used by clergy and church leaders as a "catch-all" to describe fanatics and enthusiasts for various causes, particularly pro-Israel and short horizon eschatology.
34 Both those rejecting church and those rejected by church.
35 Harvey, *Mapping Messianic Jewish Theology*.

Harvey observes that Messianic Jewish Theology (MJT): "has yet to articulate the Triune nature of God effectively"; has a number of different Christologies; has several different approaches to *Torah*, both in theory and practice; has a wide range of eschatological positions; and is still "in the process of articulating its own position" in a number of areas. His research makes it clear that there is a significant difference between MJism in Israel and MJism in the Diaspora; even within Israel, congregations differ widely from a reformed non-charismatic church format to a charismatic singing/dancing congregation, to Messianic Rabbinic Orthodoxy.[36] Some of the scholars describe themselves as Jewish Christians and lead extremely orthodox churches, while others give strong credence to Jewish tradition and *halacha*, leading streams that look very like Orthodox Jewish synagogue.

It is clear that the UK church is very wary about anything or anyone that looks too Jewish. While different churches and denominations draw their lines in different places, the interviews show that the less the overt Jewishness of a JBY, and the less they articulate their Jewishness, the more likely they are to find a level of acceptance in the UK church. What appears to be the most popular type of MJish expression—described by Harvey as "New Testament Halacha, Charismatic and Evangelical"[37] and operating in Jacob's "Separate but Open" model—might find the most acceptance among Christians in the UK and currently draws the most Gentile participation where MJish congregations exist. It appears that only very few UK church leaders would be prepared to host or embrace such expressions within their churches.

Mark Kinzer – Post-Missionary Messianic Judaism

While Harvey suggests that Mark Kinzer's "influences and assumptions place him outside the mainstream of Protestant evangelicalism,"[38] Kinzer's work attempts to move JBYs beyond simply using Jewish identity and practice as tools for evangelism, and calls them to "an observant Jewish life as an act of covenant fidelity rather than missionary expediency," yet remaining full participants in the life and work of the Body of Messiah. A key component of Kinzer's position is a "non-supersessionist ecclesiological framework," which would require the church to

---

36 Ibid., 262–5, 267–77.
37 Ibid., 270–1.
38 Ibid., 273.

repudiate supersessionism. He sees one of the JBY callings to be serving the Gentile church by "linking it to the physical descendants of Abraham, Isaac and Jacob, thereby confirming its identity as a multinational extension of the people of Israel." Kinzer makes the radical dual claim that:

> Messianic Judaism can perform its necessary ecclesiological role only if it is an embodiment of Jewish covenant fidelity at home in the Jewish world. The church of the nations can become an extension of Israel only if its Messianic Jewish partner is deeply rooted in Jewish soil.[39]

Alluding to the Olive Tree analogy, Kinzer talks of Israel's covenant enduring, the church drawing nourishment from its Jewish roots, while Yeshua "remains Messiah and Lord for both Jews and Gentiles."[40] He pursues this in his other writings, working with the Roman Catholic – Messianic Jewish Dialogue Group to reflect on "the 'mystery of Israel' and its relationship to the 'mystery of the church.'" Touching upon the One New Man, Kinzer suggests that "the corporate expression of Israel's crucified and risen Messiah, the 'one new human being' is Israel itself, reconfigured in a new eschatological form."[41] He sees the question of Yeshua's Jewish identity to be critical—"To say that Yeshua *was* a Jew is a fact of history. To say that Yeshua *is* a Jew is a fact of explosive theological consequence"[42]—and argues for Gentiles who come to faith, without becoming Jewish, to become part of that Jewish body. He argues that Israel must remain Israel, following the pattern of the first apostles.[43] This "contradicts the widespread assumption that with the death of Christ, Israel's identity markers simply expired or became purely voluntary."[44]

Kinzer's positions present a number of difficulties for JBYs attempting to be part of the UK church. As the interview data has shown, the one ground where manifestation of Jewish identity and practice is acceptable and tolerated is in a missionary context; those

---

39 Kinzer, *Post-Missionary Messianic Judaism*, 13, 15, 16.
40 Ibid., 16.
41 Kinzer, *Searching Her Own Majesty*, 21, 77.
42 Kinzer, *Israel's Messiah*, 170, original emphasis.
43 Richard Bauckham asserts that "As far as we can tell, the vast majority of Jewish Christians in the New Testament period continued to observe the whole law, taking for granted that they were still obligated to do so" (*James*, 247).
44 Dauermann, *Converging Destinies*, 190.

engaged in missionary work see their Jewish identity as perhaps their strongest asset in presenting the gospel to Jewish people. Similarly, the respondents face an uphill battle against replacement theology in its varied forms, both personal and corporate, both in being able to feel comfortable in their own Jewish identities and practices, and in the resistance many churches show to the significance of Israel and any connection with the Jewish people as the wider people of God. Likewise, many respondents reported significant opposition from those in church against the display or practice of Jewish identity markers.

David Rudolph – Introduction to Messianic Judaism

David Rudolph is a second-generation Messianic Jewish rabbi and scholar. He sees MJism as "the bridge between the Jewish people and the church, and as such it helps the church to understand better its origin and identity." Marshalling arguments by Markus Barth, John Howard Yoder, R. Kendall Soulen, and others, he urges Gentile Christians to "*come alongside* the Messianic Jewish community and assist it" in a variety of practical ways: prayer, encouragement, inclusion, affirmation, collaboration, and others.[45] Rudolph presents a case for both the first church in Jerusalem and the Matthean community being movements within first-century Judaism, and for the Acts 15 Jerusalem Council decision to be that "Yeshua-believing Jews were to remain practising Jews."[46] He briefly documents the life of JBYs until the fourth century CE and the subsequent rebirth of JBYs through the medium of missionary societies in the nineteenth and twentieth centuries. Writing from a North American context, he describes some of the changes that he has seen happening in recent years:

> The Messianic Jewish movement is growing in support among churches as New Testament scholars and theologians increasingly demonstrate that Messianic Judaism is consistent with the teachings of the Jewish apostles and the experience of the earliest communities of Yeshua-believing Jews in the Land of Israel, Syria and beyond. The movement is also winning sympathisers in the Jewish world as Messianic Jews demonstrate through their actions that Yeshua is good for the Jewish people.[47]

---

45 Rudolph, "Messianic Judaism," 14, 15, original emphasis.
46 Ibid., 22–3.
47 Ibid., 35.

Nevertheless, Rudolph sees MJism as the missing voice at the table. In a number of key ways, he documents how the MJish voice has been excluded from the table, to the detriment of both the church and the MJish movement. Making the argument that JBYs have traditionally been overlooked or ignored, he says, for example, "nothing fully substitutes for the inclusion of MJish scholars in theological forums and colloquia." By asking why they are not there, what they have to contribute, "and including Messianic Jewish scholars in the conversation, Christian theology restores an historic voice to the contemporary discussion."[48]

The situation in the UK seems to lie somewhat behind the curve as compared to Rudolph's report. The interview data records several JBYs being excluded, both from discussion groups within the UK church and from UK inter-faith liaison groups. Although some scholars do track what is being written elsewhere, adoption in the UK is slow and piecemeal. Faced with a largely Gentile church and little missionary demand for Jewishly-qualified leaders, clergy training remains overwhelmingly focussed on the Gentile majority. Jewish scholars may have their opinions quoted in colleges and academic curricula, but MJism as such does not appear to have made any impact except in a few isolated churches and parishes where individual clergy have caught a vision for the One New Man. They, in turn, report apathy at best and significant discouragement at worst from their denominations. The mainstream Jewish world is similarly unhelpful; closer to the shadow of the Holocaust and with extreme right-wing political groups on the rise in Europe, the synagogues remain trenchantly opposed to MJism or any moves towards recognition of Yeshua.

Stuart Dauermann – *Converging Destinies*

Dauermann, a veteran missionary and singer/songwriter turned congregational leader, and scholar with a PhD in Intercultural Studies from Fuller Seminary, has been proposing for some years that MJism and the church are on convergent tracks, approaching the point at which "both the Christian and Jewish worlds will be affirmed and also chastened by the God who assesses all of us."[49] He proposes a "common accountability" for both the church and the synagogue and operates within a short horizon eschatology. He expresses dissatisfaction with the attitudes and assumptions that he

---

48 Rudolph, "Messianic Jews," 84.
49 Dauermann, *Converging Destinies*, 206.

sees underpinning missions work to the Jewish people, perpetuating supersessionism in various forms and denying the importance and value of Jewish identity, practice, calling, and covenant faithfulness. As a founder of the Hashivenu organization, he speaks of five core values:

1. MJism is a Judaism, and not a cosmetically altered "Jewish style" version of what is extant in the wider Christian Community.
2. God's particular relationship with Israel is expressed in the *Torah*, God's unique covenant with the Jewish people.
3. Yeshua is the fullness of *Torah*.
4. The Jewish people are "us" not "them."
5. The richness of the rabbinic tradition is a valuable part of our heritage as Jewish people.[50]

Dauermann insists that MJish thinking and actions must be reframed around Jewish covenantal identity: "we must restore the Jewish people to their identity as a people called by God to glorify Him in the context of communal *Torah* living." He urges a major rethink about the role and purpose of *Torah* in a JBY's life, re-evaluating it as a critical and necessary part of transmitting an intergenerational Jewish identity.[51] Adding that "Israel is destined to be [the church's] senior partner in the consummation of the mission of God,"[52] although supported by some MJish leaders in Israel who are advocating for the establishment of a new apostolic leadership for the whole church based around the Messianic remnant in Jerusalem,[53] he risks offending many Gentile Christians and even taking many JBYs in church by surprise. He firmly rejects the idea that "maintaining pride in Jewish lineage, or attending periodic Jewish Yeshua-believer meetings and holiday events will sustain Jewish identity from generation to generation."[54]

As perhaps the most ambitious of the MJish scholars under consideration, Dauermann's ideas probably exceed even the

---

50 See "Principles," accessed 3:38pm 19Apr17, http://www.hashivenu.org/index.php?option=com_content&view=section&layout=blog&id=6&Itemid=54
51 Dauermann, *Son of David*, 35,37.
52 Dauermann, *Converging Destinies*, 26.
53 See for example, Asher Intrater of Revive Israel Ministries, "The New Age of the Acts of the Apostles", accessed 4:14pm 19Apr17, http://reviveisrael.org/new-age-of-acts-of-the-apostles/
54 Dauermann, *Converging Destinies*, 160.

aspirations of the most Jewish JBYs in the field interviews. Many JBYs in the UK church would simply not dare to mention them for fear of the response from their churches and church leaders. Other JBYs, who, although of Jewish heritage, have effectively assimilated to the church, would be alarmed at the implied criticism that they were not being and doing Jewish.

Bilateral Ecclesiology

One of Kinzer's most important proposals is "bilateral ecclesiology"[55]—a "crucial tool for the coherence of his re-ordered canonical narrative,"[56] upholding "the election and dignity of Israel"[57]—also referred to by Rudolph as "Torah-defined ecclesiological variegation."[58] Like Woods, by this they mean that Yeshua-believing Jewish and Gentile identities remain distinct but equal within the *ecclesia*. Dauermann also supports this proposal, linking it with a post-supersessionist missiology, a mission and outreach to Jewish people that is "best implemented by Jews living out of the obedience of Jewish faith for the sake of His name." This is to contain evangelism, but be accompanied by "humanitarian aid, social justice, ecological responsibility for Jews, living and transmitting a legacy of *Torah* obedience and much more." Kinzer and Dauermann see Yeshua as "being already in the midst of Israel, even when unacknowledged."[59]

The interview data, particularly from church leaders—Jewish and Gentile—suggest that the UK church is a very long way from being able to accede to such a major revision in the status of MJs and JBYs. Many church members, too, would struggle with a paradigm shift of such magnitude; many smaller denominations and more "evangelical" independent churches would simply reject the proposal out of hand. Even the most favorable contexts discovered by this research would balk at many of these ideas.

---

55 Kinzer, *Post-Missionary Messianic Judaism*, 151–179.
56 Harvey, *Mapping Messianic Jewish Theology*, 258.
57 Dauermann, *Converging Destinies*, 189.
58 Rudolph, "Paul's Rule."
59 Dauermann, *Converging Destinies*, 201,200,205.

Nurturing Messianic Jewish identity[60]

JBYs, whether Jewish believers in church or MJs in MJish congregations, are constantly working on defining their identity. Identity pressure comes from the church, which is urging compliance with the normal "Christian" prototype; from the synagogue, which urges abandoning faith in Yeshua; and from within where some advocate a minimum of Jewish culture and tradition and others seek a very traditional expression of Jewish life and worship. This pressure "is the result of their living in the transitional space between the Christian and Jewish worlds."[61] That pressure forges something of a community, living on the edge of both parent communities; it is a liminal community that is constantly negotiating between the Jewish and Christian cultures. Individual JBYs constantly have to ask whether they can "identify satisfactorily with two communities that traditionally call for exclusive identification."[62] One author asks, "So how are Jews supposed to maintain a Jewish identity in a heavily Christianised culture?"[63] The problem seems more acute for JBYs trying, or compelled, to live within the Gentile Christian dominant church world. Cohn-Sherbok points out that the stakes are high:

> What was at risk was total assimilation. Within Gentile churches, there was no attempt for Jewish believers to retain their separate identity, nor to ensure that their children would continue to honour their ancestral faith. Rather, it was inevitable that within a few generations Jewish believers would be totally absorbed into the life of the church.[64]

In the USA, where the MJish movement is well established, with many MJish congregations, particularly in areas of Jewish population:[65]

> Cultural constructions assist in constructing community when they define the boundaries of collective identity, establish membership

---

60 Used here to cover Jewish identity in a Jewish believer in Yeshua regardless of their context.
61 Feher, *Passing Over Easter*, 93.
62 Harris-Shapiro, *Messianic Judaism*, 14.
63 Caplin, *Confessions of a Jewish Skeptic*, 65.
64 Cohn-Sherbok, *Messianic Judaism*, 56.
65 The USA is a very young nation, with not quite 400 years of tradition, that until recently has always been open to immigration, innovation, and a strong sense of multi-cultural expression. By contrast, the UK has had an established church for more than 1,500 years and until recently has been a strongly single-faith nation.

criteria, generate a shared symbolic vocabulary and define a common purpose. The Messianic movement has done this by drawing on symbols from both parent communities and, in the process, it has created its own.[66]

But one of the significant differences between MJism and JBYs in church is that the latter have no power or control in any of these areas; the interview data shows that the church is the dominant—and controlling—culture. JBYs will always struggle to define their own identity without control of these boundary markers and conditions. This may explain why there is a high mobility among the more motivated JBYs, who are often unable to settle in a church context for very long without feeling that their identity or freedom is being questioned or constrained.

Commenting on the *Torah*'s description of the patriarch Isaac's historic "dig and move on" response to irrational opposition,[67] Jonathan Sacks maintains that this response remains correct for Jews today: "defeated once, he tries again. He digs another well; this too yields opposition. So he moves on and tries again, and eventually finds peace."[68] This is characteristic of JBY church behavior: if they can't settle in one church and instead meet with opposition or distrust, they move on to try another until they eventually, but not always, find peace and a sufficient measure of acceptance and tolerance. But at what price? Many of the respondents regretted the loss to both communities and to the church as a whole that ensues if the church of the circumcision is excluded from participation in the life and ministry of the church. Karl Barth agrees: if the church and the Jewish community become completely separated, it is the church who suffers. Without the balance of revelation in and through the Jewish people and the Hebrew Scriptures, the church can be replaced by a "Christianity of a Greek or a German or some other freely chosen kind."[69]

Hogg suggests that one way out of the dilemma between conflict and harmony, to prevent a subgroup feeling marginalized and leaving, "is for the superordinate identity to structure relations between subgroups"—in this case, respectively, the church and the Jewish and Gentile expressions of faith in Messiah—so that:

---

66 Feher, *Passing Over Easter*, 141.
67 Genesis 26:19–22.
68 Sacks, *Genesis*, 164.
69 Barth, *Dogmatics in Outline*, 66.

- the subgroups thrive as distinct and respected entities that are "playing for the same team"—which has features of both Jacob's "Church Integration" and "Separate but Open" models;
- the subgroups extend themselves to include each other's attributes as part of themselves—as Nietzsche said: "If you have your *why* for life, you can get by with almost any *how*";[70]
- the superordinate identity itself is defined by subgroup diversity —a formal acknowledgement that the church is made up of distinct and identifiable Jewish believers and Gentile believers.

Hogg admits that "this can be difficult to achieve,"[71] but perhaps this research demonstrates the need to make the effort to start. It will take significant intentionality but following the biblical mandate will draw the church closer towards the Bible's picture of the Bride of Messiah.

A Way Forward

This project suggests that there is willingness to repair the breach between the church and JBYs—at least on the part of the latter. In taking a positive decision together to be the One New Man in a full interpretation of Paul's mandate,[72] and then proclaiming that decision, JBYs and Gentiles in the church may appropriate "the power that determines the existence of the man of faith."[73]

One possible venue is the constructive connection between Paul's "faith comes by hearing" (Romans 10:17) and the proclamation of the Lord's Supper.[74] By participating as one body in the sharing of preaching and communion, the church takes again the decision to be "in Messiah" and so receives both the power and the faith for that reality to be seen. In the sharing of the word and communion, be that a *drash* after the *Torah* has been read during a *Shabbat* service followed by *matzah* and grape juice, or a sermon after the gospel reading on a Sunday morning followed by handmade stone-ground wholemeal bread and a fine heady red wine, the body of Messiah has manifested the miracle of the One

---

70 Nietzsche (1997), 6.
71 Hogg, "Social Identity Theory," 124.
72 The TJCII organisation (see http://www.tjcii.org) exists to work towards healing and reconciliation between JBYs and the church and recover the ground lost since the first century CE.
73 Bultmann, *New Testament Theology*, 302.
74 1 Corinthians 11:26.

Putting it All Together 231

New Man in unity around Yeshua's commandments. A decision has been taken and a proclamation made: we are one in him.

It is important that the One New Man operates in unity rather than in tolerance. It has been held in the past that the twin apostleship—Peter to the Jews, Paul to the Gentiles[75]—implies not only that there are two classes of mankind to be reached with the gospel, but also two kinds of churches, one for Jewish believers and one for Gentile believers.[76] While this permits Jewish expressions of worship in Messiah to thrive and develop, it nevertheless risks building a wall[77] between the two congregations of believers in Yeshua that could hinder rather than help the integration of the One New Man throughout the Body of Messiah. To prevent this, congregations should either be mixed—Jew and Gentile together in one worshipping family—or should be closely connected and interrelated, perhaps sharing some of: premises, leaders, teaching, services, to keep the channels of communication open and the people integrated. One example is the so-called dual expression congregations,[78] where both *Shabbat* and Sunday services are held with overlapping attendance; often MJs and Gentile Christians share the leadership and teaching ministry and one set of house and prayer groups serves the whole congregation. Perhaps this is what Paul had in mind.

Writing to the mixed community of Jews, JBYs and Gentiles in Romans chapter 11, Paul links $\pi\lambda\acute{\eta}\rho\omega\mu\alpha$, "fullness," with both Israel[79] and the Gentiles.[80] Fullness of both parts makes up the fullness of the One New Man. There has been an historical imbalance since the second and third centuries CE,[81] but for the One New Man to reach the fullness of the stature of Messiah (Ephesians 4:12–13), this imbalance must be addressed.

---

75 Galatians 2:7–9.
76 Robinson, "Distinction," 32.
77 Contra Ephesians 2:14.
78 Juster, *Jewish Roots*, 203.
79 Romans 11:12.
80 Romans 11:25.
81 Nanos, *The Mystery of Romans*, 10.

Bibliography

Adams, J. N. *Bilingualism and the Latin Language*. Cambridge: Cambridge University Press, 2003.
Anderson, Benedict. *Imagined Communities*. New York: Verso, 2006.
Arnold, Clinton E. *Ephesians*. Exegetical Commentary on the New Testament. Grand Rapids: Zondervan, 2010.
Assmann, Jan. "Form as a Mnemonic Device: Cultural Texts and Cultural Memory." In *Performing the Gospel: Orality, Memory and Mark*, edited by Richard A. Horsley, Jonathan A. Draper and John Miles Foley, 67–82. Minneapolis: Fortress, 2006.
———. *Religion and Cultural Memory*. Translated by Rodney Livingstone. Stanford: Stanford University Press, 2006.
Atkinson, John. "Jews and Gentiles—Metaphors of distinction and unity." Accessed 14May15 12:50. CMJ South Africa, 2008. http://cmj-sa.org/Data/Sites/1/pdf/jews-and-gentiles-metaphors-of-distinction-and-unity.pdf
Barth, Karl. *Dogmatics in Outline*. Translated by G. T. Thomson. London, SCM Press, 2001.
———. *The Epistle to the Romans*. Translated by Edwyn C. Hoskyns. New York: Oxford University Press, 1968.
Barth, Markus. *Ephesians 1-3: A New Translation with Introduction and Commentary*. Anchor Bible 34. New Haven, CT: Yale University Press, 1974.
———. *Ephesians 4-6: A New Translation with Introduction and Commentary*. Anchor Bible 34a. New Haven, CT: Yale University Press, 1974.
Bauckham, Richard. "For Whom were Gospels Written?" In *The Gospels for All Christians*, edited by Richard Bauckham, 9–48. Grand Rapids: Eerdmans, 1998.
———. *James (New Testament Readings)*, Abingdon: Routledge, 1999.
Bellos, David. *Is That a Fish in Your Ear?* London: Penguin, 2011.
Berkovits, Eliezer. *Not in Heaven: The Nature and Function of Halakha*. Hoboken: Ktav Publishing House, 1983
Bernis, Jonathan. "Where are All the Jews?" In *Awakening the One New Man*, edited by Robert F. Wolff, 173–89. Shippensburg: Destiny Image, 2011.

Bivin, David, and Roy Bilzzard Jr. *Understanding the Difficult Words of Jesus.* Shippensburg: Destiny Image, 1994.

Blenkinsopp, Joseph. *Judaism: The First Phase.* Grand Rapids: Eerdmanns, 2009).

Bockmuehl, Markus. *The Epistle to the Philippians.* Grand Rapids: Baker Academic, 1998.

———. *Seeing the Word: Refocusing New Testament Study.* Grand Rapids: Baker Academic, 2006.

Boyarin, Daniel. *Border Lines: The Partition of Judaeo-Christianity.* Philadelphia: University of Pennsylvania Press, 2004.

———. *A Radical Jew: Paul and the Politics of Identity.* Berkeley, CA: University of California Press, 1994.

Brewer, Brian. "Jewish Believers in Jesus and the New Supersessionism." In *The Jews, Modern Israel and the New Supercessionism*, edited by Calvin L. Smith, 2nd edition, 237–60. Broadstairs, King's Divinity Press, 2013.

Brown, Michael L. "Celebrating our Distinctives and Honouring the Body." In *Awakening the One New Man*, edited by Robert F. Wolff, 107–11. Shippensburg: Destiny Image, 2011.

Buell, Denise Kimber, and Johnson Hodge, Caroline. "The Politics of Interpretation: The Rhetoric of Race and Ethnicity in Paul." *JBL* 123/2 (2004): 235–51

Bultmann, Rudolph. *New Testament Theology Volume 1.* Translated by Kendrick Grobel. London: SCM, 1952.

Campbell, William S. *Unity and Diversity in Christ: Interpreting Paul in Context.* Eugene: Cascade, 2013.

———. "Unity and Diversity in the Church: Transformed identities and the peace of Christ in Ephesians." *Transformation* 24/1 (January 2008): 15–31

Caplin, Sarahbeth. *Confessions of a Jewish Skeptic.* North Charleston: Createspace, 2016.

———. *Confessions of a Prodigal Daughter.* North Charleston: Createspace, 2015.

Castelli, Elizabeth A. *Imitating Paul: A Discourse of Power.* Louisville, KY: Westminster/John Knox, 1991

Chandler, Jenny Berg. *Jew in the Pew: A Memoir.* Sself-published, Kipling House Books, 2013

Childs, Brevard S. "The Canon in Recent Biblical Studies: Reflections on an Era". In *Canon and Biblical Interpretation*, edited by Craig Bartholomew et al. Milton Keynes: Paternoster Press, 2006.

Clarke, Sir William. *The Clarke Papers: Selections from the Papers of William Clarke, Secretary to the Council of the Army, 1647–1649,*

  and to General Monck and the Commanders of the Army in Scotland, 1651–1660. Volume 2, edited by C. H. Firth. London: Camden Society, 1894.
Cohen, Elliot. "The Use of Holocaust Testimony by Jews for Jesus: A Narrative Enquiry". *Melila*, 6 (2009).
Cohen, Shaye J. D. *The Beginnings of Jewishness: Boundaries, Varieties, Uncertainties.* Los Angeles: University of California Press, 1999.
Cohn-Sherbock, Dan. *Messianic Judaism.* London: Cassell, 2000.
Cook, Michael. "Philippians." In *The Jewish Annotated New Testament*, edited by Amy-Jill Levine and Marc Zvi Brettler, 354–61. New York: Oxford University Press, 2011.
Covey, Stephen R. *Seven Habits of Highly Effective People: Restoring the Character Ethic.* New York: Simon & Schuster, 1989
Cranfield, C. E. B. *A Critical and Exegetical Commentary on The Epistle to the Romans.* Edinburgh: T&T Clark, 1979.
Danker, Frederick William, ed. *A Greek-English Lexicon of the New Testament and other Early Christian Literature.* 3rd edition. (BDAG). Chicago: University of Chicago Press, 2000.
Darko, Daniel K. "Adopted Siblings in the Household of God: Kinship Lexemes in the Social Identity Construction of Ephesians." In *T&T Handbook to Social Identity in the New Testament*, edited by Brian J. Tucker and Coleman A. Baker, 333–46. London: Bloomsbury T&T Clark, 2016.
Dauermann, Stuart. "Community of Reference." *Inconvenient Truths.* May 1, 2011. Accessed 27Dec16, 10:05. http://www.messianicjudaism.me/agenda/2011/05/01/inconvenient-truths-community-of-reference
———. *Converging Destinies: Jews, Christians and the Mission of God.* Eugene: Cascade, 2017.
———. *Keeping the Faith in Interfaith Relationships.* MJTI Messiah and Jewish Life Series #1. Eugene: Wipf and Stock, 2009.
———. "The One New Man." *Inconvenient Truths.* April 29, 2011. Accessed 27Dec16, 10:06. http://www.messianicjudaism.me/agenda/2011/04/29/inconvenient-truths-the-one-new-man
———. *Son of David: Healing the Vision of the Messianic Jewish Movement.* Eugene: Wipf and Stock, 2010.
Davis. Ellen F. "Teaching the Bible Confessionally in the Church." In *The Art of Reading Scripture*, edited by Ellen F. Davis and Richard B. Hays. Grand Rapids: Eerdmans, 2003.
Dein, Simon. "Becoming a Fulfilled Jew: An Ethnographic Study of a British Messianic Jewish Congregation." *Nova Religio: The Journal*

of Alternative and Emergent Religions, 12, no. 3 (February 2009) 77–101.

Donaldson, Terence L. *Jews and Anti-Judaism in the New Testament.* London: SPCK, 2010.

Dunn, James D. G. *The New Perspective on Paul: Revised Edition.* Grand Rapids: Eerdmans, 2005.

Durkheim, Emile. *The Elementary Forms of Religious Life.* Translated by Joseph Ward Swain. London: George Allen and Unwin, 1915.

Eisenbaum, Pamela. *Paul was Not a Christian.* New York: HarperOne, 2009.

Endelman, Todd M. *Leaving the Jewish Fold: Conversion and Radical Assimilation in Modern Jewish History.* Princeton: Princeton University Press, 2015.

Esler, Philip F. *Conflict and Identity in Romans: The Social Setting of Paul's Letter.* Minneapolis: Fortress, 2003.

Eyerman, Ron. "The Past in the Present: Culture and the Transmission of Memory." *Acta Sociologica* 47, 2 (2004) 159–69.

Feher, Shoshanah. *Passing Over Easter: Constructing the Boundaries of Messianic Judaism.* Walnut Creek: AltaMira, 1998.

Fieldsend, John Henry. *Messianic Jews: Challenging Church and Synagogue.* Tunbridge Wells: Monarch Publications, 1993.

———. *A Wondering Jew.* Thame: Radec Press, 2014.

Fischer, John. *The Olive Tree Connection.* Palm Harbour: Menorah Ministries, 1983.

Flusser, David. *Jewish Sources in Early Christianity.* Translated by John Glucker. Tel Aviv: MOD Books, 1989.

Flusser, David with R. Stephen Notley. *The Sage from Galilee: Rediscovering Jesus' Genius.* Grand Rapids: Eerdmans, 2007.

Fonrobert, Charlotte Elisheva, and Martin S. Jaffee, eds. *The Cambridge Companion to The Talmud and Rabbinic Literature.* New York: Cambridge University Press, 2007.

Foreman, Esther. "Messianic Judaism in London: A Study of a Continuum Between Judaism and Christianity." MA Dissertation, London: Kings College, 2002.

Fraade, Steven B. "Memory and Loss in Early Rabbinic Text and Ritual." In *Memory and Identity in Ancient Judaism and Early Christianity*, edited by Tom Thatcher, 113–27. Atlanta: SBL, 2014.

Friedman, Elias. *Jewish Identity.* Highland, NY: The Miriam Press, 1987.

Gale, Aaron M. "Matthew." In *The Jewish Annotated New Testament*, edited by Amy-Jill Levine and Marc Zvi Brettler, 1–54. New York: Oxford University Press, 2011.

Gaston, Lloyd. *Paul and the Torah.* Eugene: Wipf and Stock, 2006.

Gibson, Richard. "Supersessionism, Messianic Jews and the Jewish Community: A Messianic Leader's Perspective." In *The Jews, Modern Israel and the New Supercessionism*, edited by Calvin L. Smith, 2nd Ed, 261–78. Broadstairs: King's Divinity Press, 2013.

Givens, Tommy. *We the People: Israel and the Catholicity of Jesus.* Minneapolis: Fortress, 2014.

Glaser, Barney G. and Anselm L. Strauss. *The Discovery of Grounded Theory.* Piscataway: Aldine Transaction, 1976.

Glaser, Gabrielle. *Strangers to the Tribe: Portraits of Interfaith Marriage.* Boston: Houghton Mifflin, 1997.

Glasspole, Adrian. *One Size Doesn't Fit All: Issues Jewish Believers Face in the Body of Messiah.* Olive Press Research Paper, Issue 13, March 2012. Farnsfield: Olive Press, 2012.

Glenn, Susan A and Naomi B. Sokoloff. "Who and What is Jewish." In *Boundaries of Jewish Identity*, edited by Susan A. Glenn and Naomi B. Sokoloff, 3–11. Seattle: University of Washington Press, 2010.

Goel, Sharad and Matthew J. Salganik. "Assessing respondent-driven sampling." *Proceedings of the National Academy of Sciences of the United States of America*, 107, no. 15 (April 2010) 6743–47.

Goffman, Erving. *The Presentation of Self in Everyday Life.* London: Penguin, 1969.

Goldberg, Louis. "Introduction: The Rise, Disappearance and Resurgence of Messianic Congregations." In *How Jewish is Christianity?*, edited by Louis Goldberg and Stanley N. Gundry, 13–26. Grand Rapids: Zondervan, 2003.

Goldin, Rabbi Shmuel. *Unlocking the Torah Text: Bereishit.* Jerusalem: Gefen. 2007.

———. *Unlocking the Torah Text: Vayikra.* Jerusalem: Gefen, 2010.

Gombis, Timothy G. "Ephesians 2 as a Narrative of Divine Warfare." *Journal for the Study of the New Testament* 26, no. 4 (2004) 403–18.

Gruber, Dan. *The Church and the Jews.* Hagerstown: Serenity, 1997.

Guinness, Michele. *Child of the Covenant.* London: Hodder & Stoughton, 1994.

———. *Promised Land.* London: Hodder & Stoughton, 1994.

Haaland, Gunnar. "Othering the Jews from the Church Pulpit." In *Religious Stereotyping and Interreligious Relations*, edited by Jesper Svartvik and Jakob Wirén, 171–181. New York: Palgrave Macmillan, 2013.

Halbwachs, Maurice. *On Collective Memory.* Edited and translated by Lewis A. Coser. Chicago: University of Chicago Press, 1992.

Hampton, Joel E. "The Equal Ultimacy Question in Calvin's View of Reprobation: Is Predestination Really 'Double'?" *INTEGRITY: A Journal of Christian Thought* 1 (2000) 103–113.

Hardin, Justin K. "Equality in the Church." In *Introduction to Messianic Judaism: Its Ecclesial Context and Biblical Foundations*, edited by David J. Rudolph and Joel Willitts, 224–234. Grand Rapids: Zondervan, 2013.

Harink, Douglas. *Paul Among the Postliberals: Pauline Theology Beyond Christendom and Modernity.* Grand Rapids: Brazos Press, 2003.

Harnack, Adolf. *The Mission and Expansion of Christianity in the First Three Centuries.* Translated and edited by James Moffat. New York: Harper & Bros, 1962.

Harris-Shapiro, Carol. *Messianic Judaism: A Rabbi's Journey through Religious Change in America.* Boston: Beacon Press, 1999.

Harvey, Richard. *Mapping Messianic Jewish Theology.* Milton Keynes: Paternoster, 2009.

Hendriksen, William. *Philippians, Colossians & Philemon*, New Testament Commentary. Edinburgh: Banner of Truth, 1962.

———. *Romans*, New Testament Commentary. Edinburgh: Banner of Truth, 1980.

Hobsbawm, Eric. "Introduction." In *The Invention of Tradition*, Canto Edition, edited by Eric Hobsbawm and Terence Ranger. Cambridge, Cambridge University Press, 1992.

Hocken, Peter. "The Present: The Restoration of a Jewish Expression of Church," talk given at Julius Schniewind Haus, Schönebeck, Germany, February 2008. Accessed 23Mar15 18:15. http://www.peterhocken.org/mc/home.nsf/0/7E8A3D3E4C28B9DAC1257D9F006F301F?opendocument&part=1&lang=en

Hoehner, Harold W. *Ephesians: An Exegetical Commentary.* Grand Rapids: Baker Academic, 2002.

Hogg, Michael A. "Social Identity Theory." In *Contemporary Social Psychological Theories*, edited by Peter J. Burke, 111–136. Stanford: Stanford University Press, 2006.

Holmes, Michael W. *The Apostolic Fathers: Greek Texts and English Translations*, 3rd edition. Grand Rapids: Baker Academic, 2007.

Horsley, Richard A. "A Prophet Like Moses and Elijah: Popular Memory and Cultural Patterns in Mark." In *Performing the Gospel: Orality, Memory and Mark*, edited by Richard A. Horsley, Jonathan A. Draper and John Miles Foley, 166–90. Minneapolis: Fortress, 2006

Howard, George. *Hebrew Gospel of Matthew.* Macon: Mercer University Press, 1995.

Hoyt, Jane Hansen. "The Master Plan for the One New Man." In *Awakening the One New Man*, edited by Robert F. Wolff, 139–59. Shippensburg: Destiny Image, 2011.
Hughes, Aaron, W. *The Invention of Jewish Identity*. Bloomington: Indiana University Press, 2010.
Ikonen, Tuula-Hannele. *Daughters of the Vale of Tears*. PhD Thesis, University of Tampere. Tampere, Finland, 2013.
Jacob, Alex. "Root and Branch?" *Olive Press Quarterly*, Issue #6 (May 2007).
Janicki, Toby. *God-Fearers: Gentiles and the God of Israel*. Marshfield: First Fruits of Zion, 2012.
Jenkins, Philip. *The Next Christendom: The Coming of Global Christianity*. Oxford: Oxford University Press, 2002.
Jenkins, Richard. *Social Identity*. London: Routledge, 2014.
Johnson, E. Elizabeth. *The Function of Apocalyptic and Wisdom Traditions in Romans 9–11*. Atlanta: Scholars Press, 1989
Johnson Hodge, Caroline E. "Apostle to the Gentiles: Constructions of Paul's Identity." *Biblical Interpretation* 13:3 (2005) 270–88.
———. *If Sons, Then Heirs*. New York: Oxford University Press, 2007.
———. "The Question of Identity: Gentiles as Gentiles—but also Not—in Pauline Communities." In *Paul Within Judiasm: Restoring the First-Century Context to the Apostle*, edited by Mark D. Nanos and Magnus Zetterholm, 153–74. Minneapolis: Fortress, 2015.
Joseph, John E. "Identity." In *Language and Identities*, edited by Carmen Lamas and Dominic Watt, 9–17. Edinburgh: Edinburgh University Press, 2010.
Juster, Daniel C. "Denominations, Messianic Jews and the One New Man." In *Awakening the One New Man*, edited by Robert F. Wolff, 83–105. Shippensburg: Destiny Image, 2011.
———. "Do We Want the Jews to Disappear?" Accessed 12:31 pm 03Sep14. http://www.tikkunministries.org/newsletters/dj-jan06.php
———. *Jewish Roots*. Shippensburg: Destiny Image, 2013.
———. "Jews in Christian Churches." Accessed 12:32pm 12:32pm. http://www.tikkunministries.org/newsletters/dj-jul05.php
———. "When Jews Assimilate into the Christian Faith." Accessed 12:30pm 03Sep14. http://www.charismamag.com/blogs/standing-with-israel/8666-assimilating-jewish-christians
Kasdan, Barney. *God's Appointed Times*. Baltimore: Lederer Publications, 1993.
Keener, Craig S. *The Gospel of Matthew: A Socio-Rhetorical Commentary*. Grand Rapids: Eerdmans, 2009.

———. *Romans—A New Covenant Commentary.* Eugene: Cascade Books, 2010.
Kessler, Edward and Neil Wenborn, eds. *A Dictionary of Jewish-Christian Relations.* Cambridge, Cambridge University Press, 2005.
Kinbar, Carl. "Messianic Jews and Scripture." In *Introduction to Messianic Judaism: Its Ecclesial Context and Biblical Foundations*, edited by David J. Rudolph and Joel Willitts, 61–71. Grand Rapids: Zondervan, 2013.
King, Andrea. *If I'm Jewish and You're Christian, What Are the Kids?* NewYork: UAHC Press, 1993.
Kinzer, Mark S. *Israel's Messiah and the People of God*, edited by Jennifer Rosen. Eugene: Cascade Books, 2011.
———. *Post-Missionary Messianic Judaism.* Grand Rapids: Brazos Press, 2005.
———. *Searching Her Own Majesty.* Eugene: Cascade Books, 2015.
Kirk, Alan. "The Memory-Tradition Nexus in the Synoptic Tradition: Memory, Media and Symbolic Representation." In *Memory and Identity in Ancient Judaism and Early Christianity*, edited by Tom Thatcher, 131–59. Atlanta: SBL Press, 2014.
———. "Social and Cultural Memory." In *Memory, Tradition and Text: Uses of the Past in Early Christianity*, edited by Alan Kirk and Tom Thatcher, 1–24. Atlanta: SBL, 2005.
Klayman, Elliot. "Messianic Jewish Worship and Prayer." In *Introduction to Messianic Judaism: Its Ecclesial Context and Biblical Foundations*, edited by David J. Rudolph and Joel Willitts, 51–60. Grand Rapids: Zondervan, 2013.
Kleim, Jeffrey, A. and Theresa, A. Jones. "Principles of experience-dependent neural plasticity: implications for rehabilitation after brain damage." *Journal of Speech, Language and Hearing Research* 51, no. 1, (February 2008) 225–239.
Kollontai, Pauline. "Between Judaism and Christianity," *Journal of Religion and Society* 8 (2006).
———. "Messianic Jews and Jewish Identity." *Journal of Modern Jewish Studies* 3, Part 2 (2004) 195–205.
———. "Women as Leaders: Contemporary Perspectives on the Roles of Women in Messianic Judaism." *Women in Judaism: A Multidisciplinary Journal* 6 no. 1 (Spring 2009).
Lakoff, George and Mark Johnson. *Metaphors We Live By.* Chicago: University of Chicago Press, 2003.
Llamas, Carmen and Watt, Dominic. "Introduction." In *Language and Identities*, edited by Carmen Llamas and Dominic Watt, 1–5. Edinburgh: Edinburgh University Press, 2010.

Langton, Daniel R. *The Apostle Paul in the Jewish Imagination.* Cambridge: Cambridge University Press, 2010.
Lawler, Steph. *Identity: Sociological Perspectives.* Cambridge: Polity Press, 2008.
Leder, Arie C. *Waiting for the Land: The Story Line of the Pentateuch.* Phillipsburg: P&R, 2010.
Lefevere, André. *Translation, Rewriting and the Manipulation of Literary Fame.* London: Routledge, 1992.
Liberman, Paul and Jack Wasson. *Don't Call Me Christian: A Truly Jewish Story.* Arlington, TX: Tishbite Press, 2015.
Lincoln, Andrew. *Ephesians.* Word Biblical Commentary. Dallas: Word Books, 1990.
Lindsey, Robert Lisle. *A Hebrew Translation of The Gospel of Mark.* Jerusalem: Dugith, 1973.
Longenecker, Richard N. *The Epistle to the Romans.* NIGTC. Grand Rapids: Eerdmans, 2016.
MacCulloch, Diarmaid. *A History of Christianity.* London: Penguin, 2010.
Macy, Michael W. "Rational Choice." In *Contemporary Social Psychological Theories,* edited by Peter J. Burke, 70–87. Stanford: Stanford University Press, 2006.
Maltz, Steve. *Hebraic Church: Thinking Differently.* Ilford: Saffron Planet Publishing, 2016.
Martin, Ralph P. *Ephesians, Colossians and Philemon.* Interpetation. Louisville, KY: John Knox Press, 1991.
Martyn, J Louis. *Galatians: A New Translation with Introduction and Commentary.* Anchor Bible 33a. New York: Doubleday, 1997.
———. *History and Theology in the Fourth Gospel.* Louisville, KY: Westminster/John Knox Press, 2003.
Martz, Erin and Jacob D. Lindy. "Exploring the Trauma Membrane Concept." In *Trauma Rehabilitation After War and Conflict,* edited by Erin Martz, 27–54. New York: Springer-Verlag, 2010.
Mears, Carolyn Lunsford. "A Columbine Study: Giving Voice, Hearing Meaning." *The Oral History Review* 35, no. 2 (2008) 159–75
———. "Experiences of Columbine parents: Finding a way to tomorrow." Doctoral dissertation, University of Denver, 2005.
———. *Interviewing for Education and Social Science Research: The Gateway Approach.* New York: Palgrave Macmillan, 2009.
Megill, Allan. "History, Memory, Identity." In *Historical Knowledge, Historical Error: A Contemporary Guide to Practice,* 41–62. Chicago: University of Chicago Press, 1998.

Mendoza-Denton, Norma and Dana Osborne. "Two Languages, Two Identities?" In *Language and Identities*, edited by Carmen Llamas and Dominic Watt, 113–22. Edinburgh: Edinburgh University Press, 2010.

Meyer, Michael A. *Jewish Identity in the Modern World*. Seattle: University of Washington Press, 1990.

Michael, Boaz. *Tent of David: Healing the Vision of the Messianic Gentile*. Marshfield: First Fruits of Zion, 2013.

Miller, John W. *How the Bible Came to Be: Exploring the Narrative and the Message*. Mahwah: Paulist Press, 2004.

Mitton, C. Leslie. *The Epistle to the Ephesians: Its Authorship, Origin and Purpose*. Oxford: Oxford University Press, 1951.

Moberly, R. W. L. *Old Testament Theology: Reading the Hebrew Bible as Christian Scripture*. Grand Rapids: Baker Academic, 2013.

Montefiore, Hugh. *Looking Afresh: Soundings in Creative Dissent*. London: SPCK, 2002.

———. *Oh God, What Next? – An Autobiography*. London: Hodder & Stoughton, 1995.

———. *On Being a Jewish Christian: Its Blessings and Its Problems*. London: Hodder & Stoughton, 1998.

Moo, Douglas J. *The Epistle to the Romans*. NICNT. Grand Rapids: Eerdmans, 1996.

Morris, Leon. *The Epistle to the Romans*. Grand Rapids: Eerdmans, 1988.

Munday, Jeremy. *Introducing Translation Studies: Theories and Applications*. 4th edition. London: Routledge, 2016.

Nanos, Mark. *The Mystery of Romans: The Jewish Context of Paul's Letter*. Minneapolis: Augsburg Fortress, 1996.

Nanos, Mark and Magnus Zetterholm. *Paul within Judaism: Restoring the First-Century Context to the Apostle*. Minneapolis: Fortress, 2015.

Nastiti, Aulia. *Diasporic Community and European Cultural Identity*. Accessed 4:13pm 03Jun14. https://www.academia.edu/7185894/Diasporic_Community_and_European_Cultural_Identity

Neitzsche, Friedrich. *Twilight of the Idols, or, How to Philosophise with a Hammer*. Translated by Richard Polt. Indianapolis: Hackett, 1997.

Niranjana, Tejaswini. *Siting Translation: History, Post-Structuralism and the Colonial Context*. Berkeley, CA: University of California Press, 1992.

O'Brien, Peter T. *The Epistle to the Philippians*. NIGTC. Grand Rapids: Eerdmans, 1991.

Peli, Pinchas H. *On Repentance: The Thought and Oral Discourses or Rabbi Joseph Dov Soloveitchik.* Lanham: Rowman & Littlefield, 2004.

Plowden, Alison. *In a Free Republic: Life in Cromwell's England.* Thrupp: Sutton Publishing, 2006.

Ponsonby, Simon. *God is For Us.* Oxford: Monarch Books, 2015.

Porter, Stanley E. "Paul and the Process of Canonizaton." In *Exploring the Origins of the Bible*, edited by Craig E. Evans and Emmanuel Tov, 173–202. Grand Rapids, MI: Baker Academic, 2008.

Pritz, Ray A. *Nazarene Jewish Christianity.* Jerusalem: The Magnes Press, 1988.

Pym, Anthony. *Exploring Translation Theories.* 2nd edition. London: Routledge, 2014.

Robinson, D. W. B. "The Distinction Between Jewish and Gentile Believers in Galatians." *Australian Biblical Review* 8 (December 1965): 29–44.

Robinson, John A. T. *Redating the New Testament.* London: SCM Press, 1976.

Rosner, Jennifer M. *Healing the Schism: Barth, Rosenzweig, and the New Jewish-Christian Encounter.* Minneapolis: Fortress, 2016.

Rowe, C. Kavin. *World Upside Down: Reading Acts in the Graeco-Roman Age.* New York: Oxford University Press, 2009.

Rudolph, David J. *Growing Your Olive Tree Marriage.* Baltimore: Lederer Books, 2003.

———. "Messianic Jews and Christian Theology." *Pro Ecceslia* 14.1 (2005) 58–84.

———. "Messianic Judaism in Antiquity and the Modern Era." In *Introduction to Messianic Judaism: Its Ecclesial Context and Biblical Foundations*, edited by David J. Rudolph and Joel Willitts, 21–36. Grand Rapids: Zondervan, 2013.

———. "Paul's 'Rule in All the Churches' (1 Cor 7:17–24) and Torah-Defined Ecclesiological Variegation." *Studies in Christian-Jewish Relations*, 5 (2010).

Rudolph, David J. and Joel Willitts, eds. *Introduction to Messianic Judaism: Its Ecclesial Context and Biblical Foundations.* Grand Rapids: Zondervan, 2013.

Sacks, Jonathan. *Authorised Daily Prayer Book.* 4th edition. London: HarperCollins, 2006.

———. *Exodus: The Book of Redemption.* Covenant and Conversation. Jerusalem: Maggid Books, 2010.

———. *Genesis: The Book of Beginnings.* Covenant and Conversation. Jerusalem: Maggid Books, 2009.

Saldarini, Anthony J. *Matthew's Christian-Jewish Community*. Chicago: University of Chicago Press, 1994.

Samuelson, Francine K. "Messianic Judaism: Church, Denomination, Sect or Cult." *Journal of Ecumenical Studies* 37:2 (Spring 2000) 161–86.

Sanders, James A. *Canon and Community: A Guide to Canonical Criticism*. Minneapolis: Fortress, 1984.

———. *Torah and Canon*. 2nd edition. Eugene: Cascade, 2005.

Schiffman, Michael. *Return of the Remnant: The Rebirth of Messianic Judaism*. Baltimore: Lederer, 1996.

Schonfield, Hugh J. *The History of Jewish Christianity: From the First to the Twentieth Century*. Createspace; reprint of the 1936 Duckworth edition, 2009.

Schreiner, Thomas R. *Romans*. ECNT. Grand Rapids: Baker Academic, 1998.

Schudson, Michael. "Preservation of the Past in Mental Life." *The Quarterly Newsletter of the Laboratory of Comparative Human Cognition* 9, no. 1, (January 1987) 5–10.

Schwartz, Barry. "Where there's Smoke, There's Fire." In *Memory and Identity in Ancient Judaism and Early Christianity*, edited by Tom Thatcher, 7–37. Atlanta: SBL, 2014.

Scott, David and Marlene Morrison. *Key Ideas in Educational Research*. London: Continuum Books, 2006.

Shapiro, Helen. *Walking Back to Happiness*. London: Fount/HarperCollins, 1994.

Sheldrake, Philip. *Spaces for the Sacred: Place, Memory and Identity*. Baltimore: The Johns Hopkins University Press, 2001.

Shishkoff, Eitan. *What About Us?: The end-time calling of Gentiles in Israel's revival*. Bedford: Buckhart Books, 2013.

Shkul, Minna. "New Identity and Cultural Baggage: Identity and Otherness in Colossians." In *T&T Handbook to Social Identity in the New Testament*, edited by Brian J. Tucker and Coleman A. Baker, 367–88. London: Bloomsbury T&T Clark, 2016.

Shulam, Joseph with Hilary Le Cornu. *A Commentary on the Jewish Roots of Romans*. Baltimore: Lederer, 1997.

Skarsaune, Oskar. *In the Shadow of the Temple: Jewish Influences on Early Christianity*. Downers Grove: IVP, 2002.

Smith, Calvin L. "Introduction." In *The Jews, Modern Israel and the New Supercessionism*, edited by Calvin L. Smith, 2nd Ed, 1–16. Broadstairs: King's Divinity Press, 2013.

Smith, Jonathan A., Flowers, Paul and Larkin, Michael. *Interpretive Phenomenological Analysis: Theory, Method and Research.* London: Sage, 2009.

Snow, David A. and Doug McAdam. "Identity Work Processes in the Context of Social Movements: Clarifying the Identity/Movement Nexus." In *Self, Identity and Social Movements*, edited by Sheldon Stryker, Timothy J. Owens and Robert W. White. 41–67. Minneapolis: University of Minnesota Press, 2000.

Soulen, R. Kendall. *The God of Israel and Christian Theology.* Minneapolis: Fortress Press, 1996.

———. "Replacement theology." In *A Dictionary of Jewish-Christian Relations*, edited by Edward Kessler and Neil Wenborn, 375–6. Cambridge: Cambridge University Press, 2005.

———. "Supersessionism." In *A Dictionary of Jewish-Christian Relations*, edited by Edward Kessler and Neil Wenborn, 413–4. Cambridge: Cambridge University Press, 2005.

Spaulding, Mary B. *Commemorative Identities: Jewish Social Memory and the Johannine Feast of Booths.* London: T&T Clark, 2009.

Stark, Rodney. *The Rise of Christianity.* New York: Harper Collins, 1997.

Steiner, George. *After Babel: Aspects of Language and Translation.* 3rd edition. Oxford: Oxford University Press, 1998.

Steinsaltz, Rabbi Adin. *We Jews.* San Francisco: Jossey Bass, 2005.

Stendahl, Krister. *Paul Among Jews and Gentiles.* Minneapolis: Fortress, 1976.

Stern, David H. *Jewish New Testament Commentary.* Clarksville: Jewish New Testament Publications, 1992.

———. *Messianic Judaism: A Modern Movement with an Ancient Past.* Clarksville: Lederer, 2007.

———. *Restoring the Jewishness of the Gospel: A Message for Christians.* Clarksville: Lederer, 2009.

Stevenson, Angus, ed. *Oxford Dictionary of English.* Oxford: Oxford University Press, 2010.

Stets, Jan E. "Identity Theory." In *Contemporary Social Psychological Theories*, edited by Peter J. Burke, 88–110. Stanford: Stanford University Press, 2006.

Stets, Jan E. and Peter J. Burke. "Identity Theory and Social Identity Theory." *Social Psychology Quarterly* 63, no. 3 (September 2000): 224–37.

Stock, Brian. *Listening for the Text: On the Uses of the Past.* Philadelphia: University of Pennsylvania Press, 1996.

Stott, John R. W. *The Message of Ephesians.* The Bible Speaks Today. Nottingham: IVP, 1991.

Strack, H. L. and Günter Stemberger. *Introduction to the Talmud and Midrash*. Translated and edited by Markus Bockmuehl. Minneapolis: Fortress, 1996.

Svartvik, Jesper. "Introduction: 'For Six Strange Weeks They Had Acted As If They Were Friends.'" In *Religious Stereotyping and Interreligious Relations*, edited by Jesper Svartvik and Jakob Wirén,171–81. New York: Palgrave Macmillan, 2013.

Taylor, Howard. "Israel and the Purposes of God." In *The Jews, Modern Israel and the New Supercessionism*, 2nd edition, edited by Calvin L. Smith, 329–45. Broadstairs: King's Divinity Press, 2013.

Telchin, Stan. *Messianic Judaism is not Christianity*. Grand Rapids: Chosen Books, 2004.

Teplinsky, Sandra. "Ruth and Naomi: A Model of Reconciliation and Redemption." In *Awakening the One New Man*, edited by Robert F. Wolff, 119–38. Shippensburg: Destiny Image, 2011.

Thatcher, Tom, ed. *Memory and Identity in Ancient Judaism and Early Christianity*. Atlanta: SBL, 2014.

Theissen, Gerd. *The New Testament: A Literary History*. Translated by Linda M. Maloney. Minneapolis: Fortress, 2012.

Thistleton, Anthony C. *Discovering Romans: Content, Interpretation, Reception*. London: SPCK, 2016.

Thomas, Erik R. and Alicia Beckford. Wassink. "Variation and Identity in African American English." In *Language and Identities*, edited by Carmen Llamas and Dominic Watt, 157–65. Edinburgh: Edinburgh University Press, 2010.

Thomas, Gary. *How to Do Your Research Project*. London: Sage, 2013.

Thompson, John B. "Tradition and Self in a Mediated World." In *Detraditionalisation: Critical Reflections on Authority and Identity at a Time of Uncertainty*, edited by Paul Heelas, Scott Lash and Paul Morris, 89–108. Oxford: Blackwell, 1996.

Ticciati, Susannah. "The Puzzle of Israel for Christian Theology: Rereading Romans 9–11 Today." A paper presented at Trinity College, Bristol, March 17th, 2016.

Touger, Rabbi Eliyahu. *Maimonides Mishneh Torah: Hilchot Teshuvah*. Brooklyn: Moznaim Publishing Corporation, 1990.

Tucker, Brian J. and Coleman A. Baker, eds. *T&T Handbook to Social Identity in the New Testament*. London: Bloomsbury T&T Clark, 2016.

Turner, Victor. *Dramas, Fields and Metaphors*. Ithaca: Cornell University Press, 1974.

———. *The Ritual Process: Structure and Anti-Structure*. London: Routledge & Kegan Paul, 1969.

Urquhart, Cathy. *Grounded Theory for Qualitative Research: A Practical Guide*. London: Sage, 2013.
Varner, William. "Messianic Congregations are Not Necessary." In *How Jewish is Christianity*, edited by Louis Goldberg and Stanley N. Gundry, 29-49. Grand Rapids: Zondervan, 2003.
Volf, Miroslav. *Exclusion and Embrace*. Nashville: Abingdon Press, 1996.
Von Goethe, Johann Wolfgang. *Maxims and Reflections*. Translated by Elisabeth Stopp London: Penguin, 1999.
Walls, Andrew F. *The Cross-Cultural Process in Christian History*. Edinburgh: T & T Clark, 2002.
Ware, James P. *Synopsis of the Pauline Letters in Greek and English*. Grand Rapids: Baker Academic, 2010.
Weber, Max. *Economy and Society: An Outline of Interpretive Sociology*. Translated from the 4th German edition (1956). Berkeley, CA: University of California Press, 1978.
Wilson, Todd A. "The Supercession and Superfluity of the Law? Another Look at Galatians." In *Introduction to Messianic Judaism: Its Ecclesial Context and Biblical Foundations*, edited by David J. Rudolph and Joel Willitts, 235–44. Grand Rapids: Zondervan, 2013.
Winkler, Gershon. *The Way of the Boundary Crosser: An Introduction to Jewish Flexidoxy*. Northvale: Jason Aronson, 1998.
Witherington III, Ben. *The Letters to Philemon, the Colossians, and the Ephesians: A Socio-Rhetorical Commentary on the Captivity Epistles*. Grand Rapids: Eerdmans, 2007.
———. *Paul's Letter to the Romans: A Socio-Rhetorical Commentary*. Grand Rapids: Eerdmans, 2004.
Wolff, Robert F. "The Identity of the One New Man." In *Awakening the One New Man*, edited by Robert F. Wolff, 13–16. Shippensburg: Destiny Image, 2011.
Wood, Michael. "The Age of Revolution," episode seven of *The Great British Story*, originally broadcast July 27th, 2012. London: BBC, 2012.
———. *The Story of England*. Harmondsworth: Viking, 2010.
———. "Tribes to Nations", episode two of *The Great British Story*, originally broadcast June 1st, 2012. London: BBC, 2012.
Woods, David B. "Diakrino and Jew-Gentile distinction in Acts 11:12." *Conspectus* 18 (September 2014) 79–94.
———. "Does Acts 15:9 Refute Intra-ecclesial Jew-Gentile Distinction?" *Conspectus* 19 (March 2015): 105–145.
———. "Jew-Gentile Distinction in the 'One New Man' of Ephesians 2:15." *Conspectus* 18 (September 2014): 95–135.

Wright, N. T. *The Climax of the Covenant*. London: T&T Clark, 1991.
———. "The Letter to the Romans." In *The New Interpreter's Bible Commentary*, 317–664. Nashville, TN: Abingdon Press, 2015.
———. *Paul and the Faithfulness of God*. London: SPCK, 2013.
———. *Pauline Perspectives: Essays on Paul, 1978–2013*. London: SPCK, 2013.
———. *The Resurrection of the Son of God*. London: SPCK, 2003.
Wyschogrod, Michael. *Abraham's Promise*. Edited by R. Kendall Soulen. Grand Rapids: Eeerdmans, 2004.
Wyschogrod, Michael and David Berger. *Jews and Jewish Christianity*. New York: KTAV, 1978.
Yee, Tet-Lim N. *Jews, Gentiles and Ethnic Reconciliation*. Cambridge: Cambridge University Press, 2005.
Zerubavel, Eviatar. "Social Memories: Steps towards a Sociology of the Past." *Qualitative Sociology* 19 (1996): 283–299.
Zerubavel, Yael. *Recovered Roots: Collective Memory and the Making of Israeli National Tradition*. Chicago: University of Chicago Press, 1995.
Zetterholm, Magnus. "Paul within Judaism: The State of the Questions." In *Paul Within Judiasm: Restoring the First-Century Context to the Apostle*, edited by Mark D. Nanos and Magnus Zetterholm, 31–51. Minneapolis: Fortress, 2015.
Zoccali, Christopher. "Children of Abraham, the Restoration of Israel and the Eschatological Pilgrimage of the Nations: What does it mean for 'In Christ' Identity?" In *T&T Handbook to Social Identity in the New Testament*, edited by Brian J. Tucker and Coleman A. Baker, 367–88. London: Bloomsbury T&T Clark, 2016.
Zornberg, Avivah Gottlieb. *Bewilderments: Reflections on the Book of Numbers*. New York: Shocken Books, 2015.

Scripture Index

Genesis
1:1 127
1:26–27 130
1:27 125
1:28 130
2:21–23 129
10 147
12:3 144
18:18 144
42 116
42:13 79
47 116

Exodus
16:29 219
19:5–6 75
20:12 142
23:14 70

Leviticus
19:17 37
19:23–25 137
23 26
23:10 137

Numbers
15:16 41
15:21 137
15:38–39 48
22:38 110
25:6–13 141
26:55 80
33:54 80

Deuteronomy
5:16 142
6:4 77
7:3–4 80
8:3 110
8:11 129
16:16 70
21:10–14 80
28:15–46 78
29:13–14 79
29:15 82
31:10–11 102

Judges
12:5–6 116

Nehemiah
8–10 102

Psalms
19:6 37
48:2 35
52:8 138
139:13–16 84

Isaiah
2:2–4 145
11:10 138
45:23 145
49:1, 6 119
56 122
56:7 128
57:15–21 122
57:19 122

249

Jeremiah
1:5 .... 84, 120
9:24 142
11:16 139
11:16–17 139
20:9 84

Hosea
14:5–7 138

Joel
2:16 37
3:16 127

Amos
3:2 75

Micah
4:1–3 145

Zechariah
2:8 35
6:12 138
8:21–23 145
8:23 2

Matthew
2:30–34 149
4:17 129
5:35 35
7:17–19 137
10:24 125
10:37 142
13:33 137
23:1–12 79
26:20–29 97
28:18–20 .... 111, 132
28:19–20 .... 99, 131

Mark
14:17–25 97

Luke
1:6 141
1:76–77 84
17:21 129
22:14–23 97
24:36 125

John
1:3 125
5:24 216
15:2 139
19:12 144
20:19, 21 125
20:26 125

Acts
2:10 133
2:41 11
10:20 149
11:2 148
11:12 148–9
13:6 144
15:9 148–9
15:19–21 128
17:6 94
17:7 144
17:21 123
18:2 134
20:16 131
21:18–26 131
21:23–26 128
23:6 142

Romans
1–4 133
1:16 .... 126, 129, 134
2:9 129
2:14 126
3:1–2 .... 129, 141
4:17 127
5–8 133

5:15–21..............................130
8:29....................................129
8:32....................................140
9–11..................119, 133, 135, 137, 138
9:1–5..........................135, 141
9:1–11:36..........................135
9:4–5.................................125
9:6–13...............................135
9:14–33.............................135
10:1–4...............................135
10:5–13.............................136
10:12.................................143
10:14–17...........................136
10:17.................................230
10:18–21...........................136
11......................................122
11:1............................119, 141
11:1–12.............................136
11:11..................1, 131, 136, 140
11:11–17...........................136
11:11–24...........................135
11:12.........................150, 231
11:15.................................137
11:16.................................136
11:17..........................126, 141
11:17–24.....................41, 137
11:18–23...........................136
11:20.................................139
11:23.................................137
11:24...............125, 136, 139
11:25.........................150, 231
11:25–32...........................136
11:26..........................134, 135
11:29.................................150
11:33–36...........................136
12–16.................................133
14......................................131
15:12.................................138
16:3–4...............................134
16:22.................................133

1 Corinthians
5:6......................................137
5:7......................................100
7...131
7:14....................................137
7:17–24.............................120
7:18....................................145
7:20....................................128
7:24....................................145
10:11..................................214
11:1....................................133
11:23–26....................97, 100
12......................................129
12:13..........................131, 143
15:22.................................130
15:45.................................130
15:45–48...........................129

2 Corinthians
3:18....................................129
4:6......................................129
5:17....................................128
5:17–19.............................131

Galatians
1:13–14.............................141
1:15....................................119
2:7..............................132, 184
2:7–9.................................231
2:8......................................143
2:14....................................128
2:20......................................84
3:8......................................144
3:28..................127, 131, 143, 154, 215
3:28–29.............................119
3:29....................................144
4:19....................................129
5:2–6.................................145
6:16..7

Ephesians
2...151
2:1...127
2:1–3..121
2:1–10..121
2:4–7..121
2:5–6..127
2:5,7...122
2:8–10..121
2:10......................................125, 146
2:11...129
2:11–12..122
2:11–22..............................119, 122
2:12......................................126, 132
2:13...122
2:13–18..122
2:14................122–3, 125, 154, 231
2:14–15a......................................140
2:14–16..122
2:15..................68, 122–3, 125, 129, 150
2:16......................................122, 123
2:17......................................122, 129
2:18...124
2:19–22..122
2:21–22..122
3:9...125

4:7...129
4:11–12..129
4:12-13...231
4:12–14..151
4:13...147
4:15...106
4:19...129
4:24...125
5..131

Philippians
2:9–11..145
3:3–11..............................119, 141
3:8...142
3:8–9..142
3:10, 21..129
3:11...131

Colossians
1:16...125
2:16...131
3:10...129
3:11......................................131, 143

Hebrews
10:25...81

Index

A
Anti-Semitism 1, 22, 29, 42, 55, 63, 67, 73, 81, 89, 150, 155, 170, 176, 214
Assimilation 4, 8, 39, 49, 67, 87, 154, 163, 171, 175, 178, 181, 184, 187, 190, 192, 194, 198, 201, 211, 214, 218, 228, 236

B
Barth, Markus 124–30, 138, 151, 166, 212, 224
BDS – Boycott, Divest, Sanctions 42, 63
Biblical mandate 2, 4, 119, 151, 163, 166, 176, 179, 181, 183, 185, 187, 191, 194, 205, 212, 230
Bilateral ecclesiology 148, 227
Binary opposite 143

C
Calling 1, 8, 29, 34, 40, 46, 57, 62, 84, 127, 131, 136, 141, 154, 164, 167, 169, 173, 179, 182, 185, 205, 220, 226, 244
Caplin, Sarahbeth 24–5, 53, 228
Chandler, Jenny Berg 20-21, 41, 60
Christian Zionism 7, 31, 44–45, 197, 202
Christians
    Gentile 3, 5, 10, 27, 31, 47, 121, 134, 166, 192, 201, 212, 214, 218, 224, 226, 231
    Jewish 1, 19, 31, 121, 134, 220, 222
Church leader 1, 3, 9, 12, 17, 21, 29, 30, 34, 43, 47–8, 50, 53, 55, 59, 63, 69, 114, 161–2, 169, 175, 177, 184, 186, 189–90, 195–6, 198, 200–1, 204, 208, 211, 217, 222, 227
Code-switching 109, 203
Cohn-Sherbok, Dan 9, 228
Colonialism 114, 179, 193, 215, 242
Convert 78
Council of Nicea 7, 9
Countermemories 105, 170, 179, 198
Custom 101

D

Dauermann, Stuart 3, 5–6, 132–3, 140, 142, 149-150, 223, 225–7
Davis, Ellen 8, 214
Dein, Simon 9, 27
Distinction Theory (proposed by David Woods) 2, 147–9, 163, 166, 169, 174, 176, 179, 181, 183, 185, 187, 190, 194, 205, 212
Dual expression (congregations) 195, 208, 231

E

Ephesian Moment (proposed by Andrew Walls) 2, 146, 172
Ethnic collapse 124, 131
Ethnicity 8, 34, 75, 121
Eucharist 97

F

Feher, Shoshana 9–10, 228–9
Fieldsend, John 21, 27, 236

G

Gateway Approach (The, TGA) 5, 11, 13, 241
Glaser, Barney G., 13
Glass ceiling 29, 34, 43
God-fearers 134, 144
Grounded Theory Method (GTM) 3, 5, 11–3, 15, 157
Guinness, Michelle 22–3, 50

H

Halbwachs, Maurice 95–7, 100
Harris-Shapiro Carol 9–10, 228
Harvey, Richard 4, 9, 221–2
Hebrew Christian 7, 9, 21, 41, 66, 180
Holocaust 29, 42, 49, 61, 65, 68, 70, 168–9, 173, 225

I

Identity
    Christian 41, 117, 165, 168, 171, 183, 187, 202, 213
    convergence 175
    construction (methods of) 91
        amplification 92, 164, 168, 170, 182, 202
        consolidation 92–3, 164, 168, 171, 173, 175, 179, 185, 193, 202

General Index 255

> extension 23, 92–3, 119, 164, 166, 168, 173, 176, 179, 188, 223
> transformation 92, 94, 105, 124, 145, 162, 170, 175, 179, 181, 202, 213

formation 78, 96
Gentile 28, 39, 149, 153, 156, 165, 187, 190, 192, 194, 201
given 83
hierarchies 86
inheritance 78, 80, 207
Jewish 1, 7, 10, 17, 20, 23, 27, 34, 52, 59, 64, 66, 73, 86, 89, 93, 98, 100, 105, 108, 117, 122, 141, 146, 150, 152, 159, 161, 194, 198, 204, 211, 215, 222, 226, 228, 236, 239, 242
loss 20
negotiated 83
prototype 88
role partner 168, 179, 182, 184, 186, 192
roles 85, 173
self-identity 28–9
Theory 1, 3, 75, 82, 84–7, 91, 107, 189, 212
verification 13, 87, 162, 165, 168, 173, 175, 178, 185, 188, 190, 192, 194, 198, 200, 217
Interfaith relations 30, 54, 71, 194, 204

J

Jacob, Alex 69, 154-156
Jacob's Models of Church Engagement
> Church Absorption 154, 156, 163, 170, 172, 206, 214
> Church Integration 155, 169, 183, 191, 194, 206, 230
> Separate 156
> Separate but Open 155, 157, 169, 183, 187, 191, 195, 206, 222, 230

Jewish ancestry 29
Jewish continuity 66, 73, 187, 189, 196, 198, 217
Jewish heritage 24, 28, 34, 38, 45, 47, 50, 61, 66, 81, 107, 159, 171, 175, 180, 186, 203, 227
Jewish missionary activity, agencies (that is, targeting Jewish people), work 21, 29–30, 45–6, 52, 59, 111, 169, 173, 180, 186, 224
Jewish ritual 144, 172, 177, 185, 193, 197, 215
Jews for Jesus 43, 94, 235
Juster, Dan 1, 9, 15, 231

K

Kinship 78-79, 121, 144
Kinzer, Mark 2, 129, 222–3, 227
Kollontai, Pauline 9, 26–7, 240

L

Liminal 54, 105, 129, 133, 144, 163, 166, 168, 179, 181, 183, 186, 188, 191, 193, 203, 228
Liberman, Paul 23–4
Lindy, Jacob D. 14, 241

M

Maltz, Steve 25-26, 45
Marginalized 64, 73, 89–90, 103, 105–6, 132, 163–4, 166, 168, 171, 173, 175, 177–8, 181, 183, 186, 194, 198, 201, 203, 229
Mears, Carolyn Lunsford 13–14
Messianic Judaism 1, 4–5, 8–10, 27, 53, 64–5, 71, 79, 81, 112, 159, 162, 180, 204, 220–1, 229
Mimesis 133, 153, 166, 175, 190
Montefiore, Hugh 18–9, 31, 61, 68, 242

N

Narrative, commemorative 97, 105, 164, 202
Narrative, master 168, 170–1, 175, 179, 181, 185, 191, 193

O

Olive Tree 2, 119, 126, 133, 135–41, 223
    natural branches 137–8, 140–1
    wild branches 137
One New Man 2, 52, 55, 59, 65, 68, 120–1, 123–5, 140, 142, 146–7, 150–1, 153, 155–7, 163, 168–70, 174, 176–7, 179, 181, 183, 185, 187–8, 190–1, 194–5, 205, 211–2, 218, 223, 225, 230–1
Ordained clergy 29, 70

P

Passover 31, 33, 42–3, 49, 57, 61-62, 70, 97–9, 167, 190
Prominence Hierarchy 86, 162, 164, 168, 171, 178, 180, 185, 188, 200

R

Replacement theology 4, 7–8, 26, 31, 39, 44, 47, 53, 56–7, 63, 67–8, 73, 155, 161, 174, 186, 205, 215, 224
Rewriting 107, 113–5, 171, 204

General Index

Rewriting the past 103, 170, 179, 182, 191
Rudolph, David J. 10, 199, 219, 224, 227
Rules of remembrance 97

S

Salience hierarchy 86, 162, 164, 171, 180, 185, 188, 200
Samuelson, Francine 9
Sanders, James A. 102, 157–8
    extended/modified Sanders four-step process 157–9, 163, 170, 174, 179, 181, 183, 187, 189–92, 194–5, 206, 214
Shapiro, Helen 9, 17, 43
Shared vocabulary 183, 191–2, 214
Social exclusion 89, 178
Social Identity Theory 88–94, 212
Social Memory Theory 1, 75, 94–107, 212
Soulen, R. Kendall 1-2, 4-6, 15, 67–8, 224
Steiner, George 14, 55, 108
Stereotyping 89, 178, 212
Stern, David H. 9, 142
Strauss, Anselm L., 13
Supercessionism 1, 3–5, 8, 223, 226
    crypto-supersessionism 6
    economic 5
    hard 5
    Jewish 6
    puitive 5
    structural 5
    sweeping 6

T

Textual community 117, 171
Ticciati, Susannah 6
Tradition 101
    invented 102
    oral 76, 102
Translation theory 1, 3, 75, 107, 118, 212

V

Vocation 29, 150

W
Willitts, Joel 10
Worldview 83, 112
Wright, N. T. 5–6, 124–5, 130–1, 133–6, 138–9, 141
Wyschogrod, Michael 1, 15, 60, 67–8, 76

Y
Yeshua 1–3, 7–9, 11, 15, 17, 20, 27, 40, 42, 44, 50, 53, 59, 71–2, 94, 99, 102, 104, 106, 108, 119, 123–5, 127, 129–31, 137–9, 144, 146, 149–52, 154–5, 162–3, 165–7, 172, 177, 179, 182, 185, 187–8, 193, 197, 204, 218, 223–5, 231

Z
Zetterholm, Magnus 8, 71

www.ingramcontent.com/pod-product-compliance
Lightning Source LLC
Chambersburg PA
CBHW050435240426
43661CB00055B/2391